Advance Praise for *Midnight Water: A Psychedelic Memoir*

"In her vividly rendered memoir *Midnight Water*, Katherine MacLean invites us into a journey through grief, ecstasy, rejection, trauma, and triumph. This life-changing, entertaining read traverses the bardo, with much of the story arising in the spaces in between birth and death, childhood and parenthood, suffering and joy, blame and forgiveness, resistance and acceptance. Along the way, we follow MacLean through the grueling terrain of so many deaths—of sister, of father, of ego—and the ultimate rebirth of our author-heroine, who has become a spiritual warrior with the tenacity of an athlete and the scrutiny of a scientist (both identities she has worn). . . . MacLean's beautiful sharing of her quest for understanding and peace is a page turner, much like a riveting novel, but stranger, as the truth often is. *How will our heroine prevail? What might her next trip reveal? Will she find the answers she seeks?*

What unfolds is not a manual for self-discovery, but a psychedelic-fueled example of how one woman chose to live an examined life, with no time to lose. Like great fiction, this book changed my existential view. Katherine MacLean's courageous efforts to transform her path unavoidably compel us to examine our own."
—**Erika Rosenberg, Ph.D.**, Founding Faculty,
The Compassion Institute; Consulting Scientist,
Center for Mind and Brain, UC Davis

"*Midnight Water* is a truth-telling, paradigm-busting, open-hearted scholarly memoir. If that's not already a genre, then Katherine MacLean has made it one. A story told in a whip-smart, authentic and sometimes raw voice, it alternately brought tears to my eyes, fist pumps of support, and closing the book and staring into space for while—sometimes in the span of only a few pages. It's also an adventure story, tracing the author's journey of healing through realms made accessible by plant medicine and entheogens. Definitely read it."
—**Cassandra Vieten, Ph.D.**, Director of Research, Arthur C. Clarke
Center for Human Imagination, cofounder, Psychedelics and Health
Research Initiative, University of California, San Diego; Senior Fellow
and Past President, Institute of Noetic Sciences

"I had intended to ski this afternoon under the beautiful blue sky, but I started to read Katherine MacLean's *Midnight Water* and I haven't been able to put it down. I'm only half-way in and intend to finish it tonight, to have my life back. Profound, honest, somber, often makes me laugh out loud. Really some of the best writing on the psychedelic experience in all its aspects, sacred to profane, from the perspective of a mystic, psychologist, and psychedelics researcher."
　　　　—**Robert Forte**, editor of *Entheogens and the Future of Religion*

"A moving and mysterious memoir of life, death and rebirth from the frontlines of the psychedelic renaissance."
　　　　—**Jules Evans**, author of *The Art of Losing Control: A Philosopher's Search for Ecstatic Experience*

"Through the gift of *Midnight Water*, Katherine MacLean shares a story that offers meaningful help for readers who have lost a loved one, faced an unbearable truth, or yearned to find meaning in chaos. It is a beacon for those of us who have had to learn how to keep going after profound loss, and then make the return journey to joy and awe."
　　　　—**Alicia Danforth, Ph.D.**, clinical psychologist and psychedelics researcher

"I truly enjoyed reading Katherine MacLean's memoir. It was a pleasantly easy read; it went down smooth, like an iced, aged whiskey. What was in this cocktail? Not just her challenging experiences at Johns Hopkins, holding space for, and sometimes wrangling her research participants, her triumphs in publishing groundbreaking work on the personality component of 'Openness,' but also in moving the needle, pushing the whole psychedelic ecosystem forward, championing end-of-life care, caregiver support, and especially: accountability and equity."
　　　　—**Julie Holland, M.D.**, psychiatrist and author of *Good Chemistry: The Science of Connection, from Soul to Psychedelics*

"With prose that is both irreverent and numinous, honesty that is both scathing and tender, and vulnerability that is both brave and hypnotic, Katherine MacLean has shared a story that is unique and deeply personal and yet somehow also my story. For those who dare to read this book you will be rewarded with a funny, bracing, and profound glimpse into the depths of a soul grappling with the pain, mystery, and beauty of human incarnation."
　　　　—**Margaret Cullen, MFT**, meditation teacher; founder of Compassion Corps, Founding Faculty of Compassion Institute, Founding Board Member of Compassion Education Alliance

"In *Midnight Water*, neuroscientist and noted psychedelics researcher Katherine MacLean, Ph.D. has crafted a gripping personal narrative of grief, trauma and healing. She welcomes the reader into her interior life with grace and bold honesty, revealing how her journey with a variety of entheogens, along with meditation and other therapeutic modalities, has brought her to a wise and liberating understanding of the harms and loss that have powerfully shaped, but not determined, her life. Bookended by her accounts of the early death of her twenty-nine-year-old younger sister and six years later the death of her father, the story draws on her experience as a guide during psychedelic research sessions to become an inspiring spiritual guide for loved ones in their final days. This remarkable account will surely resonate with a broad readership, from those who seek a career path of meaning and whole-person embrace, to those challenged with the unhealed effects of deep trauma. It will be of particular note to those in the helping professions interested in integrating psychedelic therapy into their practice. This is an eye- and heart-opening book for anyone interested in forging their own spiritual path and exploring what can be learned when that path includes entheogenic medicines."

—**Clifford Saron, Ph.D.**, neuroscientist at Center for Mind and Brain and MIND Institute, University of California, Davis

"Katherine MacLean, in her professional life, has helped guide people on life-changing psilocybin journeys, and this relentlessly raw, deeply compassionate, and heart-wrenching memoir takes us on a kaleidoscopic tour through birth, death, sisterhood, motherhood, and the non-ordinary spaces where real magic happens. And, like the best psychedelic trips, her journey leaves us quaking in awe at the fearsome depths and exquisite ecstasies we carry within. Jump into the dark waters and trust that currents will carry you through to the heart of a beautiful mystery. Highly recommended.""

—**Michael M. Hughes**, author of *The Blackwater Lights* trilogy and *Magic for the Resistance: Rituals and Spells for Change*

"This brutally beautiful book takes you on a wild and wise journey of heartbreak, insight, and awe. Dr. Katherine MacLean's words are like the psilocybin she describes: captivating, connecting, and transportive. Make sure to clear your schedule and pay attention to set and setting because once you begin the journey of reading, you will be unable to put it down."

—**Amishi Jha, Ph.D.**, neuroscientist and author of the national bestseller, *Peak Mind*

"Katherine MacLean didn't just influence the field of psychedelic therapy with her impeccable science and unyielding care of those suffering, she herself is an embodiment of fierce compassion and authenticity, transformed in the very fires that almost took her down. This book is a testament to the power of psychedelics to heal and help us all grow."
—**Michael Sapiro, Psy.D.**, clinical psychologist and psychedelic psychotherapist

"Katherine MacLean gives us a wild ride through a life devoted to discovering what truly matters. She describes her scientific work at Johns Hopkins elucidating the importance of psychedelic mystical experience in healing, while also revealing the fear, trembling, and joy of her own underground psychedelic explorations. She brings us into the birth experience, with all its pain and joy, as well as into the world of the dying, where she holds space for presence and compassion during her sister's and father's passings—fiercely protecting them both from the routine medicalization of death in hospitals. In this very personal and sweeping revelation of life, we meet a Mother Bear who is stubbornly devoted to her parents, children, husband, and friends—and to searching for the magic that makes our time on this planet truly meaningful."
—**Erik F. Storlie, Ph.D.**, author of *Nothing on My Mind: Berkeley, LSD, Two Zen Masters*

MIDNIGHT WATER

☾

A Psychedelic Memoir

KATHERINE MACLEAN, Ph.D.

MIDNIGHT

WATER

☾

A Psychedelic Memoir

GREEN WRITERS PRESS | *Brattleboro, Vermont*

Printed in the United States.

10 9 8 7 6 5 4 3 2 1

Green Writers Press is a Vermont-based publisher whose mission is to spread a message of hope and renewal through the words and images we publish. Throughout we will adhere to our commitment to preserving and protecting the natural resources of the earth. To that end, a percentage of our proceeds will be donated to environmental and social-activist groups. Green Writers Press gratefully acknowledges support from individual donors, friends, and readers to help support the environment and our publishing initiative.

GREEN
wriTers
press
Giving Voice to Writers & Artists Who Will Make the World a Better Place
Green Writers Press | Brattleboro, Vermont
www.greenwriterspress.com

ISBN: 979-8-9865324-7-9

Song lyrics "Immunity (Asleep Version)" written by Jon Hopkins and Kenny Anderson. Courtesy of Domino Publishing Company Limited.

COVER ARTWORK & DESIGN: Eileen Hall / www.eileen-hall.com

AUTHOR'S WEBSITE: www.katherinemaclean.org

PRINTED AT SHERIDAN

AUTHOR'S NOTE

Dear Reader: The contents of this book are not for the faint of heart. In the spirit of harm reduction, I want you to be prepared and informed before embarking on this journey. It is important for you to know that the story is true, and I survived it, but it may be painful and hard to read, especially if you have endured similar life events. Through my story, you will visit realms of physical and mental illness, death, sexual abuse, and the often unspoken pain and suffering of birth, child-rearing and motherhood. I encourage you to read the legal disclaimers, as well as the Introduction, and decide whether you have the resources and support in place to read this story now. If you are deep in personal grief, or seeking treatment for a mental health condition, abuse, or trauma, please consult a trusted professional before reading. If you do decide to begin reading this story, I implore you to finish it. Like any spiritual journey or psychedelic trip, there is a beginning, middle, and end; and the middle is often the hardest part. Unlike in life, I can promise you that this story has a happy ending.

PUBLISHER'S NOTE

CONTENTS

INTRODUCTION

MY DAD started seeing a psychic the year my sister got diagnosed with breast cancer. He was a corporate attorney, so this was a bit out of character for him, to say the least. I suppose he wanted to know if my sister was going to survive, or if he was going to get cancer too. His father and grandmother had both died of breast cancer, and his brother had already suffered through it, so the fear was warranted. Breast cancer was like our special family curse, although it wasn't the only one. The psychic charged a lot of money but provided remarkably specific predictions about the future. She described a vision of my sister's face on a huge screen. And she told him about the book I was going to write.

So, this is that book. I distinctly remember the first two thoughts I had after my sister died: "I am here to help people die." And, "This is the book I'm going to write." That was nine years ago. I've helped a few more people die since then, including my dad. And now I'm finally ready to tell our story.

The psychic was right about the big screen too. One year after my sister's first grueling bout with surgery and chemo and radiation, at the age of twenty-eight, she was promoted to one of the top executive positions in an international company, and her face was beamed out on one of those huge screens in Times Square. There she was, with her brilliant smile and bright blond hair and classic magenta top . . . and her brand-new breasts. She always told me that the best part about facing Stage 3 breast cancer in her mid-twenties was that she could get the boobs she'd always dreamed of. She said, "God, I don't even know why I waited so long."

Which is a funny thing for a twenty-eight-year-old to say: "Waited so long." But this was my sister. She was born an adult. By the age of twelve, she was so ready to move out of the house. By twenty-five, she had already finished college, gotten married, started her own business and had her first kid. She had even bought herself life insurance, which absolutely no person in their early twenties ever does. But then, she got a terminal diagnosis out of nowhere and was dead by thirty, so I guess her precociousness was practical.

My sister died in Room 37 on the 17th floor of a fancy cancer hospital on the Upper East Side of New York City. By the grace of God, and one particularly stubborn and kind young doctor who helped us sign the necessary paperwork at the last minute, she was able to receive palliative sedation during her final hours. What this means is that the patient is delivered higher and higher doses of morphine through an IV until their respiration and heart rate slows down so much that they die, which sounds gruesome until you have seen someone awake and suffering through end-stage cancer, and then you realize that this morphine protocol is sent straight from Heaven. The doctors will say that high-dose morphine simply enhances comfort by relieving the awareness and sensations of suffocation which happen during the course of a natural death. And they will insist that morphine doesn't speed up the dying process. But they also know that many patients and families choose this approach because it absolutely does. It is the best kept secret in palliative care.

For most of those final, quiet hours, it was just me and my sister and her husband. The nurses encouraged us to talk to her, because many patients can still hear what's happening in the room around them even when they appear comatose. We told her about the funniest and cutest things her daughter was doing back home. We reminisced about the early days when she first met her husband in Vermont. Then my parents and husband joined us at the very end. We were all circled around her, watching every breath and holding her hands. It was a prayerful time, even though none of us were specifically religious. We were listening to the only music my sister could tolerate during her time in the hospital: Jackie Evancho, who was an eight-year-old operatic prodigy. Her angelic, soprano voice filled the space of the room, drowning out the beeping machines and masking the horror of this beautiful, healthy-looking, mother-of-a-young-daughter dying before our eyes.

My sister's final breaths came in a specific pattern: in, in, out—gasp, gasp, sigh—with long pauses between the sigh and the next gasp. I got so used to this rhythm that it took me nearly half a minute to realize that the last sigh had happened. No more gasps came. My mom made some unintelligible expression and my dad said, "Ohhhhhhh." I looked down at my watch. It was one minute after midnight. My eyes searched the room, looking for some sign, some confirmation that this impossible thing had actually happened. All I saw was half-full cups of water everywhere.

Suddenly, my mind transports me to an exquisitely beautiful meditation lodge in the American Southwest, where an old Zen teacher is explaining how she had once tried to escape a peyote ceremony. There was too much pain; she wanted out. She fled during the midnight water break and hid in her car. But the Road Man, who was in charge of leading everyone through the ceremony, startled her awake with a loud pounding on the window. "You need to come back! Ceremony cannot continue until everyone is back." The Road Man marched her straight back to the tipi and made her walk slowly around the whole circle, past every single member of the community until she arrived back at her seat. It was humiliating and humbling, and ultimately life changing. Sitting next to my dead sister, I hear the Zen teacher's final lesson echoing in my mind: You don't get to decide whether to finish the ceremony.

But my sister left at midnight and never came back. She broke the most important rule. How are we supposed to finish without her? I suppose that this book is my way of trying to finish.

Years ago, when I first envisioned this story, it was all about me and my sister: our lives growing up together, our dramas, our fights, our moments of connection when she was sick and dying in the hospital. It was all very sentimental and moving and heartbreaking and beautiful. It was a real love story, in the sacred tradition of Rumi and his Beloved. But I learned quite quickly that the love she showed me as she was dying was just the beginning. Her love opened a portal into the underworld, showing me the necessity of coming face to face with the darkness as well as the light. In order to write this book, I finally had to face my monsters.

For a long time, I thought the monster in my life was my dad, or at least my dad in his worst moments. Then, I thought the monster was me, everything wretched and hateful and hurtful that I couldn't seem to change about myself. Toward the end of my journey, I started to see The Monster everywhere—omnipotent, waiting in ambush, laughing, ready to pounce. I nearly concluded that this life on Earth was just an entertaining horror show, and we were the unwitting villains and victims, hurting ourselves and each other in our desperate, ignorant attempts to carve out a modicum of safety and happiness while waiting to be swallowed up by an endless, heartless void.

Luckily, a wise friend posed the right question at the right time: "What if you find out there is a serial killer in your neighborhood, and there's nothing you can do to stop him. He will kill your friends, your parents, your siblings, your children. He will take every single thing from you that you hold dear, and then he will kill you too. In the face of that reality, what do you do?"

And I surprised myself when I blurted out, "I'd make friends with him."

The epic love story I really want to tell is about making friends with a monster. Which, as you can imagine, involves some pretty hard truths. When I met a famous science fiction author who shares my name, she advised me to tell the truth but call it fiction so that people would believe me. I suppose she was also suggesting that the veil of fiction would protect me. It's hard to hang your own laundry out to dry for everyone to examine and remark upon the patterns of the stains. Her advice challenged me to confront my shadow, those things I was hiding from everyone, including myself. The things I never wanted to say out loud. The things I thought, if others knew of them, would make me permanently unlovable. But I finally came to accept that I had been bargaining with the truth too long to try to hide it anymore. And honestly, the weight of carrying this shit on my own is just too much. So, now, if you decide to read this book, you get to carry it with me. Lucky you!

Mark Twain had a famous quote, "If you always tell the truth, you never have to remember anything." But what about telling the truth about things you can't quite remember? Well, this book documents my many attempts to remember, and tell the truth, and remember again, and tell the truth again, honing ever closer to some ultimate reality where everything is Known and Seen. I'm not sure I ever get there, but maybe this process will help you get there in your own life. My greatest wish is that this imperfect but sincere truth-telling will liberate you, too, in ways I can't possibly predict.

Some of the truths in this book may seem fictional to you. Some of them do not cast people in my life in the best light. I have tried to tell even the hardest and ugliest truths with respect and compassion. I got as many permissions as I could, including from my dad, although he had just died at the time, so I guess we can debate how he feels about the whole thing. The descriptions reflect my experience, as best I can remember it. I might have been wrong in places, although my husband always likes to remind people of my "steel-trap mind." I struggled for many years with how some of these truths might cause unnecessary suffering and harm to myself and others. I have made my peace with that outcome.

Before we dive in, I should warn you that this book has a lot to do with drugs. I've spent the greater part of my adult life exploring the world of psychoactive substances, both personally and professionally. For four years, I was one of the only women in the world studying psychedelic compounds as part of a world-class team of researchers and clinicians at the Johns Hopkins School of Medicine. Despite never fitting in with the conservative culture there, I managed to maneuver my way onto faculty. I had secured private funding to conduct my dream study of the effects of psilocybin (the main chemical in magic mushrooms) in long-term meditators. I had even finagled a personal meeting with the head of the Psychiatry Department to pitch a new experimental model for assessing the effects of psilocybin in people with depression. But I walked away from all of it.

The truth of it was, my job was killing me. By my third year at Hopkins, I was having regular anxiety attacks and terrible asthma and I didn't always recognize myself when I looked in the mirror. I couldn't tell if it was the 60-hour work weeks or spending most of my time in a small room with people on super high doses of mind-bending chemicals. But as I looked around at my colleagues, I could only find one or two people who seemed healthy, both physically and mentally. I mean, Christ, one of the guys who started the postdoc program with me had an actual heart attack during his first year. I saw how much my own health had deteriorated in such a short period of time. What was the point of doing this for another forty years? To be at the cutting edge of the next major breakthrough in psychiatric medicine? Well, yeah, it was actually hard to walk away from that.

But after my sister died, I knew I had to leave. Her death shocked me out of my complacency. I mean, there she was, twenty-nine years old, with a four-year-old daughter and a happy marriage and a beautiful home in the suburbs, poised to step into one of the top positions in a hugely successfully international company. But death doesn't give a shit about your family life or career goals. I hate to break it to you, but the Grim Reaper is so not interested in your bank account or your CV. If death came unexpectedly for me, I certainly didn't want my final months to be spent on that Hopkins research treadmill.

There's a warning I've since taken to heart: Be careful when you are climbing the ladder of success, because you might get to the top and realize it's leaning against the wrong wall. Thankfully, my sister's death helped me jump off half-way up.

I may not actively climb that ladder anymore, but I still have a lot to say about psychedelics. There are jewels of psychedelic wisdom scattered like breadcrumbs throughout this story, and I hope you enjoy discovering them. The main thing I hope to convey is that there are million right ways to take drugs, and there are also a million ways to screw it up. For better or worse, joining a clinical trial or paying $20,000 for a fancy clinic experience with certified guides and boutique drug selection won't ensure your success. But I'll leave that to you to figure out. I recommend always listening to many different viewpoints before deciding what works best for you—as long as you do your research and take your drugs safely. I am by no means encouraging you or advising you to take any substance, illegal or legal. I am simply sharing my story. Through my own adventures and mishaps and spiritual tight-rope walks, I hope to illustrate just how fun and illuminating psychedelics can be, especially when no one is looking over your shoulder and telling you how to do it.

Some of my best, early experiences with psychedelics were "recreational"—in other words, I did it because it was fun and interesting. I'm sure some healing happened too, but that wasn't the point. I liked MDMA the most and did it too much. I liked mushrooms, too, for the most part, but they were always weird and spooky. And then, they got downright terrifying. I kept feeling like I was dying, or that someone was trying to kill me, and I couldn't understand why. Then, after my sister died, I became desperate and depressed enough to finally ask the mushrooms for help. And wouldn't you know it: I showed up with all my shit and the mushrooms helped me turn it into gold. Not by fixing me, or healing me, but by shining a light into all my dark places and teaching me about relationship.

I used to think that human relationships ended when someone died or left. But the mushrooms showed me how easy it was to have a conversation with my dead sister or my yet-to-be-born daughter, and I really had to revise my limited worldview. During the course of my re-education, one of the relationships that seemed to stump even the mushrooms was the one between me and my dad. There was just so much anger there, and we were both stubborn, difficult people. As my dad's cancer progressed and he got really sick, I asked a good friend, "What happens if I can't forgive my dad before he's gone?" And she said, "Well, I found that my relationship with my father really blossomed after he died!" And now I know what she meant.

The bonds that connect us with our loved ones are not broken upon death. Our lives continue to weave together, between Earth and Heaven, between Human and Ancestor, between Body and Spirit. My relationships with my sister and my dad live on. Which also means, for better or for worse, that unless we keep healing, the old wounds will keep festering. We'll just keep showing up, making the same mistakes over and over again. This book is my prayer that we stop making the same mistakes. That we learn to forgive each other. The prayer won't work without an audience, so thank you for joining me on this ambitious journey. I promise you won't be disappointed.

DEDICATION

Rᴇʙᴇᴄᴄᴀ. Becky. Becca. I called her Bec. She was my sister. Younger than me in age but always so much older.

I knew my sister for twenty-nine years. And yet I only really knew her for a few weeks one winter before she died. There is an openness that comes with proximity to death. And that openness showed me that, in spite of all the ways I thought we were so different, we were the same in every way that mattered.

I have heard that twins often feel like they are sharing one extended body. Sometimes one twin will spontaneously cry when the other is harmed, as if it is their own body that is being violated. As a child, this is how my sister felt; she felt everything around her, as if the world was an extension of her body. My mom used to say that my sister refused to accept "time-outs" and would throw herself against the door, wailing, unable to accept the separation. When our parents got divorced and my dad left the house, my sister was so distraught that she climbed up on the kitchen table and just stood there, screaming. As an adult, she always claimed that she couldn't remember anything from our childhood. But I have to believe her body remembered.

I met a psychiatrist once who insisted that there was a reason that my sister got cancer and I didn't. And I said, "Yeah, 'cuz she has the genetic mutation, and I don't." And he said, "No. Trauma." I was pissed at him for saying this, not knowing us at all. But it made me wonder. What was it like to go your whole life feeling every single thing around you? What happens to the body when it's always absorbing the pain of others? What happens when you can't remember?

Although my sister and I were not close in a conventional sense, I always felt like she belonged to me, in the way that I still believe my children belong to me (though I know they're just on loan). During one of our final conversations in the hospital, I got up the nerve to tell my sister how sorry I was that we spent so many years apart, sorry that I could never show her how much I truly loved her. And she said, simply, "It's OK. We love deeply." Which kind of reminds me of how mushrooms are connected to each other, deep underground, through an invisible woven net.

My sister and I spent a lot of our lives fighting. There were times I thought we might never speak again. But she saved my life at least once. And now, there is a part of me that lives on the other side. Other side of what? I still don't know. But that's where my sister is. When I gave the eulogy at her funeral, her daughter reminded me, "Mommy will hear everything you say, you know." And I hope she still can. This one's for you, Bec.

MIDNIGHT WATER

☾

A Psychedelic Memoir

CHAPTER 1

❨

One Missing

When I am rowing you across a dark and bottomless lake
to the shores of another world,
we shall look back on these next few moments and laugh.

—MATT ADRIAN

M Y SISTER came to visit me in Baltimore about a week after completing her first round of chemotherapy. This was a big deal because she never came to visit me. And even this time, she only came because there was some business conference downtown that she had to attend. But it was an even bigger deal because of how shitty she felt. We had been texting and calling every once in a while during her treatment, and she seemed to be toughing it out OK. So I was unprepared for how sick and exhausted she would be when she arrived. She told me it was basically like having a terrible hangover every single day for months. And yet, when we went out for dinner that first night, she chose a killer red mini-dress and high heels, and ditched her wig. I had never seen a bald woman get whistled at before.

I was still living in Baltimore two years later when I knew my sister was going to die. I had just gotten back from my first silent meditation retreat, and the world was still all sparkly and swirly and bursting with extra color, like Van Goghs' *Starry Night*. I remember the date—12/12/12—because everyone had been joking about it being the end of the world. My husband, John, and I decided to go out to one of our favorite neighborhood restaurants in case the world did actually end, and in the middle of my meal I suddenly looked up and said, "I have to go to New York. She's gonna die." This wasn't a rational thought, not a careful analysis of her new symptoms alongside the doctor's prognosis. Just a sudden, obtrusive ping from the Universe. At that time, everyone was still pretending/hoping/claiming she would be OK. No one had even said out loud that the cancer had definitely come back. But I knew. And I was on a train the next morning.

She had been having trouble breathing for maybe a week or so when she finally stopped by a local ER because she couldn't walk up a flight of stairs. She thought she had bronchitis or pneumonia or something. They scanned her lungs and freaked and sent her by ambulance to the cancer hospital in New York where she had been going for her oncology follow-ups. It took them days to run all the tests and scans they needed to confirm what had suddenly made my sister so sick. Everyone was dumbfounded because her workup from earlier in the fall had shown no sign of cancer. She was only a couple months away from getting the green light—three years cancer free—which means, you're cured.

I got to my sister's hospital room just in time for a sweet, young female doctor to come in and announce that her cancer levels were "very high." Both my sister and her husband broke down in tears, hugging each other, while I just stared out the window at the twinkling lights along the East River, floating slightly above my body like I had been practicing my whole life. My sister said, "I need to know. Are we talking weeks, months or years?"

The doctor was definitely caught off guard by the question but quickly reassured her, "No, no, no. Definitely not weeks or months."

Temporarily satisfied with this answer, my sister sent me and her husband home and said she'd be fine on her own.

We were in shock the whole drive. Rebecca and Ryan had just bought a beautiful home in Connecticut, one town over from my mom, so that Rebecca could start her new position as Director of Operations at the Subway headquarters. The house had a ton of bedrooms, and it seemed like they were ready to try for more kids. They had both always dreamed of a big family, and one of the more practical things my sister had managed to do before her cancer treatment began was freeze her eggs. It felt unnecessarily cruel that the cancer would come back right then, right when they were ready to start their new life.

Ryan went back to the hospital early the next morning and I stayed home with their daughter, my niece. Anya and I had always had a special bond, and she was at least as into magic and mystery as I was. As her godmother, I was allegedly in charge of her spiritual upbringing, but Ryan always used to admonish me, "no mushrooms, OK?" It was easy to forget about everything that was happening back at the hospital, and just immerse ourselves in our fantasy world. We jumped on the trampoline and hiked around the woods and drank hot chocolate. Later that afternoon, I played her a video from her mom, singing, "I'm coming home, coming home, tell my girl I'm coming home." And this four-year-old looks at me, reaching toward me to hold my cheeks in her tiny hands, and says,

"I can't wait to see the smile on mom's face when she sees her sister is here."

On Christmas Eve morning, I accompanied Bec to the hospital for her pre-op appointment. A few days later she would be getting her ovaries removed, which the doctors thought would halt this new round of rapid disease progression. Hardly anyone was there, and the appointment went much smoother and faster than she was used to. She seemed calm, and I thought we weren't going to get a better chance, just the two of us, so I decided to ask her about her end-of-life wishes.

"I can't think about that right now," she said. "I'm leaving everything up to Ryan.

"Well, what about after life?" I pressed. "Do you have any fears or hopes or anything?"

And she snapped back, "As long as Ryan and Anya are happy, I don't care if I end up in hell."

Her response shocked me in its decisiveness and supreme selflessness. I had been agonizing about my own end-of-life for years now, and I definitely didn't trust someone else to decide for me. Up until that moment, I had suspected that my sister was a superhero, but now I thought she might actually be a saint.

Later that evening, we were sitting around laughing about how Anya had told her mom to stop sleeping on the couch so that Santa would come. Rebecca's cough had gotten so bad that she had taken to sleeping downstairs so that she wouldn't wake anyone. And Rebecca and I were both joking about needing nebulizers now, her for her cancer and me for my asthma that had gotten so bad in Baltimore.

"Well, I guess this is Dad's gift that keeps on giving, huh?" I said.

And Rebecca, seeing that Ryan and John didn't understand the full picture, explained, "You guys don't understand. Kath had such bad asthma and allergies growing up, but Dad refused to get rid of his cat. And he smoked all the time. She couldn't even breathe! Can you imagine doing that to your own child? He's the most selfish person I've ever met." I felt my heart swell with sadness and pride. So, she did remember. She was the only person in the world who really knew what it was like.

Thankfully, Santa did come, and my sister somehow managed to host the extended family for Christmas dinner (see: earlier remark about superhero status). As a Christmas present to everyone, my dad decided to plan a family vacation to the Florida Keys in January, I guess hoping that we could squeeze it in before Rebecca had to start chemo again. John and I stayed until the day after her surgery, and when all seemed as good as it was going to get, headed back to Baltimore.

We weren't home for long before I got the text from my sister: "Feels like I'm suffocating. Nebulizer not working. Going back to hospital." Despite finding numerous tumors in her ovaries, lymph nodes, and lungs, the doctors didn't seem sufficiently concerned about the breathing difficulties. Her oncologist insisted she still had "years, not months." They diagnosed her with pneumonia and gave her antibiotics and some oxygen, and suggested that, since she was already back in the hospital, she could start the next round of chemo. This is when everything went quickly downhill.

After all these years, it's still difficult to accept that my sister's life could have been extended, or at the very least improved, if she had had the right information. If she knew she was facing the final weeks of her life, she might have chosen to go on that Florida vacation with her daughter, or at least go home and enjoy time with her friends and family. But the doctors had her believing that she still had years left to live. Like, let's just get through this next round of chemo and you'll be good to go! My mom and I always suspected that the chemo was the thing that finally put her body over the edge. It took all that remained of her life force. But ultimately, this is just what cancer does. Cancer almost always wins.

I arrived at the hospital to find my mom sitting at the foot of my sister's bed, nervously looking through a newspaper. The mood in the room was tense. The woman who shared the room was equally young, but in even more dire straits than my sister. From what we could gather, her cancer had spread to her spinal cord, and she was in so much pain she could barely sleep. I saw her later that night, roaming the hallways, delirious with insomnia. Whenever her husband would call, she kept talking about the meeting she was supposed to have with "the pain team." All of this was just annoying background chatter; I couldn't even bring myself to empathize with what this woman was going through. I didn't realize that "pain team" meant palliative care, and that she was dying. It didn't register that the arguments with her husband on the phone were about whether her kids would be allowed to come up to visit her, or whether she would have to make the shameful, and painful, journey down to the main waiting area on the ground floor. We didn't know it at the time, but we were about to step into this very same reality. But for now, it was someone else's problem. Cancer wards are a peculiar version of survival of the fittest. Each person is just trying to get through the day, and then the next day, and then the day after that until they are out. Or until they die. You can't waste your energy worrying about your roommate.

But all that background chatter seemed to help change my sister's perspective on important conversations. Or maybe she had finally started to fit all the pieces together. Because she was suddenly very open to having that end-of-life talk I had tried to initiate before Christmas. She was the primary breadwinner in the family, so she was very concerned about finances. She wanted to make sure her husband and daughter would be taken care of, and I assured her that between her life insurance policy and Dad, we could figure out the financial piece. "What else?" I asked. "Can you tell me more about your hopes for Anya?" And she said: "I've always tried to give her a perfect life. If I could just see her through high school graduation, you know?" And I said, "What. So she can be a shit to you the way you were to mom?" And she laughed, because she knew it was true. And then she said, "It's just crazy. We should be doing this when we're eighty." And I replied, "Yeah, but if I were eighty years old, I wouldn't be nearly as helpful as I am now."

It was getting late, but I wasn't sure how to leave. I asked Rebecca if I could hold her hand, the way I had been trained to do in the psilocybin sessions at Hopkins. I was surprised by how much grief and love welled up as I sat there. And then she said, "I love you. It's OK for you to leave." And in my mind, I decided that, from here on out, leaving was an affirmation, an agreement: "Let's do this again tomorrow." I thought to myself, "I'll know it's the end when I can't leave."

John arrived in true heroic fashion the next day with the only food my sister agreed to eat: mac n' cheese from the diner around the corner. She'd barely had a meal in days because of the chemo effects, but after the mac n' cheese miracle she finally got some of her energy back. We sat around joking and chatting. She even agreed to try a guided meditation with us, as the resident hospital musician strummed her guitar while I played the xylophone. I guess John and I were used to this sort of thing from hippie festivals, but I know it was way beyond my sister's comfort zone. I had asked her a bunch of times if she was open to trying mushrooms, or at least low-dose MDMA, and she just could not be bothered. If it didn't cure her, it was a waste of time.

My dad and brother came to visit the next day. Ed was only in high school, and Dad clearly had not prepared him for how sick Rebecca was. Rebecca later told me Ed was in total shock when he walked in the room. So my sister sent my dad for pizza and basically explained the whole family cancer situation to Ed. "There's a genetic mutation that I have and Dad has and one day, when you're ready, you should get tested too, to make sure you don't have it. It's really important. Don't listen to what Dad tells you about it."

Actually, she was only inferring our dad's status, because he had refused to get tested. When our uncle got breast cancer in his early fifties, he explained to the docs that his father and grandma had died of the same disease. So they suggested he get a blood test for the major genetic mutations that had been linked to breast cancer. At the time, no one really understood whether male breast cancer was related to female breast cancer, and many of the doctors were still learning about all the mutations. But my uncle did the right thing, got screened, and when he received his positive result, shared it with his siblings and recommended that they all get tested, too. My dad was the only one who refused.

But then his daughter got diagnosed with Stage 3 breast cancer at twenty-six and tested positive for the exact same mutation as our uncle, so I guess my dad couldn't really pretend anymore. I remember sitting with Rebecca in her post-op room after her double mastectomy. She was disoriented from the pain meds and kept asking for Dad. When he finally came in, she pulled her robe down to her hips, exposing her bandaged chest and just said, "Look. Look." Her chest was so flat, it made her seem like a prepubescent child. If she could have, she might have pulled all the bandages off, too, to make him look at the scars. I felt her saying, "Don't look away. You have to see what you've done."

I know it seems harsh to hold the man accountable for his genes. It's not like he chose them or anything. But if he had gotten tested when my uncle first shared his results, then my sister could have gotten tested too. You see, having a grandfather and an uncle with breast cancer isn't a "good enough" reason to screen a healthy woman in her early twenties, but having a father with a confirmed BRCA2 mutation, now THAT was compelling to the healthcare industry. And if she had been tested even six months earlier, they might have discovered the tumor at Stage 1, or 2. Heck, maybe they could've gotten to her before the tumor started growing at all. And I'm almost certain that those test results would've made her country bumpkin doctor take her more seriously when she first showed him the lump, rather than dismissing her concerns because she was "too young" to get breast cancer. She might have still lost her breasts, but she could've been cancer free. She could still be alive today. My dad never saw it that way. To this day, I don't know what went on in his head, refusing to know his status. I even found some paperwork in his desk after he died, about getting screened for various genetic mutations linked to both breast and lung cancer. He never followed through.

As for me, I got the test as soon as I found out my sister was positive. Luckily, I had just started my job at Hopkins, which came with great health insurance and access to a world class breast and ovarian screening program for families with cancer. There was no doubt in my mind that I wanted to know my status, especially before I had kids. If I was positive, I don't think I would have taken the chance of potentially passing the gene to my children. I remember talking about it with my new mentor, right before getting on the bus to go up to New York for my sister's surgery. "Well, if I'm positive, I'll probably just adopt," I said. "You know, it's a 50/50 chance. It's not worth the risk."

The day after my dad and brother's awkward visit was the last good day of my sister's life. We had been planning to bring her daughter in for a visit, but that night, her heart rate shot up and Ryan had to race back to the hospital. She was moved to a private room and given a morphine drip, because the normal pain meds were just not cutting it. So John and I were left to get Anya ready in the morning, which neither of us knew how to do. Luckily, she agreed to let John do her hair and had a dress already picked out, one that would match the character in the musical we were going to see before heading to the hospital. My sister had coordinated the whole day so that Anya would only remember it as a fun trip to the city.

The hospital visit was like a rocket launch. We had to time it exactly so that my sister wouldn't be zonked out on her meds, and Anya wouldn't fall asleep in the car, and none of the security guards would notice and prevent us from bringing a child into the patient wing. As we walked quietly and quickly through the corridors, I held Anya close to my chest and whispered in her ear about where we were and what we were doing. She was so serious and attentive.

When we got to the waiting area, I was shocked to see Rebecca sitting up, bright-eyed, perfect ponytail, no IV. She was putting on the best show she possibly could for her daughter. She still couldn't get by without oxygen, so Anya was nervous at first, wanting to know what that big tank was next to mommy. But she eventually relaxed, and they sat there eating ice cream together out of one of those little cardboard cups with the tiny spoons. It was the sweetest, most heartbreaking thing. And I was just in awe of my sister, laughing, keeping the mood light, never once betraying how deathly ill she was. After maybe fifteen minutes or so, Anya walked her mom back to her room and left her a drawing of a rainbow, with the words, "I love you" scrawled over the top.

On the drive back to Baltimore, I looked at John and said, "What's the best day in the history of the world?"

He said, "What, I don't know."

And I replied, "Today."

I was only in Baltimore for two days before my sister asked me to come back. Her anxiety was getting worse, and she didn't trust the meds that the psychiatrist was giving her. She sent me a photo of one—Haldol—which is an antipsychotic tranquilizer used for schizophrenic patients.

"Do they think I'm crazy?" she said on the phone. "Kath, I need you here. You have to talk to the doctors. They won't tell me what's going on."

I found her in her hospital bed, face flushed, frantically picking at the navy-blue gel nail polish on her fingers. She looked like she had just run a marathon.

"Are you OK?" I asked.

And she said, "I'm freaking out. My heart rate is so high, all the time. I can't find a focal point."

I did the only thing I knew would help in that moment, which was go find a nail salon that would give me a tiny bit of the chemical solution that would get that stupid nail polish off.

As I gently swabbed her fingers, she started to relax. "I want you to talk to my oncologist tomorrow," she said. "I have a lot of questions that they're not answering. It's some guy I haven't met before. My real doctor won't even come to meet with me. Everyone is acting like the chemo will start working any day now, but something doesn't feel right."

I stayed with her all afternoon and into the night. Normally, they kick visitors out around 10 P.M., but the rules on this floor seemed different. My sister asked if I would help her take a walk, with her IV and oxygen tank wheeling next to her. And as we slowly made our way past the other rooms, it was pretty obvious that no one on this floor was doing well. It took a bit of sleuthing, but we finally figured out that she was back in the ICU. If they thought she was going to die, why wouldn't they tell her?

After a few laps, I said, "It's getting late, Bec. You should try to get some sleep. I need to go." I was still in a bit of denial myself and was planning to go meet some friends who were in town for a meditation conference. And this was the first night I saw that look in her eyes, like when a kid knows there's a monster under their bed and can't figure out why their parents are acting like it's no big deal. What? So you're just gonna leave me here to get eaten alive?

Her eyes pleaded with me, "Please don't go; don't go."

"But I have to—remember? If I stay, it's because you're going to die."

The next day, my sister's husband and I finally corralled the oncologist into a formal meeting, to go over the questions my sister had about her treatment. He kept perseverating on the median response time for the current round of chemo, which was three and a half months. As far as I could tell, there was no way, given my sister's current state, that she was making it to three and a half months. But there was also no way to get the doctor to admit this, so we had to get creative. I showed him a video I had taken of my sister sleeping and said, "She's an athlete, you know. She's really struggling to breathe, even with the oxygen. Even when she's asleep. Can you show us the most recent scan of her lungs?"

His voice started shaking as he pulled up the scan and said, "As you can see, there are tumors throughout her lungs. They are ... too numerous to count." And then he said, "In New York State, the patient needs to have their wishes in writing, regarding things like life support and resuscitation. Do I think it's too early to get that paperwork and other legal affairs in order? No." Ah, so now we're getting somewhere.

I persisted, "Under what conditions will she be dead in a week?"

After the initial shock passed, he said, "Well, I don't have a crystal ball. I'm an eternal optimist."

I interrupted, "Well, that's lovely. But under what conditions will she be dead in a week?"

"OK," he said.

And the answer he supplied sounded like he was reading out of his med school textbook: "Ummmm, she could get an infection, or she could experience a pulmonary embolism, which would be rare in someone so young, or the cancer could metastasize to her brain, where the chemo can't work." None of his conditions included the reality that was staring him straight in the face: the cancer had already taken over her lungs and would suffocate her to death in a matter of days.

I didn't have to tell Bec what the doctor said. I could see it in her eyes; she knew it was over. I said, "You know, Bec, if you still want to go home, we can get you home. Just say the word."

"But what if something happens? I don't want Anya to have to see that," she said.

So we managed to get Anya into the hospital for one more visit, but Rebecca was so exhausted she could barely keep her eyes open. They mostly just snuggled together in her hospital bed. As Anya walked out the door, she confidently proclaimed, "Bye, Mommy! I'll see you next weekend!" and never looked back.

In the waiting room, she told me, "Mommy was so tired she could only half-smile. But I know she was smiling in her heart."

A few hours later, I received a text from my mom. On the drive home, Anya had made her pull over to take a picture of the sunset to send to mommy back at the hospital. Then, when they got back to the house, Anya happily reported that "mommy's hospital bed" had arrived and she could come home now. But it was too late. The delirium had already set in.

John and I stayed with Rebecca the whole night. She was anxious and paranoid and now even I was struggling to find a focal point. It was like we were trapped in some unending bad acid trip. We tried taking a walk to the patient "rec center," but it felt like a low-budget psych ward. They tried to make it cheerful, but it felt more like prison. This creepy feeling slowly worked its way through my body: we were guiding my sister on her death march through enemy territory, through some highly sanitized version of hell. There was no way out. No way back to the dark night sky or the cold winter air or water or trees. Her sacred body, born of the stars and Earth, loved into life, would be sacrificed on this altar of modern medicine; she would become just another statistic.

Back in her room, we tried everything to help her relax. We turned on the nature documentary, *Blue Planet*—no good. I tried the Hopkins psilocybin playlist—terrible. My period had been late, again, and I even thought about lying and telling her I was pregnant, because she was always so excited for me to become a mom. Anything to make her smile and ease her mind. But nothing worked. None of the meds even helped anymore. I was getting a very quick lesson in how absolutely abysmal end-of-life care is in our medical system. And just when we had given up hope, my sister's guardian angel managed to sneak through the gates of hell to help us.

Leo arrived early Sunday morning before his shift ended to see how Rebecca was doing. (Dear Reader, please note that some names have been changed throughout the book. When you first encounter a new name in italics, that means it's a pseudonym. All other names are real). Leo was a visiting doctor-in-training and had taken a keen interest in my sister's case. He kept going out of his way to check on her and really listen to her questions. He challenged the oncologist when he didn't think the treatment plan was adequate. And when the anti-nausea meds weren't helping, he gave my sister a green vial of some experimental herbal treatment they were testing back at his home hospital. It smelled of pine needles and was strangely soothing. (I still carry that bottle with me. I think it's actually a magic potion, and there's no way in hell I'm gonna be caught dead without it.) We didn't know until afterward, but Leo had been working hard to get my sister transferred to the palliative care team. But the oncologists couldn't accept their failure, so they wouldn't approve the transfer. He could easily see what they wouldn't: she was dying, quickly.

Leo immediately assessed that things were rapidly devolving. We had a quick conference outside her room. "Her sodium levels are really low," he explained. "She's losing lucidity, which means that soon, she won't be considered competent to make her own healthcare decisions. If she stops breathing, we have to resuscitate her, and initiate life support. We don't have a choice, unless her wishes and a DNR order have been documented." "Oh, shit," I said. "This is what the other doctor was talking about. We never got that paper signed." And Leo said, "As her doctor, I can testify to her wishes, as long as she can say out loud what she wants. I'll take care of it."

He went back in her room, just the two of them. And when he came out, he said, "She confirmed. She doesn't want to be resuscitated. I'll update her chart." And I suddenly felt like someone was on our side. The gate was open, we were going through!

Spiritually speaking, things started to move rather quickly after that. I don't remember who made the phone calls, but suddenly the whole family was spilling into Rebecca's tiny hospital room. My mom ran to her side and said, "Oh, Rebecca, you were always so good. Don't worry. Gram's here to help." My mom later told me that when she walked in the room, she saw her mother, my gram, who had been dead for over ten years, and a bunch of other people she didn't recognize gathered around my sister. In my mother's vision, my gram kept shaking her head, "No, no, no! It can't be Rebecca!" And my mom told her, "Yes, it's Rebecca. You have to help her across."

In the midst of the flurry of final goodbyes, my sister announced, "OK, I'm ready to go. I trust you guys. I'm not worried at all." And then she looked at me and said, "I want her!" and grabbed me, pulling me so close I was practically laying on top of her. My mouth was right next to her right ear, and she said, "Describe it." And I suddenly realized that I had really, really screwed up.

I had first heard about the *Tibetan Book of the Dead* when I was a grad student working on a big meditation study in the Rocky Mountains of Colorado. It was a guidebook for lay (non-monastic) Buddhists on how to navigate the bardos, or the stages of transition of consciousness after death. According to this book, if you manage to follow the instructions, you can be enlightened on the spot, even if you've never meditated a day in your life. But most dying people are so bewildered by fear and confusion that they forget the instructions as soon as they get close to death. So the book clearly states that you're supposed to have a calm, neutral, experienced practitioner nearby to recite the instructions in your ear and keep reminding you what you're supposed to be doing. I had studied this text and contemplated it and wondered to myself a thousand times, "What will it be like when I die? Will I recognize the bardos? Will I be able to choose my next life?" It had never occurred to me that I would need to recite the instructions for someone else, least of all my extremely non-Buddhist, anti-psychedelic, couldn't-give-a-shit about New Age spirituality sister. And I had forgotten the damn guidebook. I didn't even have the version that had been adapted back in the '60s to guide psychedelic sessions.

Then a lightbulb went off. I had just been to a Zen center. And every day and night, we would recite a million prayers, called sutras, in both Japanese and English. Out of all those recitations, I remembered the four words used to describe the awakened mind. So, I took a chance. I said into my sister's ear, "Your only job is to look for the clear light. Become one with it. Do not be distracted. You will recognize it when you see it. You cannot mistake it. It is *eternal, intimate, pure, and joyful.* You're gonna live forever, Bec." "Wow," she replied. "That sounds great."

By evening, everyone had gone home except me, John and my mom. We had booked a hotel room across the street, but we all stayed with Rebecca in her room instead. The doctors had finally agreed to increase her morphine, and between that and the full oxygen mask, she was able to get some sleep. The night was quiet and calm. We had her favorite opera music playing, and walking into her room felt like stepping into a small chapel for midnight mass on Christmas Eve.

For most of those peaceful hours, John and I held her hands and meditated next to her. My mom slept on and off in the recliner chair in the corner. Then, sometime around two or three in the morning, something shifted, and I knew she was about to die. I started to hear her heartbeat as if it were my own, echoing in my mind, and then that sound became a rapid drumbeat, like you would hear at a carnival right before the daredevil gets shot out of a canon. I closed my eyes and saw a dark lake at twilight. A murmuration of swallows came swooping down from one corner of my vision and continued their flight path out across the lake. And I knew she was headed to the other shore. "That's it, Bec, you can do it. Just let go," I remember thinking to myself. I saw Death like a soft, billowing curtain coming down over her face.

She had been completely asleep, but suddenly she shook her head and tried to turn away, as if she could feel this fabric of death brushing up against her face. She sat up in bed and shifted her body into a kind of royal posture, as if sitting on a throne, with one leg outstretched and the other tucked underneath her. In a graceful, purposeful way, she extended both of her hands until her arms lay one on top of each thigh, her palms turned upward toward the ceiling. The air took on the iridescent, fractal quality I remembered from so many mushroom trips. It looked like there were delicate, sparkling threads connecting every single object in the room, and us. And with that oxygen mask on her face and the tube coming down from it, my sister kind of looked like an elephant. And then I really saw her. Or him, I guess I should say.

Ganesha. Great Hindu deity. Remover of obstacles. Likes to hang out in the charnel grounds and help souls navigate the afterlife. He was so beautiful when he was born that his father, Shiva, got jealous and cut off his head, and when his mother, Parvati, found out, she went into a rage and made Shiva replace it. So he killed an elephant and stuck that head on his son's body. Ganesha, the great elephant-headed god. This deity sure knew a lot about family trauma, and difficult fathers.

Of course, I didn't know any of this at the time; I had to look it up later. I just knew what Ganesha told me. "I'm your sister, and I'm dying. But I'm also a supreme deity who's been meditating in bliss since beginningless time. It's cool." And I looked at John, still calmly meditating. And my mom, sleeping in the corner. And then back at my sister/Ganesha. Let me tell you, it's quite a strange thing to realize you've lived your whole life with a deity as your sibling. No wonder she always seemed super-human.

As miraculously as the vision appeared, it dissolved again.

And my sister's eyes popped open, and she said, out loud, "Not yet."

Selfishly, I wish she had decided to die that night. It would have been way more peaceful than the horror show that unfolded over the next 24 hours. But she had unfinished business.

If Sunday was all about letting go, Monday was all about fighting. Mostly fighting with the oncology team to withdraw her from all her medications and hand her over to palliative care. The rage was palpable.

When my sister's oncologist finally came to say goodbye—which was also the first time she had bothered to pull herself away from her office work in two full weeks—I almost threw her against the wall. She walked in as if she owned the place, "Hello. I'm your sister's doctor. I don't think we've met." And before I could kill her or she could reach out to touch Rebecca's hand, Ryan deftly escorted her out. "Don't you dare touch her," I thought. "She doesn't belong to you. Get the fuck out."

But it wasn't just fighting the doctors. An epic battle of wills was underway between my sister and my dad. When he first entered my sister's room that morning, I could see her whole body tense up with adrenaline. It wasn't like she was preparing to defend herself, it was more like she was trying to pretend everything was normal, that she wasn't actually that sick. She couldn't let my dad see her vulnerable. I could see how uncomfortable she was as he held her hand and sang to her. She was just as skilled at putting up walls as he was, and she refused to let him in. She even tried to take off her oxygen mask, to show him how fine she was. But I knew from a very close call the previous night that her oxygen levels would plummet within thirty seconds of having the mask off.

I reached in between them to put the mask back on, trying

my best to mediate this stand-off. But it blew up in my face. My dad pushed my hand away and said, "She's fine." I said, "Dad, you need to tell her it's OK to let go." And he stormed out of the room. I found him in the family waiting area, looking up funeral homes on the internet, in full-blown aggressive work mode. I said, "Dad, what's going on in there has nothing to do with me or you. It's not personal." And he snapped back, "She's just trying to control her environment." The whole day he kept telling her to keep fighting—the way people always tell cancer patients to fight their disease—oblivious that this was indeed the final battle of the war she'd been waging with him her whole life.

I knew this was important for both of them, but I hated seeing it play out. So, John and I left and took a long walk along the East River. "This is torture," I cried. "I can't take it anymore. I can't watch her do this! I don't even care if I'm there when she dies." Back at the hotel, I fell into a fitful sleep. By the time I woke up, I was distraught, literally screaming, "Who's with her? Is she OK?" I asked John to go back to the hospital to make sure she was OK, and called my old mentor from grad school, the one who had led that big meditation study. And his calm, humorous voice immediately broke through my spiral of grief.

Cliff was a caricature of a rational, logical scientist, and he worked way too much to have time for real meditation; he always joked that his daily meditation was his two-hour commute. But he was one of the most self-accepting, jovial people I had ever met. Sure, he could get frustrated and stressed out, but that was mostly around grant writing deadlines and lab work. In regular life, he was a wise, contented soul. He was one of my best friends, and like a surrogate father. And Cliff was the one who finally explained the morphine protocol.

"They've got her on a morphine drip, right? OK, listen. We did this with my mom," he said. "There's a whole procedure."

And I felt like he was letting me in on some big, well-kept secret in the medical field. His voice was slow and measured as he went on, "Morphine is prescribed for pain and for trouble breathing. Now that the palliative care team is in charge of her care, you can request palliative sedation, which is just a constant, high dose of morphine rather than the drip." "But here's the important part," he continued, "Once that's in place, they can only increase the morphine dose if she's having trouble breathing or seems like she's in pain." And he didn't have to explain any further. I knew exactly where he was going. "I got it," I said. "Jesus Christ, this changes everything. We can do this."

I threw on the outfit I always wore for psilocybin sessions at Hopkins, including a hand-made beaded necklace with a special Hindu seed that hung at the center of my chest, directly over my heart. Maggie, the study coordinator at Hopkins, had made it for me for my wedding, and it became like a magical, mystical, good luck charm in all of my sessions after that. Just as I was about to head back to the hospital, my mom came in. She had brought me dinner, and said, softly, "Rebecca really needs you. She's having a hard time. I think this is it." And I ate that sandwich like it was my last meal before execution.

My heart pounded as I walked through the whipping wind across the street to the hospital. I knew at a rational level that it was my sister who was dying, but at a deeper level, it felt like I was going to die too. I remembered this feeling from my Zen retreat, and from so many psychedelic trips. The Katherine who walks into that room will not be the same Katherine who walks out. And I also wondered about the woman I was about to encounter. My sister, Rebecca. But also, a woman who had suddenly remembered she needed Tibetan death instructions. Maybe also a deity. I was so inexperienced; I had just been stumbling along, looking for answers, hoping for some relief from the endless parade of death anxiety and psychotic fantasies. How could I help her get through this final threshold? Could it really be as easy as they said? Maybe there was nothing any of us needed to do. Just be with her. Bear witness. Trust that something greater, and more mysterious, was coming.

I found Ryan as soon as I arrived and explained the morphine protocol. And this wave of relief went over his face when he realized there was a dignified, peaceful way out. Then I went to find the head palliative care doctor. She was a petite, warm Indian woman, and when we first met, she noticed the mala beads around my wrist and joked, "I don't know much about the Buddha, except that he came from my country." When she and her team took over, it was like night and day from the confusion and fear that surrounded the oncology team. Her peaceful, serene energy filled the room and I said to myself, *Finally, the professionals have arrived. Where have you been all my life?*

I chose my words carefully. I knew that she knew about the morphine protocol. And I also knew that according to her oath as a doctor, she couldn't do anything that she believed would hasten death. So I said, "Doctor. My sister has been in a lot of pain and distress all day. She almost died last night. She keeps saying she wants it to be easy. She's coughing up blood, and it's really hard for her to breathe, even with the oxygen mask. As her health proxies, her husband and I would like to request palliative sedation."

"I've been keeping a close eye on your sister all day," the doctor said. "She's amazingly strong; she must have a very high pain threshold. I think it was important for her to remain awake enough to see her friends and family who came by earlier. But now, we are in the final hours. I think your assessment is correct. Of course, it's up to you, and her wishes. But if you believe that she's ready, we can get everything set up."

And then it was time for our final goodbye. The same opera music—Jackie Evancho—had been on repeat for two days, but it didn't match the current mood in the room. Rebecca was frantic with pain and kept trying to get out of bed. It took all of Ryan's strength just to hold her down.

"Let me try," I said. And as I sat on the edge of her bed and wrapped my arms around her.

She recognized me as her sister, and said, "Kath, you know it's me, right? They'll know it's me," like she was on some VIP list to Heaven and just needed the bodyguards to get the heck out of the way so she could make it through the door.

And I said, "Honey, I know it's you. But you gotta stay in bed. This is all gonna be over real soon." And I held her, the way you would hold a child who's just woken from a nightmare, stroking her back, saying "It's OK. It's OK. You're safe."

To this day, I can still smell the sweet baby-like fragrance of sweat and urine on her body, feel her breath on the bare skin of my cheek and shoulder. She had taken over my entire mind, my whole heart. I felt her love, her life force, just flowing into me, like a channel. Her frequency was high and clear; just pure, unadulterated love. I had no idea it was possible to love someone this much. With her mouth only inches away from my ear, she said, "Listen. Listen." And I briefly registered the song that was playing in the background before she pushed me away and threw herself into Ryan's arms.

It was hard to tell if she was wrestling him to get out of her way or trying to hug him as she finally screamed, "You guys have to let me go!" And we thought she was still trying to make her escape, but Ryan said, "Alright. Alright." and released her and stepped back from her bed. And she just sat there. A few moments ticked by. Right. We have to let her go.

The morphine protocol was like a football play. Ryan had been a star player and head coach back in Vermont, so he knew the drill. A nurse would come in to check on us every twenty minutes or so, and each time the nurse would ask, "How does she seem?" And Ryan and I would take turns saying, "Her respiration seems a little fast" or "Her heart rate seems high" or "She's moaning a bit, I think she's still in pain." And each time, when we said those magic words, they would increase the morphine. At one point, my dad was there for one of the check-ins, and when they asked how she seemed, he said, "She seems fine." And Ryan and I both looked at each other and communicated telepathically, "No, Richard. That's not the protocol!" and laughed. The mood in the room was light-hearted and pleasant. Just before we invited the family in for the final vigil, Ryan looked at her with his eyes beaming, just so in awe and in love, and said, "She's so fucking tough. Look at her. I can just hear her saying, 'Go ahead. Keep giving me morphine. Hit me with your best shot. I'm gonna go when I'm ready.'"

My sister released her final breath just after midnight. It felt purposeful, like she had waited for everyone in the room to give her permission to die. Ryan and I bet that my dad was the last holdout. They called the attending doctor, Leo, her guardian angel, and he came all the way from his home to be the one to pronounce her. By the time he arrived, it had been half an hour after her death, but he still went through all the formal motions of checking for her pulse and heartbeat. He was graceful and respectful, like he was blessing her body on its final voyage. He asked me, "What was the time of death?" And I said, "12:01 A.M. You know, yesterday was the holiday for MLK. I don't think she wanted to intrude on Dr. King's day." And what I thought to myself was, "Another great saint. She deserves her own day."

None of us really knew what to do after that. I removed the

soft contacts from her eyes and pushed her eyelids down. My dad cut off a lock of her hair. I had never been present for a death before, and I was shocked at how quickly she left. I knew the Buddhists always talked about it taking some time for the final energies to leave the body, but she was just . . . gone. Her body went cold and her head drooped to the side and all the color drained from her face, and she was just no longer Rebecca. But where did she go?

The hospital still felt like Mordor to me, and I hated leaving her body with the enemy. But Leo promised me he would take good care of her and would make sure she was transferred home to Connecticut as soon as possible. As we stood by the elevators, I held the pink orchid that had been with her all those days in the hospital and found myself automatically counting but coming up short. "One missing. One missing." I wasn't doing it intentionally; it was like some ancient tracking device in my brain had just turned on, some old piece of humanoid machinery from the days when we traveled as nomadic tribes through the great deserts of Africa. The tribe is too small. Someone's missing. Who's missing?

☽

Many months after my sister died, I met a former ICU nurse who had been learning a lot about psychedelics. We met for breakfast at a tiny cafe in downtown Sacramento, while John and I were back visiting friends. She was one of the first people who was able to help me process and understand what had happened with my sister in the hospital.

"It was the most important thing I've ever done in my entire life," I said. "And now it's just over. I felt this otherworldly love filling up my body, 24/7, for months after she died. And then one morning, that was gone too. I just don't think anyone understands."

She smiled and replied, "Well, you should know this from your own research. You had a mystical experience. Your sister was like your psilocybin. I've seen it happen before, but not everyone is open to it."

"It was just crazy how the oncologists were so oblivious to the fact she was dying," I continued. "But the palliative care docs were a godsend. When I met them, I thought, that's what I want to be when I grow up." Then I asked her why she left the ICU.

"It was a really hard decision," she said. "It was always an honor to be there with people as they were dying, and to support their families. It was sacred work. But I always felt like I was fighting the man. There was love literally pouring out of the walls, but I couldn't keep watching people get tortured to death."

"Yeah. I know what you mean."

I've learned a lot about intentional dying and hospice and sacred death rituals since then. I learned more about what happens to people's consciousness as they're dying. Apparently, those death-bed visions that my mom had are actually a thing, a recognized medical phenomenon; although they usually only happen to the dying person, not to the people around them. I learned more about euthanasia and was honored to meet the man who was known as the Canadian Jack Kevorkian, shortly before he underwent his own intentional death in Switzerland. I even tried to help start a psychedelic hospice once, but it didn't work out. Big business ruined it, the way it usually does. You can't commodify the sacred. It just slips through your hands. Which is probably for the best. I think that dying should be left up to regular people, not doctors and experts; we can trust people with their own death. I like the idea of helping people die the way they want to, which is usually at home, surrounded by family, and without a lot of drugs. Morphine really seems to help, though. And psychedelics can help, too, but mostly for the people who have to figure out how to keep living afterward. Which is what most of the rest of this book is about.

My sister's death was my trial by fire. I thought I knew a lot, just from sitting with people in psilocybin sessions. But I was so naive. I agonized about leaving her body, alone. For all sorts of reasons I still don't understand, she sat in a morgue in the basement of that stupid hospital for nearly a week. At the time, I didn't know that there are legal protections in all fifty states that allow you to keep your loved one's body in your home for up to three days. We can all thank our Jewish and Buddhist friends for that one. But I didn't know what I was doing. I didn't stay with her body. I didn't do the right rituals. Sure, we pulled off a beautiful funeral, but that was for us. It wasn't for her.

She kept coming to me in dreams, even entering my body. One night I woke up as her, in her hospital bed, with sharp pains in my chest, and it took real effort to re-instantiate my own consciousness into my body. Another night, I woke up convinced she was sleeping in the bed next to me, and when I reached over, knowing that the body belonged to John, all I could feel was her tiny shoulders and her bony back against the palm of my hand. I could even smell that sweet, baby fragrance that her body had taken on in the hospital.

The final night before her body was cremated, Ryan and I had a tense conversation with my dad about legal and financial issues. Rebecca hadn't left a will, so I could feel her frustration and anger pushing through as we speculated about her wishes. Well, to be clear, I felt her fighting with Dad, like always. Later that night, she showed us just how mad she was by throwing her daughter's trampoline into the woods. We woke up to find it mangled, completely destroyed, hundreds of feet away from where it had stood the previous evening. Yeah, of course the wind was strong that night. But not that strong. And who started ringing the doorbell incessantly at six in the morning? The doorbell that had never worked? It was a proper haunting, and let me tell you, I never want to piss off a dead person ever again. Also, for what it's worth, write your will. That way, no one has to risk pissing YOU off either.

Ryan did the only reasonable thing a parent should do in that situation, which was scoop up Anya and leave the house. I tried to follow, but my sister's car refused to play along. It was the first fancy car she bought herself, with no help from my dad. The Girl Rocket, she called it. It was her absolute favorite. When I went to open the driver's side door, all the doors suddenly locked. For the life of me, I couldn't get the electronic key system to grant me access. I was stuck there, alone, in her house, with the doorbell still ringing, pleading with her, "Bec, I'm so so sorry. We're doing the best we can! Can't you see we're doing the best we can?"

In all of my grief and confusion, it took me several months to finally look up which song had been playing when she begged me to listen, during our final goodbye in the hospital. And it took me years to learn that it was actually a very famous song from *Phantom of the Opera*. Those words were her final gift to me and have carried me through my darkest hours. Those words gave me the courage and the freedom to tell my story. "Love me. That's all I ask of you."

Now, it's your turn . . . Listen.

CHAPTER 2

((

Mushroom Night in Freedom

A S IT TURNS OUT, Freedom really is a place. I had stumbled upon it a few times but never felt welcome. Like Goldilocks with her perfect bowl of porridge, I had enjoyed a few bites of freedom before, but it was always somebody else's living room, and the bears were at the door. I certainly didn't believe it could be my permanent residence.

I met *Sarah* during a trek through the Himalayan mountain range of Nepal. We were on an annual medical service trip led by a famous American Zen teacher, but mostly I was there to get over my dead sister. Sarah was traveling with all her kids, and this alone seemed like a miracle to me, that a family could get along so well—could actually enjoy each other's company so much—that they would travel halfway around the globe just to spend a month in the middle of nowhere together. I was traveling that far to get away from my family, away from everything that reminded me of my past. But I was still carrying my sister.

Sarah was one of the first people on the trek who approached me in a kind and unassuming way when I first shared that my sister had died and that I was really struggling to get over it and get on with my life. Sarah wasn't a stranger to loss. Her sister had died, alone in a hospital, when Sarah was only five years old. Sarah herself had a near-death experience when she almost drowned in a river in Colorado, and she worked as a hospice chaplain in Boston. She was one of those people who just wasn't scared of anything, least of all death. But most importantly for my situation, she didn't let my initial attempts to scare her away from me work.

Sarah and I first connected over the fact that we had both shaved off our beautiful long locks before the journey began. But we really got to know each other in the "pharmacy," which was the place we stored and organized and doled out all the donated medicines and first aid supplies and surgical equipment for our temporary medical camps. Neither of us were clinicians or doctors, so it wasn't appropriate for us to be caring for patients. Although Sarah's background as a chaplain did come in handy a few times, particularly with the older women who weren't sure how to safely talk about the big challenges in their lives, including domestic abuse. The pharmacy was the only place that made sense for me to be—I knew a lot about drugs. I used to joke that based on my training, I should never be trusted around another human being except if they were on powerful psychoactive substances. Then I was the best person for the job. Honestly, though, giving other people drugs remains one of my favorite pastimes. Even on a Buddhist trip in a devoutly religious country, I couldn't resist. On the first day in the pharmacy, I offered Sarah half a Modafinil from my drug stash to try to prove I was actually cool and not just the depressed lady carrying her dead sister's ashes around.

Being in this part of Nepal just south of the Tibetan border didn't just feel like traveling back in time; it felt like space travel. Like arriving on planet Earth for the first time, pure and unadulterated, not Earth all done up with plastic and air conditioners and cars and money. We'd set up our medical camp in an empty schoolhouse or open field, our blue tents scattered across the rocky landscape, usually just beyond a nearby town that looked like it was straight out of the Middle Ages. Villagers would line up early in the morning and wait patiently to receive a shot of cortisone in their knee that would get them through another harvest, and kids would get their multivitamins and de-worming meds, and teeth would be extracted without Novocain, and the women would finally receive basic, necessary gynecological care.

I didn't realize that I had traveled to another planet until I was on my final return path. Flying from Kathmandu to Dubai is like dying and waking up in the afterlife only to realize that the Buddhist monks were definitely not correct and actually the Egyptians had it right all along and how the fuck did I forget all my gold and servants and shit? Nepal had emptied out my tomb. And I was the happiest I had ever been in my life. This emptiness was the only thing on Earth more powerful than grief. Maybe even more powerful than love.

My life before Nepal was the opposite of empty. I had been working way too many hours at my alleged dream job, and the work was so compelling and cutting edge and even fun that it was easy to be there ten, twelve hours a day, including clocking in a few hours on the weekend writing research grants and academic papers. This whole routine was awesome until it wasn't.

About a year before my sister died, I started having panic attacks and borderline-psychotic episodes. Reality started warping in a really-not-fun way. For those of you lucky folks who've never dabbled in mind-altering substances or sat a silent Zen retreat or got struck by lightning as a child and realized maybe those alien abduction stories weren't entirely made up, let me put it this way: psychedelics and the supernatural are super fun when you still believe you're the one in charge. But suddenly one day, you start to feel like maybe THEY are the ones in charge, or certainly something else is, and it doesn't really matter if you take the drugs or not, but this new reality is not going away and it doesn't really care if you believe it or not, because it's just there and it's unavoidable so what are you going to do about it? Wait until you're on your death bed to face it? Not me. I kept facing it and facing it and facing it until I found myself in the middle of an abyss with no life raft and no captain and no map for getting back. And that's right about when I heard Sarah call out, "Katherine, are you OK? I'm worried about you."

By the time Sarah and I took mushrooms together, we'd been through quite a lot. We hadn't even known each other six months, but we must have been clocking in some serious, quality time across past lives or something because the cosmic clock was ticking quite fast by the time we located each other in these current bodies. At the end of our trek, one of the young sherpas and medical translators named Tsering, a dear friend and amazing human being, drowned while saving the life of a palliative care doctor on our trip, also a dear friend and amazing human being, who had fallen into a raging river. I was the only person there when she fell in, and through the distortion filter of PTSD, I had come to accept that I was personally responsible for the young sherpa's death because I was the one who called for help. If I had just stayed silent, then he would have stayed happily sipping tea and laughing at the lodge just up the trail. But instead, I did what any decent human would do, which is call for help. And he did what only a natural hero would do: he ran to the scene of the accident and dove in and swam with the woman and kept her afloat in this crazy, slow-churning whirlpool (yes, it was an actual whirlpool), and then somehow managed to push her close enough to the riverbank so that we could pull her onto shore. But he got sucked back into the whirlpool and never came out.

The aftermath of Tsering's death was pure chaos: the Zen teacher yelling at everyone to get back on the trail; the grueling final stretch through mud and slippery rocks in the darkening night; one of the medical doctors handing out benzos to help lessen our inevitable PTSD. And Sarah, thank God, stepping up and somehow chaplain-ing our butts back to America and into our lives, which were still waiting for us dammit. Except the life I returned to seemed to be some kind of hell-on-earth carnival horror show that everyone else seemed to be enjoying but I definitely was not. If Nepal is the place of Never-ending Peace and Love, then America is A Magnificent Eden Ruined in Capitalism, Amen. All I wanted to do was stay in Nepal and leave behind my old life for good.

But they don't have mushrooms in Nepal. Well, they have them, but it's impossible to determine if anyone takes them. The monks certainly claim not to, but have you read any Tibetan scriptures? Come on. Of course they are taking all the drugs! Our trip leader, Prem, was the one who helped me bridge this cultural gap. Prem was not only a skilled mountaineer who had summited Everest, but also an amateur psychologist who had incidentally become a bit of an expert on the American mind, from leading all those treks and having to deal with annoying, hungry, out-of-shape, know-it-all Americans all the time. He was one of the few Nepalis who really understood my work, and I could tell he understood it when he said, "Americans need mushrooms, because they're so unhappy. Nepalis, we don't need them. We are already here, connected with Nature, together."

So, America had that going for it. All the drugs, that is. It's kind of simplistic and lame but I've come to decide that the best thing we have to offer the world is our drugs, including our best medicines. And for better or worse, drugs are what I dove back into when I returned.

I hadn't exactly been taking great care of myself before Nepal. There was that short period of time before my sister went into the hospital when I gave up drinking and meditated every day for at least an hour and even survived my first silent Zen retreat. I remember walking into town on the evening the retreat ended. It was Christmas time, and the shops and stands along the square were glowing and dazzling with Native American crafts and jewelry, and the church was all lit up and I thought, "My God! I've finally found the ticket to ecstasy without the Ecstasy." In that moment, I loved my family so much and could finally breathe again without wheezing (you see, trauma masquerades as all sorts of physical ailments, like chronic asthma). I felt so grateful for my moderately fucked up and very privileged life and had even forgiven my dad (or so I thought at the time). But then, of course, my sister went into the hospital, and I knew she was going to die. So, I guess that's what emptiness gives you: total clarity, which includes great joy and beauty, as well as great and unavoidable awareness of reality.

People often wonder how shamans and spiritual adepts can appear to read your thoughts and see the future, and really, it comes down to experiencing reality as it is. We often get the future, and other people's thoughts, wrong because our own totally distorted, chatterbox story is mucking up the channel. Too much noise, too little signal. But when you clean up the channel, and the background noise softens to a whisper, you momentarily think you're one of the lucky ones because wow, that signal is just so perfect and beautiful and clear and heavenly. Reality is not, in fact, about suffering! And it's not even about me! How glorious! And then you quickly realize that that clear signal now also contains the Truth, whether you like it or not. And you have to hear it.

☾

Mushrooms, like Sarah in Nepal, had walked with me through many a dark night. I wouldn't say they were the most reliable companions, but at least they told me the truth and made me laugh. But they could also be such assholes! They were the kind of friends who would trick you into walking into a cemetery at night only to hide behind a gravestone and jump out and yell, "Boo!" But they were surprising you with your worst memories. Like, "Hey! Look at this one! Did you remember THAT? Maybe that's why you hate your dad and are so mad at your boss." They didn't understand that friendship was supposed to be fun, or maybe their version of fun was just different. So instead of asking you to take a walk in the graveyard—which you have to know is a pretty spooky idea—they invite you to a party instead. You think it's gonna be fun, although your stomach is turned in knots and you say to yourself, "I'm just gonna have one drink and then leave." But before you can slip out the back door, everyone jumps out from behind the sofa and screams your worst trauma at you and throws confetti at the same time. The mushrooms think they're helping. They think this is fun. They have such a fucked up sense of humor.

People often ask me how mushrooms work, or if they can work for them. After all these years, I can say that I honestly don't know. It's always a bit of a crap shoot. But I can also say that the true magic of mushrooms is that you are creating an opening, an invitation, for dialogue with a complex intelligence that is totally alien and totally Earthly at the same time. I don't believe it's possible to fix individuals with this medicine, despite what psychedelic psychotherapists claim. I have come to learn that mushrooms work at the level of connections and relationships—in the spaces *between*. They will do their work of weaving and connecting even where you don't wish them to. They will shine a light on all the dark corners, not just the ones you picked. Sometimes, you'll get better; other times, you'll get worse. You will definitely learn and see things that you wish you hadn't. In this way, it's a lot like the path to enlightenment. You don't start down that road because you want to feel better about yourself. Or, as one of my favorite tortured authors, David Foster Wallace, once put it, "The Truth will set you free, but not until it is finished with you."

Which brings me back to Freedom. Sarah was one of the first actual adults I had ever met in my life. I had always wanted to believe adults were real like I wanted mermaids to be real. But most people between the ages of thirty-five and seventy were clearly just playing dress up with fake mermaid tails, pretending they could swim in the deep ocean while actually clawing to stay afloat and accidentally drowning anyone who came near them. Sarah was the real deal. Which made it even more confusing and happily surprising when she agreed to take mushrooms with me.

Now, being a real adult, Sarah had a lot of questions. Sarah had taken mushrooms before, when she was younger, but they weren't entirely positive experiences. This is a very common excuse I hear from grown-ups: "I already tried mushrooms; they just weren't for me." And then I come along and basically convince them to give it one last college try.

But I wanted this to be different than college, so I arranged for an honest-to-goodness shaman to meet us at Sarah's family farmhouse. Although spring was blooming just about everywhere else, New England was still socked in with mud and never-ending grayness and cold nights; in other words, mushroom weather. It reminded me of vampire-mother Morticia of the *Addams Family* proclaiming, "What a miserable night! Perfect for a seance."

The family home was perched at the top of a long, steep, dirt driveway flanked by huge hay fields and an ancient burial plot. The house appeared elegant and dignified at first glance, with its all-white exterior typical of old New England. On the inside, it was old and spooky and had many levels and tiny rooms tucked at the end of narrow hallways and creaky steps and old furniture, including a grand piano and warped mirrors, of course. It would be a real shocker if there weren't at least eight ghosts permanently residing there. Now, I would normally say that a ghost-filled location is perfect mushroom territory, but I had the feeling that these were not the kind of spirits who were fans of psychedelics. So we decided to sleep and eat and conduct the ceremony in the small caretaker's abode at the bottom of the driveway, where Sarah and her kids usually stayed when they visited the farm.

The first night, we made dinner and chatted and watched a movie called *Spirited Away*, which is a Japanese animated fantasy film about a little girl who loses her parents and has to sneak into a supernatural world to get them back. The whole time in this "bath-house for spirits," the little girl follows the advice of a sympathetic gatekeeper who tells her to focus on one goal. No matter how many times the boss lady tells her no, or she gets turned away or scared, she just states her mantra: "I'm here for a job!" Screams it if need be. Anyway, it's a fantastic movie, but maybe not the best movie to watch the night before taking mushrooms.

Between the hilltop ghosts and the bathhouse spirits, I had a hard time finding restful sleep that first night, and I was definitely feeling on edge when I woke up the next morning. Thinking back, I probably would've bailed if not for Sarah's presence. Which brings me to one of the only important pieces of advice I can offer regarding healthy psychedelic use: Choose your companions wisely. Make sure there's at least one real adult in the room and it's not you. This adult should be the kind of person who is willing to call an ambulance or put a warm blanket over you or simply break the rules of the game by speaking in the middle of the ceremony to ask if you're OK, because you definitely do not seem OK at all.

The morning of the ceremony, we attempted a short stroll up to the main house, but the weather was still crappy, and the muddy ice severely slowed our progression up the steep driveway, so this single outing didn't last long. We had a light lunch and then planned to fast until after the ceremony was over. The mushroom shaman said it was a good idea to begin just before sunset, when the veil between worlds was thin.

Wait a minute. How does one find a mushroom shaman anyway? (People are always asking me this by the way). Well, in my case, it was by accident. I met *Patrick* at a fancy dinner at the one and only board meeting I attended for the non-profit research organization that funded my psilocybin research. I was one of maybe two or three female researchers who had ever been invited to such a meeting at the time, as this group was not-so-affectionately referred to as The Boys' Club. Well, the whole psychedelic research world was basically a boys' club back then, so this distinction of being THE boys' club within the larger boys' club should give you a sense of how pleasant it was to be a young woman at this gathering. I was there to receive a privately funded research award, the first of its kind, which would be my ticket onto the faculty in the Department of Psychiatry at the Johns Hopkins University School of Medicine (sounds fancy, right?). The award would cover my salary for the next three years while I competed for an extremely small pool of public government grants. Luckily, the same wealthy benefactor who had funded the award I was receiving had also committed to funding a new long-term meditator study that I had designed and was preparing to launch later that year.

Anyway, I was all decked out in my best impress-the-hell-out-of-all-the-old-white-men-in-the-room work persona, and then I was seated next to Patrick for dinner. And all we could talk about was my dead sister and supernatural experiences. As dinner wrapped up, I remember Patrick gently touching the center of my chest, just above my heart, and saying, "Trust your experience with your sister. It's real. It's not a figment of your imagination."

I didn't know very much about Patrick when I invited him to Freedom, but I knew from our short interaction during dinner that, like Sarah, he was not afraid of death, or me. He had a real gravitas about him when he spoke about his ceremonial work. I didn't really understand what he meant when he talked about "the mushroom altar," but I somehow knew that this experience had been waiting for me for fifteen long years since I had first dabbled with mushrooms by the side of a friend's pool one warm summer night.

Patrick was very quiet during the hour or so before the ceremony began. Earlier, he had led us through an "intention-setting" exercise that neither Sarah nor I completely understood. I had lofty spiritual goals, which Patrick gently steered me away from. He said, "Your intention should be simple." The idea was to reduce your aspirations and goals into a single, short phrase that you could repeat to yourself during the experience to keep your mind on track. What came out of the exercise was the mantra I would use during the ceremony, like the girl had used in *Spirited Away*. This would be the thread I dragged behind me as I entered the labyrinth to meet the Minotaur, and it would ideally get me out again in one piece. I had never used this approach before, which, looking back, maybe explains why my mushroom experiences were so all over the place and often quite bad. No, please, don't just drag me around the room introducing me to every single person you invited to your spooky party. I'm here to see the little girl.

I had encountered this little girl only once before, during a "soul retrieval" exercise guided by a witchy hermit. In the vision, a dry, scaly, slithering rattlesnake led me into a desert cave somewhere in the American southwest, and hiding there, all curled up, was this small child, maybe three years old. She had clearly been abandoned, or maybe she intentionally ran away, but she was all alone and wanted nothing to do with me. The woman who fell in the river in Nepal had also mentioned soul retrieval when she described the process of her psychological healing after returning to the States. She had no memories from the accident, including the life-saving measures she had received on the riverbank or the helicopter ride to Kathmandu. She just remembered being on the trail one minute, and then waking up in the hospital the next. How do you go about healing a trauma you don't even remember?

Well, I learned that adult traumatic brain injury isn't so much different than very early childhood trauma. We were there when it happened, but it never got clearly encoded as a memory. Our minds don't remember, but our bodies do. So, what some modern psychologists call trauma therapy, witches and shamans call soul retrieval. In both cases, you are engaged in the process of re-collecting the parts of yourself that have been broken off and scattered as a result of life events that involved too much pain or fear to fully bear at the time. Perhaps, this mushroom ceremony was my chance to finally re-collect myself, in contrast to my historic practice of blowing up and scattering every part of myself all over the Universe.

The first time I realized how far my soul could travel away from my body was during my initiatory experience with the toad medicine, 5-MeO-DMT (I know, I know! Now everyone's got a 5-MeO story, but this was back when only like two people knew how to get it or administer it.). This was right after I had returned from Nepal and had fallen into a deep depression, so I had nothing to lose by trying a totally obscure drug. Let's just say that I stumbled into myself by storming Heaven. Right before inhaling, I told my friend I wanted to know if I was already dead, because I felt like I was. And within about four seconds of exhaling, I did die, and oh so briefly said hi to my sister and Tsering as I flew through the gates of Heaven or Nirvana or whatever you want to call the place where suffering has been obliterated, snuffed out, GONE. Gone beyond. That's what the Buddhists say. Nirvana literally means "blown out," extinguished. There was no remainder, nothing outside of or missing or left out. I was all there was and what WAS, was Love. I know, sounds super cheesy, right? But it's not. I hope you get to experience it one day, too.

I came out of that experience knowing for sure that I was not dead. It was a straight-up miracle, but it didn't last. Within a few days I was basically suicidal. Not like counting benzos and calculating lethal doses or anything, but like maybe if I accidentally fell on a knife while cooking or wandered into the woods one cold, winter night like Charlize Theron in that horrific post-apocalyptic movie, *The Road*, I could just trip on out of here and never have to answer to Earth and its miseries again. Because Death now meant Life. Death meant Love. Death meant Freedom.

I now understand that this is one of the classic misinterpretations of a unity experience. Our materially trained minds can't grasp the Oneness when we're trapped in these little, pain-filled, grieving bodies, so we choose one or the other. We latch onto Body or God. Heaven or Earth. Life or Death. It can't possibly be both, can it? So I chose Death. I was done with whatever Earth and this body had to offer. After all, I had seen the other side and it was WAY better. Plus, death meant getting to be with my sister again.

Luckily, I had enough faith in drugs to try at least one more before jumping through the escape hatch. If 5-MeO was the drug that showed me Heaven, ketamine was the one that pulled me back to Earth. Ketamine showed me that my desire to die was just a temporary state of mind, not a signed-sealed-delivered invitation from my sister to the afterlife. Ketamine reminded me that there was a more sensible path, albeit one that I didn't really want to walk, and it involved finally coming to terms with my past. Ketamine oh so gently told me that I would, eventually, get over my sister, and I would even get over what happened by that river in Nepal. She reminded me that my life was worth living, but I should probably finally go see a therapist.

The first time I walked into *Dana*'s office, I knew I was out of my depth. It was like she had some kind of X-ray vision for psychological wounds. She could immediately see all those nasty, shameful secrets and heavy baggage I'd been carrying around trying to pretend wasn't there. I was not happy to be in her office. I told her I had decided to come because my sister had died a year before and I was super depressed and I had a niece and a younger brother who I really wanted to stay alive for. But she saw through all that and got right to the heart of the matter. This isn't about staying alive for your family, hon, this is about staying alive for you.

Dana had moved her practice to Newtown, Connecticut after the Sandy Hook school shooting, which occurred in the town where my mom lived. The tragedy happened on the very day I was babysitting my niece while my sister was in the hospital with her husband, right after they got the news that the cancer had come back. My sister's memorial bench ended up being placed right next to a bunch of gravestones for those little kids who died that day. Her life, and our family's mourning, became permanently bound up with the lives of those kids and their families. One time when we visited the cemetery, my daughter saw all the little teddy bears and purple decorations around one of the stones and asked me how old the person was who had died. When I told her, she exclaimed, "Wow! That little girl was only five! That's how old I am."

Dana was skilled in a few different forms of somatic, or body-based, therapy that are really helpful for kids and adults who have experienced a traumatic life event. When a person survives trauma, their nervous system can get all out of whack; their sense of self, their emotions, their thoughts, and their sense of their physical body, all become disconnected, or split apart. As the trauma is unfolding, it can actually be self-protective to disconnect or dissociate from your body and your emotions, while you are hearing gunshots and seeing people run for their lives, for example. But over time, it can be hard to reconnect your sense of self, and your emotions, within your physical body. In my experience, you don't need a diagnosis of post-traumatic stress disorder (PTSD) to suffer this way. Even relatively minor childhood traumas can get twisted into all sorts of issues later on, like depression and chronic pain and anger. Until we understand the original wounding, and practice staying with the feelings and thoughts and body sensations that are attached to that life event, the wound will just keep masquerading as all sorts of physical ailments and mundane psychological issues, like hating your boss because you're still angry at your dad.

It is not an overstatement to say that Dana showing up in the place and time she did, with the skillset that she had, probably saved my life. And the fact that she arrived in Newtown only because of the horrific tragedy that had occurred made me understand what religious Christians mean when they say that God acts in mysterious ways. I had always cringed when I heard that. Same with grace. What do you mean you were saved by grace? Well, I was, and by the senseless deaths of those poor little kids. What a mind-fuck.

Dana's therapeutic presence was the first real-life healing I had experienced outside of drugs. She actually couldn't give a crap about psychedelics. She cared about me, and listened to my stories, but the stories were not the point. She was like this really calm, cool detective who had already solved the mystery but was trying to keep you in the room long enough for YOU to solve the mystery. Her training was to pay attention to changes in my body, like posture, respiration, and muscle tension, while I was sharing my memories. Often, we would focus on a single memory for the whole session, like watching Tsering drown, or making a blanket cave in my sister's closet when I was four, or seething with rage as my dad tried to hold my sister's hand in her hospital room. And as I shared each memory, she would teach me how to take "time outs" to check in with my body and notice my own sensations and feelings. Dana was so full of love and so grounded, and her goal was to use this grounded loving presence to teach me how to also love being in my body, on Earth, without needing to transcend or avoid anything. She was teaching me how to be alive, how to accept myself, and how to grieve.

A big part of my weekly sessions with Dana involved trying to process my anger toward my dad. For most of my life before my sister died, my dad and I mostly got along and gave each other space to do our own thing. We had a lot of fun the couple times a year we would get together. We skied, we traveled, we told sarcastic jokes. He was known for having angry outbursts that I never understood as a kid but kind of grew to tolerate and even find endearing as an adult. I honestly believed I had already forgiven him for whatever mistakes he had made when I was growing up. One morning during the silent Zen retreat, before my sister went into the hospital, I held my dad in my mind and witnessed some of the hardest interactions between us, including things that happened when I was too little to understand what was really going on. I looked at it all from a neutral vantage point, and I simply forgave him. No big deal. What a relief! Now I could get on with my adult life without therapy! Ha ha ha. But when my sister's cancer came back and she died, something broke in me. It's like a big, friendly, amusement park facade had been constructed in front of a long, dark, twisting, super terrifying wormhole, and my sister being alive was the last thing holding up the facade. As I got pulled into that wormhole, I careened straight back into both our childhoods, without the Adult Rationalization Filter of what I wanted to believe had happened. Straight to the heart of the matter. And the heart of the matter was hate.

The rage I felt toward my dad after my sister died was unquenchable. His angry outbursts had gotten worse, too (shocker! He was also deep in grief and facing one of his own worst nightmares). It felt like a big magnifying glass was directing the full power of the sun onto our relationship. There was a real possibility that we were just going to roast to death in this pit of hatred, but quietly, and while pretending everything was actually OK on the surface. Luckily, my mom was familiar with this sort of scenario, and on the year anniversary of my sister's death, when I shared with her that I sometimes hated Dad so much I wished he would die, she assured me that it was totally normal for my father to inspire such feelings in a person. But it all felt really unhealthy to me. In one of my early therapy sessions, I envisioned my dad in the middle of a forest fire, desperate for help, alone, and I just watched as the fire consumed him. Yikes.

Thank God Dana knew what she was doing. Like Sarah and Patrick, she was familiar with these nightmarish landscapes of the human mind. She had already walked through them herself and alongside many others, so nothing I could conjure up could make her scared of m e, or disgusted by me, or hateful toward me. It's actually a shocking thing to be met with unconditional love when you are trying your best to freak someone out by proving how monstrous you are. You see, I thought that in order to be happy, I needed to defeat the monster, who I believed was my dad, and also probably kill off the monster in me that had learned to be like him. But through all of our sessions, Dana kept gently showing me that there was a little girl hiding behind the monster, and it was this little girl I needed to get to know and love. My idea of The Monster was just getting in the way.

So there I was, in a spooky, but also friendly, old farmhouse in Freedom, prepared to finally meet this little girl. Patrick had said he saw a little girl running through the house at different points throughout the day, so he was hopeful that she would feel safe enough to make contact. Yes, shamans see and hear stuff that the rest of us don't. If you're skeptical about this, you may just want to stop reading right now, because it's only going to get worse as we go. I certainly don't want to be responsible for upending your comfortable world view. Just so you know, I was also skeptical once, and then life served me a whole plate of unbelievable shit, and I had to accept it. If it makes you feel any better, Patrick always said that most of us are born with these extra-sensory abilities. We used to be able to see and hear all sorts of apparently magical and supernatural stuff when we were kids, but it was trained (or scared, or shamed) out of us by our culture. Another term for this de-mystifying process is called formal education. Paraphrasing Tom Robbins, it's never too late for a magical, mystical childhood, and I was prepared to reclaim mine that night.

While Sarah and I arranged our blankets and cups of water and various ritual items in our separate, cozy little personal areas of the room, Patrick started a fire in the ground-level brick fireplace. He said he would stay near the fire throughout the ceremony and would not be directly engaging with us. His training was quite hands-off. He told us that we would hear him singing or using other shamanic props like the rattle, to help keep us focused and keep the energy moving, but he also said, "I won't be holding your hand and giving you a pep talk like in those Hopkins sessions." In many indigenous traditions, a healing ceremony is not the place for talk therapy. It is a place to be quiet, go inward, and receive whatever communication or treatment might be offered by the beings and spirits who feel inclined to help you. The shaman is not there to fix you. Their job is to hold the space, invite the spirits in, and act as an intermediary if need be to keep the communication flowing.

Patrick asked us to keep the center of the room clear, as that's where he would be setting up the altar. I figured the altar was some kind of low, wooden table upon which he would place all sorts of meaningful and mysterious talismans. But instead, he brought out a small, rolled up piece of fabric. When he first opened it up and laid it on the floor, I was confused. It was literally just a dark blue piece of felt, with some very subtle grey markings emanating like beams of broken starlight from the center. I mean, it was beautiful, in an understated way, but it was so . . . ordinary. It did not feel magical or special at all. Patrick took out a small stone that he placed on one of the markings toward the outer edge, at about 11:55 if the markings were oriented like a clock. As he placed the stone, I saw the line at 11:50 light up and suddenly got a weird feeling in my body that said, "No. That's not the right place." But I didn't say anything and let Patrick continue setting things up.

To begin, Patrick ritually cleansed us with burning sage, moving and wafting the smoky, pungent material about six inches from our skin, even under the soles of our feet. He also used an eagle feather to ritually brush off any remaining impurities along our arms, legs, head and back. Then we sat down, and he used the sage to cleanse the bag of mushrooms. He started counting and creating little piles of mushrooms on the piece of fabric, one in front of me and one in front of Sarah. He would reach into the plastic baggie and withdraw a single, small, dried up little grey-brown mushroom, hold it in his hand, and then delicately place it in one of the piles. I had read enough about the traditional Mazatec mushroom ceremony to know that the mushrooms are believed to be divine oracles and can speak to the healer, so perhaps Patrick was allowing them to tell him where they wanted to go. But as the piles grew larger, I started to really hate mine and covet Sarah's. Sarah's mushrooms looked beautiful and sweet and delicious. Mine were simply repulsive, like some grotesque, twisted, dead thing by the side of the road. I did my best to breathe into my belly and stay aware of my sensations as the counting continued. After the piles were complete, Patrick asked each of us, "Does that amount seem about right?" Sarah was good with hers, but I was surprised to hear myself saying, "Just a little more."

Patrick then asked us to stand up and join him in welcoming in the directions—North, South, East, West, Above (Heavens), and Below (Earth). As we turned to face each direction, Patrick recited a beautiful, simple prayer honoring the attributes of that direction and inviting in the beings and energies associated with it. He ended each prayer by saying, "Be not far away." Then, we each took a pinch of cornmeal from a small pouch in his hand and tossed the cornmeal in that direction and said, "Aho."

Once the space had been ritually prepared and opened, Patrick invited us to eat the mushrooms in our pile. He had left one or two small mushrooms aside for himself, although he said he didn't like to take too much when he was leading a ceremony. He had also prepared hot chocolate, which he claimed the spirits enjoy; it helps encourage them to show up. In my experience, chocolate is also the only accompaniment that makes mushrooms even remotely edible. As I put the first mushroom in my mouth, it didn't seem that bad, just dry, but as I chewed it, that old familiar taste took over my mouth and I almost vomited. It's like opening an old tomb. Everything in my body was saying, "Don't go in. Back away. Spit it out." But I had done this enough times before to know that the entry was always the hardest part. I kept reminding myself that Sarah was there, and I was safe.

And then Patrick told us a sweet, old myth from his Celtic background. About a woman who was really a witch but had to pretend to be a gardener. The story seemed kind of pointless, even as I searched for some larger meaning in it, and I realized that this was a bit like telling a child a story before bedtime. Patrick was lulling us into dreamtime. And then, he started singing, and it sounded like the most beautiful lullaby I had ever heard. "Over the mountain . . . Across the river . . . showing us the way home . . ." Quickly, more quickly than I was prepared for, the room started to shift. The song started to sound a bit threatening, and the fire seemed ominous, and my head started spinning and I had to lie down.

The mushroom visions immediately started forming and bursting behind my closed eyelids. The colors and swirls were entertaining, and they momentarily took my mind off the creepy vibes in the room. The energy in my body was building, fueled by the sound of the rattle as Patrick used it to help us enter our trance. I heard a male voice call me by my family nickname: Kath. Then I remembered my intention. "You know why I'm here. I'm here to see the little girl." I had to say it a few times for the mushrooms to pay attention. But shortly, the visions stopped and a terrible, stabbing pain began in my stomach. Ah yes, I know this pain. I had had all sorts of anxiety and stomach issues as a kid, and also, mushrooms didn't really agree with my physiology. The last few times I had tried other psychoactive plant medicines, it was the same thing. So I just chalked it up to nerves, and the challenge of processing those nasty dry mushrooms.

I had my hand on my belly, with my eyes closed, just trying to ride it out. But the pain wouldn't subside. I opened my eyes at one point to get a sense of where Patrick and Sarah were, and while Sarah seemed totally fine, just lying on her back on the couch across the room, Patrick seemed way spookier than I was prepared for. He was tending the fire with a stick, and I suddenly saw him as one of the characters from the movie we had watched the previous day. The first "person" the little girl encountered on her journey was an elderly spider-human whose job it was to man the fires in the boiler room that fuel the bathhouse. In Japanese folklore, this humanoid spider character lives underground, covered in dirt. Like mushrooms. The boiler man is initially quite unfriendly to the little girl, but finally helps her get a job and even claims to be her grandfather at one point to protect her. In my mushroom-infused mind, Patrick became this spider-fire-keeper, and I had a sneaking suspicion that maybe I was trapped in hell and about to get boiled.

I did my best to shunt these associations out of my mind, closed my eyes, and went back into my interior world. But it was no better than before. The pain was unbearable, and I felt paralyzed. How do these people not see how much pain I'm in? How can they not hear me calling out? Begging for help? I found myself pleading with the little girl. "I'm so sorry. I'll do whatever it takes." I felt her standing next to me and I turned over onto my right side to face her, curling into the fetal position, hugging a pillow. And then the tears came.

Wracking sobs. I can't breathe. "I'm so sorry." I don't even know who I'm crying for. Initially it feels like it's still about my sister, but then I realize it's way deeper than that. I am starting to whimper, clutching the pillow. The pain is so intense, straight through the middle of my stomach. I am clutching and grabbing at my stomach now, trying to push the pain out.

My throat hurts too, like pressure around my esophagus. It's so hot in the room. The air is thick and hard to pull into my lungs. I feel trapped in my own head, in this terrible body. Then a single clear thought pierces my consciousness. It is what I have always known. What I have always known was at the root of this pain. I'm too ashamed to stay with the thought so I heave myself up from the couch and lurch toward the bathroom. Hovering over the toilet, I vomit up this dark black goop and stare at it. It contains all the evil and shame and pain of what happened to me. What the fuck! I was just a little girl! It smells so bad. I am wretched. Disgusting. I flush the toilet and collapse on the cold floor. I am on my knees on the cold tile, banging the tile with my hands. My forehead is pushed against the cold. I am pulling at my hair. SO. ANGRY. Then, I hear the sound of the rattle coming from the other room. I know it's for me. I don't want to go back. I'm not ready to go back. But it's calling me. I manage to slowly get up from the ground and make my way back to the couch. I curl up onto my knees, face pressed into the couch cushion.

Monster!

The dragon has awoken. My hot breath is filling the space between my mouth and the pillow. I keep smelling the vomit. Pure rage. I am no longer the victim. I am fierce! I am now the dragon mother, protecting her child. A monster-mother who no one understands. Breathing literal fire. My power is building. I will lash out at anyone who comes close to her.

And then Sarah's kind, calm voice breaks through my monstrous fantasy world.

"Katherine? Are you OK? I'm worried about you."

She comes over to me and places her hand on my shoulder. Oh my God. She has cut through. She sees me. She understands. I can be the little girl.

"So. There's something I need to say. I tried to tell John once. I thought no one would believe me. But I have to say it out loud, right?" And Sarah and Patrick, in unison, go "Yes."

"I think my dad sexually abused me. I was only three years old. What the fuck! I just want someone to believe me. It wasn't OK."

I had never said those words out loud before, not even to myself. But I had thought them a million times. I had been so good at silently holding onto this confusing, scary, shameful secret for thirty years. It was confusing because I didn't know the truth; I couldn't remember exactly what had happened, maybe because I was too young or because I had blocked it out at the time. It was scary because I thought I'd ruin my dad's life and all our relationships with my family if I ever told anyone. It was shameful because I still really loved my dad and could never reconcile who he was now with who he must have been in order for my thoughts to be true. But this was just that Adult Rationalization Filter hard at work again. The mushrooms are immune to that filter. They just kept showing me how it felt in my body until it was so painful and obvious that I had to blurt it out. Carrying the secret inside me had finally become too much to bear. In that moment, it didn't even matter if the words were true, in some ultimate sense, but they were true for me, and they had been slowly killing me.

I wish I could remember what wise and kind things Sarah and Patrick said or did in that moment, but all I remember was the rush of relief from the pain leaving my body and the air becoming cool and refreshing, and my lucid mind returning. I no longer saw Patrick as a threatening spider-man from Japanese folklore but as a supremely gentle and gracious protector, tending the fire and this space of healing. An awesome, wonderful, healing energy flowed through me now. It was unstoppable. I started talking to my little girl: "I'm so sorry. I'm really screwed up. I don't know how to love. But I'm going to try my best. I love you so much. Thank you for coming back."

Sarah and I spent the next period of time sharing and supporting each other, but also analyzing the ways in which trauma seems to screw up people's lives. We were on the verge of solving all the world's problems when Patrick abruptly interrupted our conversation. He said, "Excuse me, but it's time to say thank you to the altar." And I was a bit shocked that the ceremony was over and said, "Wow. Already?" But we shut up and let Patrick sing his "thank you" prayer. And then he said, "OK. You can go back to whatever it is you were talking about."

And I looked at that weird little piece of fabric at the center of the room, "the altar."

And suddenly, I remember who I am and why I am here.

This has so little to do with me and my dad, or my sister, or Nepal. I am finally staring straight into the face of God. How embarrassing that I've been bellyaching (literally) and lamenting and bitching and theorizing right at the feet of this divine being.

"Ohhhhhhh!"

I get down on the floor, on my hands and knees right at the edge of the fabric. My body remembers this pose, kneeling in prayer at church as a kid, and I laugh, realizing that I was totally missing the point. You don't kneel on purpose to talk to God! You kneel without thinking because it is the only thing your body can rightfully do in God's presence.

"Ohhhhhhh!"

I don't have much time to stay embarrassed, because She doesn't care. She's kind of chuckling and just thrilled that I finally got with the program.

God the Mother. Not the Father.

She is so beautiful. She is me, too. I am beautiful. I am Her. We are simply regarding each other, as would a child looking in a mirror for the first time and seeing herself looking back, and knowing it is herself, not some imposter hiding behind the glass.

"I've looked all over the world for you. And you've been hiding in plain sight!" I say out loud.

Sarah looks straight at me and says, "Yes, Katherine. Why have you been hiding?"

The ordinary piece of fabric has now morphed into the most cosmically beautiful gateway to the Beyond. The little grey markings are elegant hieroglyphs of some ancient language. There is an iridescent rainbow encircling the altar and I am staring into the great void. I am literally perched on the edge of infinity, peering into this unimaginably exquisite abyss.

Death. Void. Cosmic eternity. 5-MeO had rocketed me straight into the center of this portal, but I couldn't track how I had gotten there. I had been missing the thread. Now I had it.

This is my labyrinth. This is my whirlpool, now.

"Thank you. Thank you. Thank you."

The simple grey markings against the dark blue felt appear as stars in a vast galaxy, and the space of the altar is a map to this vastness. Everything is contained in this space. And everyone has their place on the cosmic map. There's Rebecca! And Tsering. He's at 11:50, the place that glowed when Patrick was placing the stone at the beginning of our ceremony. Patrick touches the mark, and it shimmers. A radiant smudge.

"Tsering! It's so good to see you again!"

Just like with my little girl, I am finally able to speak with him. "I wish I was standing next to you at the river. I wouldn't have let you go in. I would have stopped you. You didn't have to leave. It was someone else's time. But you saved her and went in her place. I see you now, Tsering. I understand your choice."

Time is starting to congeal and flow in a linear direction again, and the mystical reality is giving way to historical reality. The altar now appears to be offering a view of Earth, of human life, but from a great height. Me, Patrick, Sarah—we are like three Greek gods sitting by the cosmic fire. Above it all. Looking down from the Heavens, laughing at this great, messy human affair; entertained by the theatre of it all. Lounging, luxuriating. Mischievous in our enjoyment of human suffering. After all, it's not that big a deal. A young hero dives into a raging river to save the damsel in distress? Same old story. Been told a thousand times.

But I'm still here for the little girl. So I practice speaking up for her, and for the rest of these poor humans. "We're here," I say to Patrick and Sarah, as I sweep my arm over the altar, indicating the level of the Gods, "But *that* is still true," pointing into the center of the circle, indicating the level of the humans. "The world of suffering. How can we make it better?"

And now time is really slowing down, and we are back to the level of our bodies and our personal biographies. We spend some very sweet time thanking our spouses and partners, our human allies. We name and offer forgiveness and gratitude to the people we've harmed, and the lives that have been lost.

We throw a bunch of shit in the fire, like Deserve. And Guilt. And Shame. We ask the fire to eat it up for us, get rid of it. Be gone!

Thank you, Sarah, my psychedelic mom. Thank you, Patrick, great fire keeper and medicine weaver.

I say one last goodbye to the altar. To Her. I bow down with my hands together in front of my face and blow a kiss through the air. "I can't wait to see you again. I love you!"

And I hear that Beatles song playing in my head: "I've just seen a face . . ."

CHAPTER 3

((

Open Wide and Say Awe

ow is Baltimore like a high-dose psychedelic? What exactly transpired in that tiny fake living room in the middle of a war zone? How does a person get trapped in a vortex thinking they are living their best life while actually being devoured by God? These are the questions I am left with all these years later, since walking away from my former life. I have often reflected on the riddle of my time at Hopkins, as a psychedelic researcher, before it was a popular or well-paid job to have. Before psychedelic researchers were respected or taken seriously. When it was just a handful of crazy people trying to do the impossible, which was study psychoactive drugs that were actually good for you.

Every day at work was a performance, an elaborate magic act within a system of institutions designed to make sure everyone believed that drugs were bad. Every day, we said hello to the security guard and swiped our IDs—once, twice, three times—to enter the inner sanctum. We signed our names as we picked up the blue capsules from the high-security pharmacy, knowing that the amount of psilocybin had been exactly weighed out and catalogued in case the DEA showed up. We wrote our grants begging money from agencies that called our chemicals "drugs of abuse." We ran our statistical analyses and submitted papers that were laughed at and rejected by mainstream science journals. We persisted because we were the true believers. Our solace was that we already knew the drugs worked. We would be the ones laughing last. At least that's how it felt to me.

I knew from the time I was a nineteen-year-old college kid that psychedelics would be a defining feature of my life, maybe even the central feature. My obsession with altered states of consciousness was a bit of an unexpected detour from captain of the track team and valedictorian, but I embraced it. After so many years of excelling and achieving and finally getting into an Ivy League school, my mind was yearning for freedom. I had dabbled a bit in mushrooms and weed, but it was my first sweet taste of pure Molly that blew me open for good. A rich frat kid had brought some mystery capsules up from New York: "It's called MDMA," he announced. "It's supposed to feel like a combination of acid and heroin. It's like the best drug ever made!" I asked around. I researched extensively on Erowid. I hemmed and hawed. The final decision, on the night of a big party, was like jumping out of an airplane. The first strange thing I noticed was that I felt completely at ease on the dance floor (I didn't know I had social anxiety until that moment). Pure bliss! Endless energy! Grandiose visions! 12+ hours later (yes, I am very sensitive to serotonin), I was hooked.

I promptly quit training for the Heptathlon and did as much E as I could handle (which my brain does not necessarily thank me for now). My main partner in crime was my best friend Jared (of course, there were many others who joined in the escapades, but they shall remain nameless in deference to their current very professional titles and respectable lives). Jared and I tried just about every chemical we could find. When we bought random pills from the designated drug dealer in our favorite Montreal club, we called it the "drug grab bag"—you never know what you're gonna get! One time, Jared left the club early to find our friend's car had been broken into, and he just sat in the back seat amidst the shattered, glistening glass, snacking on Goldfish and watching a river of naked people gather for some kind of art demonstration (true story, actually confirmed). Another time I took a pill that didn't kick in until maybe seven hours later, on the drive home. I had huge pupils and *Truman Show*-level delusions all the way through the Ausable Chasm outside of Plattsburgh, New York. I became convinced that an old phone by the ferry terminal would transport me out of the matrix (finally!). I continued to hear voices into the following night. It seems foolish in retrospect but at the time, all of this psychedelic risk-taking felt important. It was our form of basic training; Dartmouth was our proving ground. Jared still claims our self-experimentation was what saved him from psychosis; instead of drowning, he learned to swim in the deep end. He likes to refer to himself as "patient zero" when he meets my work colleagues.

Believe it or not, throughout all of this playful insanity, I was still managing to excel in my classes and hold tight to my ultimate dream of being a psychedelic researcher (which wasn't even a real thing at the time). I remember proclaiming to my undergrad advisor, "One day, I'm gonna record people's brains while they're on ayahuasca in the middle of the jungle!" He laughed and replied, "Come on, KMac. Stick to monkey brains. They're much easier."

The Dartmouth monkey lab was a mostly well-kept secret housed in the basement of the Psych building, behind many locked doors accessible only by key card (not unlike the Hopkins psilocybin room). The rhesus macaque I primarily worked with was named Sassafrass, which is another name for Ecstasy (oh, the irony). Sassafrass was both scary-looking and scared of the world. Before arriving at the Dartmouth lab, she had been injured in a fight with another monkey and was missing her lower lip. Then, she endured an accidental and severe burn during a routine surgical procedure. When I arrived, she was clearly the lowest monkey in the lab-group hierarchy. And I became the one responsible for tending to her wounds.

I remember how terrified Sassafrass was the first time I walked in the room, how resistant she was to human contact. Everything recognizably primate about me had been covered up behind a lab coat and hair cap and goggles and mask, so why shouldn't she be afraid.

She bares her teeth and clings to the back of the cage. I fumble as I attempt to hook the end of a medieval-looking metal rod onto the metal collar around her neck. I muscle her into the plexiglass chair, and lock the latch at her back, allowing only her head to stick out the top. I wheel the squeaky chair down the hall to the medical room. I fill up a syringe with ketamine and mark the dose down in the three-ring binder. As I reach the needle through one of the tiny holes in the clear side of the chair to pierce the muscle of her thigh, everything shifts.

I have to get the timing just right so that I can safely remove her from the chair as she loses the ability to control her body. She is momentarily a skinny, limp baby in my arms. I lay her down on the medical table. I have about ten minutes to remove the old bandages, clean the gaping, raw wound on her soft, tiny belly, and wrap her back up before carrying her to her cage. I need to do all of this while she is fully in the K hole, unaware of what is going on around her. I bring her back to her prison home. The ketamine will gradually wear off, usually in about an hour.

Each time after the first time is easier. She quickly comes to associate me with ketamine. I no longer have to use the chair. She jumps to the front of the cage and presses her thigh against the bars, anticipating the injection. I carry her in my arms, back and forth, and watch as the wound heals. This is our special dance, and her brief reprieve from hell.

At the time, I thought that I was the powerful one, a compassionate savior to this poor, pathetic creature. But I now recognize Sassafrass as my savior, my first Buddhist teacher. In her unassuming way, she showed up in my life to teach me about the first and second noble truths: Life is suffering. There is a way out. The summer of wound-tending was also the summer of my worst drug binge. Following an exceptional weekend of alternating bouts of MDMA + cocaine, and a lot of alcohol, I found myself physically on the bank of a beautiful pond at the edge of campus, but existentially at the edge of a very deep, dark, inviting abyss. It was the first time I thought, "Maybe I don't want to be on Earth anymore." It was also the first time I became conscious of a very tender, raw, wounded place in me. My underbelly. The part I kept hidden and was trying so desperately to tend in all the wrong ways.

During the year after college, I lived with one of my best, non-drug-taking friends in a quiet Vermont town just across the river from my college campus. For an entire month that winter, it never got above zero degrees: perfect conditions for hibernation and self-care. I kept working in the monkey lab and applied to grad schools. I wasn't able to give up all my chemical addictions, but I slowly began to realize that maybe taking drugs all the time was not going to produce everlasting peace and joy in my life. A wise climbing instructor invited me to join him in sitting meditation with a group of visiting monks from Bhutan. I broke up with my alcoholic, med-school-obsessed boyfriend. I got into all the grad schools I wanted and rekindled an always-elusive romance with my now husband. And, after nearly fainting while assisting in a monkey surgery, I realized I was not cut out to be a primate neuroscientist. I was off to California, to study . . . human consciousness.

Given my bizarre interests, I arrived at UC Davis at just the right time and with just the right people. The Psychology and Neuroscience departments had recently joined forces to build a state-of-the-art center for the study of consciousness (although no one in academia was allowed to say that word in 2004, so they called it "The Center for Mind and Brain"). My mentor, Ron Mangun, was not only the top of his field—the neuroscience of attention—but a gregarious man who made everyone feel part of a family. As the director of the center, he was tasked with hiring all kinds of young, creative scientists and inspiring them to try out their most unusual, groundbreaking ideas. We had people studying music and the brain with fMRI; multisensory processing with EEG; and even social cognition and emotion regulation in children and their caregivers. And lucky for me, there was one particularly wild project that was about to be launched: we were going to enlist people of all ages, vocations and backgrounds and turn them into monks, while tracking changes in their physiology, brain activity, cognitive ability, and behavioral performance. It would turn out to be the most comprehensive study of intensive meditation ever conducted in the West.

The person responsible for this study was Cliff Saron, one of wackiest and most brilliant people I had ever met. He was obsessed with meditation and the brain the way I was obsessed with psychedelics. During my grad school interview, Cliff didn't bat an eye when I mentioned my ultimate dream of becoming a psychedelic researcher. This was quite the opposite reaction to the one I received from the head of the Neuroscience department at UC Berkeley, who basically told me that psychedelic research would only ever happen there over his dead body (side note: It's been nearly twenty years since that conversation. I don't know if this man is dead yet, but psychedelic research is now, in fact, happening at Berkeley).

The meditation study was called the Shamatha Project, and it probably deserves its own book. There is no easy way to summarize what it is like to harness over a million dollars in private foundation funding, 10+ experts in psychology and neuroscience, a Tibetan-trained Buddhist teacher, and sixty people who want to give up their lives for three months to live silently in a monastery. I was there; I saw the whole thing happen; and I still don't believe it.

Getting to be a part of the Shamatha Project meant becoming an expert in something that other scientists would care about even if they thought meditation was a bunch of New Age woo. Every faculty member involved in the project had already established themselves in their respective fields, and they warned me that I couldn't make a career out of studying meditation (remember when mindfulness was taboo, just like psychedelics?). I had to develop an independent body of work that would lead to a Ph.D. and a job after grad school, whether or not this crazy meditation study ever got off the ground.

During those early years, I worked alongside a young, pensive woman from Poland, named Ewa Wojciulik. She was one of the earliest researchers to map the human visual-attention system using fMRI and had published her findings in *Nature*. Impressive on paper and intense in person, Ewa was very hard to work for. She challenged me to come up with the perfect sustained attention task to test whether meditation "actually did anything." I had to navigate nearly a hundred years' worth of ancient papers about the "vigilance decrement" and "sensory thresholds" and WWII radar operators taking methamphetamine to stay focused on their mission. I learned to code experiments. I sat in a darkened room for hours upon hours, tweaking variables and trying out the task myself: long line, long line, long line, long line, just-barely-noticeably-shorter short line (click) . . . I struggled to motivate extremely bored undergrads to stay awake while they watched the unending series of lines flashing on the screen. Somehow, on the other end of this gauntlet, I had developed a nearly impossible, universally hated thirty-minute visual sustained attention task that every normal person failed. This task would become a cornerstone of the Shamatha Project and, ironically, my ticket to Hopkins.

How do you go about building a state-of-the-art biomedical laboratory in the middle of nowhere at 8,000 feet? The answer, in our case, was very quickly and with a huge amount of help. When the first research team showed up at Shambhala Mountain Center (SMC) in Red Feather Lakes, Colorado it was the dead of winter. Over the holiday break, Cliff had designed the labs along with the head of building and grounds, an elfin jack-of-all-trades named Dickie, and volunteer carpenters had built soundproof modular sections that we would use to put the labs together. We Fedex'd dozens of boxes ahead of us from California full of computers and EEG equipment, which had been dutifully off-loaded and stored in the basement of one of the meditation halls by SMC staff.

When we arrived, we began by creating makeshift living quarters for ourselves using silk-screen dividers to separate one large basement room into four roughly equivalent cells. Yes, we all slept in the same room for four months; yes, the mattresses were on the ground. In the room next door, we built the lab. We installed computers, speakers, special low-light color video cameras, EEG and physiology equipment, wiring, lighting, and even interior finishing using black commando cloth from the film industry and reflective scrim on the ceiling. After many arguments and countless two-hour trips back and forth to the nearest Home Depot, we managed to erect two identical sound-proof booths in about a month.

I didn't know much about meditation at that point, but I had resigned myself to the reality that meditation was the closest I was going to get to psychedelics for a while. My occasional mushroom trips had become unbearably gloomy and para-noia-inducing since leaving my Dartmouth bubble, so I stuck to tried-and-true binge drinking with my fellow grad students. But I was curious. Could a meditation retreat really compare to a psychedelic journey? What was it going to be like for our study participants, in total silence (for the most part), meditating for six to ten hours each day? Always the fan of self-experimenta-tion, I decided to find out.

During the summer before the Shamatha Project began, I attended a week-long meditation retreat with the contempla-tive director of our study, B. Alan Wallace. I was enamored with his charisma and quick mind; he was born and raised in Santa Barbara but had studied with and translated for the Dalai Lama and other top Tibetan teachers. I took it as a challenge when he said that *shamatha* (aka, the first stage of total concentra-tion on the path to enlightenment) had not been achieved by a Westerner (I always assumed he wasn't counting himself). I found it adorable that he hated all drugs, so I made sure to talk about psychedelics with every retreat-goer who would tolerate it (thankfully, this was not a silent retreat). I learned to do yoga for the first time and was convinced I'd never do it again. I did chores alongside an ex-military dude who told me that meditation helped him give up alcohol and eased his PTSD. It all felt like fun and games until the final evening of the retreat, when Alan gifted me with what Tibetans call "transmission," which is when the teacher temporarily shares his consciousness with you so that you can finally understand what the hell he's been talking about. For approximately thirty seconds of clock time and an eternity of spiritual time, I experienced absorption. Everything dropped away and it was just me and my focal point. No fireworks, no fancy visions, just total, one-pointed attention. My scientist mind was fascinated by the quality of my awareness, but what I wasn't prepared for was how good it felt. Why had none of the literature mentioned that sustained attention could be euphoric? Aha, I thought. Maybe this is why Ram Dass gave up LSD.

The Shamatha Project went on to become a huge success, a truly historic study resulting in fourteen widely cited empirical papers and many spin-off studies. We found that full-time, daily meditation does, in fact, improve many aspects of health and human performance, including sustained attention (I do hope the poor undergrads who helped me develop the task are now proud of their contribution to such important science). You can read all the papers and watch some truly amazing TED talks on the website for the Saron Lab at UC Davis (currently: https://saronlab.ucdavis.edu/shamatha-project). It's all very impressive, professionally speaking. But for me, the Shamatha Project was a personal gateway, a giant leap into the unknown.

Up until that point, I had believed that I was making choices about my life: choosing to do my homework, choosing to play field hockey and run track, choosing Dartmouth, choosing drugs, choosing grad school, choosing meditation. It hadn't fully sunk in that perhaps my life was following a path guided by unimaginably mysterious forces. But right around the time of my first meditation retreat was when the first Hopkins psilocybin study was published. I remember rushing to Cliff with the paper in my hand, "This is totally where I'm going next!"

((

I met Roland Griffiths on a supremely drab and depressing day in late November. I had emailed him a few weeks before a trip to Washington, DC, where I would be presenting the results of the meditation study at a huge neuroscience conference. It went something like this: "Hello Dr. Griffiths . . . I really admire your psilocybin research . . . my childhood best friend lives in Baltimore . . . can I maybe swing by and meet you after the conference?" I was basically a nobody Ph.D. student; it was totally an amateur cold call. I was in the manic final year phase of graduate school—sorting and analyzing behavioral performance and EEG data like my life depended on it—but I didn't have a published meditation paper to hang my hat on yet. So, I was beyond surprised when he invited me for a full-on job interview in the psychopharmacology research program at Johns Hopkins. I learned many years later that the main reason he responded so positively to my email was because he had just sat a meditation retreat with the very same Tibetan teacher from our study, and both the teacher and Cliff had put in a good word for me.

I had no idea what to expect at Hopkins, but I knew I had to buy my first suit and try to act like an actual grown-up. I scanned my two-day interview schedule, recognizing exactly zero names, and quickly became terrified to meet all of Roland's colleagues. I knew nothing about their world, except that they were all very important people who had published many, many articles about how drugs were very, very bad for you. Roland, too, was a legend in the world of drug abuse research—mostly studying the effects of sedatives and caffeine—but that wasn't the reason I accepted his invitation. I was determined to study psilocybin. I would do anything to get a shot at my dream.

In the years before I joined the psilocybin research team, the Hopkins group had resuscitated an old line of research investigating the spiritual effects of psilocybin, picking up where an infamous group of researchers had left off in the late 1950s. The Good Friday Study—so-called because it was conducted in an actual chapel on the Friday before Easter—was orchestrated by a medical doctor and theology student named Dr. Walter Pahnke. Pahnke was a graduate student working with Dr. Timothy Leary and Dr. Richard Alpert (who would both soon leave academia, one to start a revolution and the other to meet his guru and become Ram Dass). They had been investigating the effects of psilocybin on personality and behavior change and had tried giving the drug to men in prison. They sometimes even took psilocybin alongside their study participants! The research world was a lot less regulated back then, I guess. Suffice to say, the Good Friday Study proved what indigenous cultures had known for thousands of years, which is that mushrooms can show you the face of God.

Beginning with that seminal paper in 2006—the one that pinged into my brain like a homing beacon during the Shamatha Project—Roland and the Hopkins group had continued to solidify their main finding: High-dose psilocybin can produce mystical experiences that are indistinguishable from the experiences of unity and oneness described by saints across the ages. You can imagine how excited the director of The National Institute on Drug Abuse was when the Hopkins team started churning out paper after paper showing how good psilocybin was for you. As good as God! Yikes. That was definitely not in the mission. Drugs are bad! No more money for you!

So this was the environment I walked into. I had never met real-life behaviorists before—scientists who think that all of our actions are dictated by reward and punishment, and that the only outcomes that matter are behaviors that another person can observe. From the behaviorist perspective, thoughts and feelings are right out; humans are no different than animals. Based on my Intro Psych textbooks, I thought behaviorists had gone extinct shortly after World War II. Of course, they thought I was the alien—a new-age, meditating drug enthusiast from California. I was pretty sure I had lost the job before I even got halfway through the first day. During the research presentation portion of the interview, I felt confident and self-assured. Then, the questions came. I knew I was one of the smartest people in the room, and I could defend every technical aspect of my research. But I wasn't prepared to defend the very premise of why a person would study meditation and consciousness in the first place. From within my NorCal bubble, I had momentarily forgotten how much the rest of the research world did not give two shits about consciousness.

I spent one night in a fancy, lonely hotel down by the harbor, slogged through a second day of interviews, and then said goodbye to Roland as it was getting dark. He seemed optimistic about my chances, despite how terribly I thought my other interviews had gone. "I don't know," I said. "Maybe I should just stay in California." I couldn't have known at the time that Roland always got his way, so I suppose he knew it didn't matter what his colleagues thought.

That night, I stayed with my best friend, Gaby, before flying out the next morning. Gaby was the first person who had befriended me when my mom and stepdad moved me and my sister to a new town the summer before I started middle school. Over dinner, we reminisced about jumping off cliffs and doing handsprings over Revolutionary War gravestones in our rural hometown. Gaby loved Baltimore and her job as a physical therapist at Hopkins Hospital. I couldn't see it yet, everything that I, too, would grow to love about this crazy city. Baltimore felt like the underworld to me. I was still quite naive, so I didn't know about things like spiritual initiation or dark nights or trials by fire. But my gut told me that if Gaby was there, maybe it could all work out if I got offered the job.

((

The first rule of fight club is you don't talk about fight club. In the Behavioral Pharmacology Research Unit on the Bayview Campus of the Johns Hopkins Hospital & School of Medicine, I had to learn to be two people. I had to dress up, every day. Wear the right shoes ("I better not hear your sandals flip-flopping down the hallway!"). No jeans, not even on Fridays (Fridays were bow-tie day for the MDs). And above all, don't talk about drug use! "Remember," Roland would always coach me, "If someone asks you about your own experiences with psychedelics, just say no."

Our research building was a relic of days gone by. As the myth goes, some former King of Drug Abuse Research, whose face was framed in fake gold above the faculty conference table, saved the building from demolition in order to create a permanent home for behavioral pharmacology research. The Department of Psychiatry wanted nothing to do with us. We were exiled to the east end of the city, along with a bunch of rats and primates (even baboons!)

I was given the shittiest office I had ever seen. No windows. Old carpet. Harsh, grey metal furniture. Maybe 6x6 ft. Oh, how I had been spoiled in those brand-new, thoughtfully decorated research buildings at Dartmouth and UC Davis! I couldn't help but laugh when I learned that the original patriarch of LSD, Tim Leary himself, had once worked out of a converted closet at Harvard. The only beautiful thing about my new postdoc position was a MacBook Pro laptop. It was pretty clear that the whole point of my life now was to work, all the time, and not get distracted by my surroundings. It's really too bad they made the psilocybin session space so pretty (more on that in a moment). If not for that room, I could have been an excellent workaholic for at least three or four decades.

I did not arrive at Hopkins thinking I would become a psychedelic guide. Literally every participant in the first Hopkins psilocybin study had the same guides during their day-long sessions: Bill Richards (as lead guide) and Mary Cosimano (as the assistant). Then Mary became the only other lead guide in the studies that followed. We even joked that maybe Bill and Mary were the ones responsible for the mystical results, not the drug. But again, I guess I arrived at the right time. It was clear that we needed to expand the number of sessions we were running in order to complete a new, massive study, and there was no way Roland was going to pay a bunch of therapists an hourly wage to sit in a room for eight hours. Begrudgingly, he asked Bill if someone without therapist training could be a guide. And Bill's response was telling: "It doesn't matter so much if she has a particular license. It matters if she has the gift."

The new project had a big, impressive title but we always referred to it as the Spiritual Practices study. It was going to be a combination of daily meditation and high-dose psilocybin. Roland was curious if having a regular meditation practice would enhance or change the long-term effects of psilocybin (especially pro-social behaviors like compassion and forgiveness). He also wanted to find out if high-dose psilocybin and regular integration (in the form of one-on-one meetings with your guides plus peer support groups) could inspire more commitment to daily meditation in the months after a big experience. The study was privately funded by the same organization—the Fetzer Institute— that had funded the Shamatha Project.

I initially advocated for us to teach mindfulness meditation, which is a secular spin-off of traditional *Vipassana* (or insight) meditation that was developed by Jon Kabat-Zinn for use in medical settings. But Roland and Bill ultimately went with a Christian-inspired practice called "passage meditation." Each participant in the study memorized the "Prayer of St. Francis" and recited it to themselves for ten minutes every morning. As the study went on, people started choosing other passages that aligned more with their personal views, but St. Francis's prayer was the foundation: "Lord, make me an instrument of your peace . . ." Looking back, I can totally understand why some people think we were biased toward spiritual outcomes.

The psilocybin session room was like an oasis in the Sahara. A technicolor refuge in the middle of a black-and-white wasteland. I was told it had originally been part of a lab space designed to train astronauts for social and biological isolation. There was the session room itself, a small kitchen, and a bathroom. Soon after my arrival, we turned the closet next to the session room into a behavioral experiment space where more people could be tortured with my sustained attention task.

The design of the session room had been inspired by Bill's early days at the Maryland Psychiatric Research Center in Spring Grove, where he worked with Stan Grof and his team studying LSD. To me, it seemed straight out of Huxley's mescaline visions in *Doors of Perception* (which was the first trip report I had ever read). It was a privileged white man's dream of a perfect living room. Gorgeous paintings on the wall (one classic, one abstract). A pristine white couch with tastefully decorated end tables. All of the smartest-sounding spiritual and philosophical texts in the bookshelf. And one of the trippiest Oriental rugs you'd ever seen.

Oh. There was also a mushroom statue—a grey stone block hidden partially out of view, just behind the couch. The statue had been gifted to the study by the strange and mysterious person who had introduced Roland and Bill and encouraged them to restart the old research. When the mycology expert Paul Stamets came to visit our team at Hopkins, he immediately recognized the statue and said he had a few of his own (don't ask me how all these white guys had the same "authentic" Mexican mushroom relics.) While enjoying Chinese take-out at Roland's house, Paul got the perfect fortune cookie: "You will have a pleasant trip." The next morning, I taped his fortune under the mushroom statue for good luck; maybe it's still there (can someone please check for me?)

I spent as much time as I possibly could in that session room. It was a space to breathe and relax and be myself. Mary held guided meditation sessions there on days when no one was using the room for psilocybin. We sometimes had team meetings in the session room because we could safely talk about whatever we wanted, and we could also get away from our dreary office surroundings (even the nicer window offices had terrible views). Plus, the magic in the air was palpable—almost as if psilocybin was alive.

Of course, we weren't using live mushrooms. We were using a form of pure psilocybin that a chemist named David Nichols had synthesized in a lab, for research purposes only. All of it was stored in a small vault in the pharmacy, which met the exact dimensions that would satisfy the DEA that none of the drug could escape (which they call "diversion"). Whenever we ran a session, one of the head investigators would bring a special code down to the pharmacy and then the pharmacist would weigh out the right amount of psilocybin or placebo filler (so that all the capsules looked and felt the same from the outside) and deliver it back to the researchers. The guides in the Spiritual Practices study, including me, were blind to dose and study design (e.g., who got how much psilocybin when), except we and the participants knew that each capsule contained some amount of psilocybin. The highest doses in the studies were equivalent to about 4 to 5 grams of dried mushrooms: a heroic dose, in the words of the underground.

At the time, I took it for granted that the psilocybin we were giving people was the same as the magic mushrooms I had taken so many times before. I accepted the white man's myth about synthetic drugs being just as good if not better than natural sources. I didn't know much about the godmother of mushrooms, María Sabina, except that her name was often invoked when the guys talked about their mushroom statues. I knew that she had given magic mushrooms to a white banker named Gordon Wasson, who then wrote about his experiences and shared the mushrooms with the Swiss chemist, Albert Hofmann, who had discovered LSD. As the story goes, Gordon brought the synthesized psilocybin back to María Sabina and she proclaimed that it still had the spirit of the mushrooms in it. After I left Hopkins, a woman who knew the Wassons shared an old newspaper article with me, revealing that it was actually Gordon's wife, Valentina, who was the brains in the relationship and the mushroom enthusiast. I learned that the Wassons had lied to María Sabina in order to convince her to give them the mushrooms in the first place, and that her life had been ruined by all the hippies and American elites who flooded her village, searching for spiritual salvation. Most importantly, I learned that María said that after the white people showed up, the mushrooms would no longer work as a portal to God.

But psilocybin seemed to be alive and well at Hopkins. This was pretty obvious from the first few sessions I ran alongside Bill. Bill's approach was very laissez-faire, trusting, spiritually informed. Apart from holding the participant's hand during "take-off" (the first ten or so minutes after the participant laid down on the couch), he hardly said a word or moved from his seat unless the participant asked for help. He trusted the musical playlist—an emotionally evocative blend of Christian choral pieces, opera, and classical music—like it was a holy book; divinely crafted and impeccably delivered through a pair of classic, electrostatic Stax headphones. I quickly came to see that he truly believed nothing could ever go wrong with psilocybin. He was like a jovial grandfather on Christmas morning; no gift was a bad gift!

Bill had been inspired by his first mystical experience in a German psychedelic research study when he was a young student and went on to become a pastoral counselor, working in a variety of clinical settings alongside doctors and nurses. One of those nurses was his wife, Ilse, who also worked at the psychedelic research center at Spring Grove. He told me that she was the best at helping people feel safe and loved, especially if they were nearing the end of life, and I always got the sense that Bill's psilocybin mantra—Trust, Let Go, Be Open—was imbued with her spirit.

Tragically, Ilse died of cancer shortly after the Spring Grove research center was forced to close its doors in the late 1970s, following President Richard Nixon's decision to create the DEA and make all drugs illegal. After losing his wife, Bill had to face the "psychedelic dark ages" mostly alone. He patiently waited out the long decades between the shuttering of Spring Grove and the invitation to start the research program at Hopkins (around 2000). Unlike his former colleagues, many of whom were still practicing psychedelic therapy illegally in the underground, Bill filled his cup by raising his sons and helping regular people find more meaning and purpose in their lives.

If Bill was the mystical mind of the Hopkins program, Mary was its beating heart. She meditated every day, in the peaceful, simple tradition of Thich Nath Han. She had trained as a social worker and was skilled in establishing an emotional connection with strangers and helping them feel at home. Mary was the main gatekeeper to all the psilocybin studies. She was responsible for interviewing every single person who walked through the Hopkins doors claiming they wanted to try psilocybin. Over the course of two days of psychological evaluations disguised as casual conversation, she assessed people's basic competence and mental health. Her warm personality and big, open laugh were disarming. Even the people who had prepared to fib to get into the studies couldn't help but spill their guts after an hour or so with Mary. Everyone loved her, even the folks who didn't pass her test. She hugged everyone goodbye. She was one of the main reasons I stayed for as long as I did. Everything I needed to know to help my sister die, I learned from Mary. Mostly, she taught me how to hold someone's hand and have that be enough.

People often ask me now what the best training is for someone who wants to be a psychedelic therapist. And I think the answer is quite simple: sit with as many different tripping people as possible and learn from an expert. In other words, the only way to learn is to do. Of course, I disclaim this as my opinioned advice only, but I still believe it is good advice, and I spent years learning this way; the answer is simple, but the process is not. I was one of the lucky ones to apprentice with two of the most experienced clinical psychedelic guides in the world. I was a direct beneficiary of their lifetimes of wisdom.

Hundreds of people have now experienced the magic of the Hopkins psilocybin protocol. But when the first study began, Roland was skeptical of the grandiose stories Bill had been sharing about the Spring Grove days. As participants started making their way through the study, it became clear that Bill wasn't exaggerating. People were saying that it was "the most spiritual experience of their life"; on par with the birth of their first child or the death of their parent. Luckily, Bill also had a bit of science on his side. Back in the early research days, Bill and Walter (Pahnke) had developed a 100-item survey to categorize and quantify the types of experiences someone could have during a psychedelic journey, including the mystical nature of someone's trip. The questionnaire helped make the participants' self-reports more concrete and believable. When I arrived and started crunching the numbers through a proper psychometric analysis—with the help of an amazing young statistician named Jeannie-Marie Leoutsakos—it became clear that about thirty of the one hundred questions were driving the life-changing results that Hopkins had become known for. These thirty questions can differentiate between a mystical, or unity, experience and other types of equally profound and meaningful, but not spiritual, trips. And people who have mystical experiences go on to show greater benefits and more change on most of the outcomes you've probably heard about in mainstream media. The now-famous Mystical Experience Questionnaire (or MEQ) has been translated into tens of languages and is used in research all over the world.

The MEQ was just the beginning. I could regale you with so

many stories about being a researcher at Hopkins: how I discovered that a psilocybin-induced mystical experience can change someone's personality; how my research was featured in every major news outlet and even mentioned by Bill Maher on his late night show; how Roland and I met with the head of psychiatry to pitch a groundbreaking neuroimaging study of the role of glutamate in the anti-depressive effects of both psilocybin and ketamine (nearly ten years before the FDA gave psilocybin "breakthrough" status as a potential treatment for depression); how we gave high-dose psilocybin to Zen masters and Tibetan meditation teachers who had never taken a drug before in their life. But these are not the stories that have stayed with me, informing and bettering my life.

What I remember, most of all, is sitting with regular people in that tiny room, watching new possibilities blossom with the help of psilocybin. I remember a young Trinidadian woman who almost went to the ER after her blood pressure skyrocketed during her first psilocybin session; in the midst of her cardiac crisis, she proclaimed how much she loved us and that she didn't even care if she died because she was One with the Universe. (She was OK by the way.) I remember the young father who brought his guitar to the session out of concern he might be bored with the music, but instead starting chanting in tongues along with one particular Indian raga. And the young man who had grown up in a cult and chose to face every one of his worst fears during his high dose session, and eventually was inspired by his experience to reconcile with his estranged father. And the young woman writer who had bad anxiety and two small children who kept her up at night and had lost her sister in a tragic accident at a young age. I remember these people because they remind me of myself. I realize now that they were holding up a mirror—a sacred mirror, not unlike the mushroom altar—so that I could learn better how to love others and, ultimately, myself.

In contrast to the sacred memories of the session room, I remember the endless, invisible war that dragged on between us (the psychedelic researchers) and the rest of the department. I remember watching Roland ridiculed in front of all our Psychiatry colleagues during Grand Rounds when the former chair told him his research was a bunch of nonsense and that he was probably just high on his own drugs. I remember trying to pitch new federal grant ideas—like an emergency medication I called the Trippy-Pen that medics could use when someone was having a bad trip that wouldn't stop—and getting laughed at by my fellow faculty members. I remember the new head pharmacist interrogating me in his small, windowless office, making veiled threats about what would happen to a young faculty member if they found out she was stealing Schedule I drugs.

As if that wasn't bad enough, there was also the internal war that raged between me and Roland and one of the other investigators. I remember the heated meetings in Roland's cramped office, papers everywhere, the huge, looming brick facade of the NIDA research building dominating the view from his window; and the ever-present plastic Diet Coke bottle next to a small timer that Roland used to keep track of his work time (he always hit the button on the top when I would walk in to chat). I remember disagreeing about almost everything and still somehow feeling like we were karmic friends who had ended up in a weird DMT portal together.

There were moments of pure joy, like the first time Roland offered me a ride home through the bumpy streets of East Baltimore in his yellow Lotus sports car, or the time I played Lady Gaga's song *Edge of Glory* for him as I tried to pitch a new study about music and psychedelics and awe. And there were moments of terror, like when one young man trashed the session room in a dissociated frenzy and a very experienced psychonaut refused to take the final dose of a strange drug we were studying (a high-dose extraction of *Salvia divinorum*) because he wasn't convinced he would make it back to his body. Toward the end, I told Roland that I didn't think I could manage being a psychedelic researcher anymore. I remember being completely torn between two worlds.

Everyone assumes I left Hopkins because my sister died, which is not entirely true. Her death just gave me a totally understandable reason to get the hell out of there. During the year before Rebecca died, my mind started changing in ways I couldn't control. On top of 60-hour work weeks and guiding all of those high-dose sessions, I had been meditating every day and repeating a silent mantra—*Om mani padme hum*—as I walked and bussed and biked through the streets of Baltimore, just like our participants had been doing. A spiritual reality that felt vaguely psychotic but also quite lovely began opening up alongside a growing realization that our elite psychedelic lab was surrounded by a vast sea of poverty and suffering. I couldn't reconcile the two, so I kept trying to focus on the spiritual dimension. *Om mani padme hum, om mani padme hum* ... may all beings be free of suffering.

My spiritual balancing act fell apart in quite spectacular fashion during a work trip to Tucson, Arizona in the Spring of 2012. My paradigm-shifting openness paper had been published a few months prior and I was on top of the world. My paper demonstrated that people who had had a full-blown mystical experience on psilocybin showed increases in the domain of personality linked to imagination, creativity, flexible thinking, and tolerance of others; and these personality changes lasted for more than a year after receiving their high dose of psilocybin!

Everyone was talking about how psilocybin could permanently change your personality, something that psychology researchers had previously concluded was nearly impossible. The Tucson trip was the first time I had been invited to present my psychedelic research at a big conference, and I would be speaking next to now-famous neuroimaging researcher Robin Carhart-Harris. It was a dream come true on every level! As I walked through the halls of the gorgeous conference center, Roland's tempered congratulations echoed in my mind, "This is your fifteen minutes. Soak it up."

Because it was a conference on the science of spirituality, there were plenty of weirdo meditator types there, including some actual experts, like Deepak Chopra (interestingly, he was quite anti-drugs at the time. I guess he's changed his tune now). Robin and I were sitting out by the pool finalizing our PowerPoint slides when a tiny, grey-haired leprechaun of a man called out from his balcony "Hey Robin! It's me! God! I'm real!" The man's name was Gary Weber. His claim to fame was that he had gotten all his thoughts to stop, for good. He was at the conference to present his "N-of-1" findings and I suppose convince a few others that they could also get enlightened in this lifetime.

Running into Gary on a small path behind the conference center turned out to be one of the most pivotal moments of my life. He was kind and funny and unassuming up close. He didn't seem any different from the outside, having lost his train of thought. I remember him telling me about some special kind of wine that the Zen folks used to drink at the Japanese monastery he trained at. I told him how I had been practicing mindfulness of breathing, which I learned from Alan Wallace, and how my mind felt like a volcano that could burst through the top of my skull at any minute. He suggested I continue up the path and enjoy the view of the waterfall. And he offered a new technique for me to try. "Just sit quietly and ask yourself 'Where am I?' and see what happens."

I arrive at the end of the path and see a pretty normal-looking waterfall, which is only slightly unusual because we are in the middle of the desert. Huge Saguaro cactuses rise up all around me. The sky is growing grey, as if a thunderstorm may be rolling in. I find a small nook in the rocks, maybe twenty feet above the landing, and watch as an adorable couple and their small child arrive and take pictures. "This is where we met," I hear the woman say to her child. "You wouldn't exist if not for this spot."

I close my eyes and take a few deep breaths. My body is buzzing with a strange energy, as if I'm plugged into a wall socket. I remember Gary's suggestion, which seems quaint. I decide to try it out. "Where am I?" I ask, thinking I will keep repeating it like my *Om mani padme hum* mantra. My heart starts racing and it feels like my body is quickly disappearing. My mouth goes dry, and I instinctively part my lips to maximize the available oxygen. It feels like I am in a rocket ship. Then, a bomb goes off, and I am very far away from planet Earth, the only remnant of life left in the cosmos. I am watching the aftermath of what seems like a nuclear explosion, realizing that the roiling mass of energy that remains does not give a shit about humans, or life, or Earth. I am terrified.

When I open my eyes, I am back in my body and overjoyed. My hands reach down to pat my legs and ensure that all of my parts are still there. The world is glistening with beauty. Every single detail is like a jewel. Each tiny desert flower and green plant pushing through the rocky ground. The delicious molecules of oxygen and water flowing into my lungs. "I'm alive!" I exclaim. "Holy shit!"

The afterglow of this experience carries me through my talk and the fancy dinner afterward. I briefly run into Gary as I am leaving for the airport and try to tell him about what happened by the waterfall. "Forget about it," he says. "Just keep going. Keep asking the question and let everything else go."

I have spoken publicly a few times about the plane-death-ride that happened next. You can hear all about it in my TED talk. I don't like remembering it, let alone writing about it for posterity. It was one of the scariest things I've ever endured. The nightmare lasted for months afterward, though it feels like a figment now. When I returned to Hopkins, I knew I had to leave. I tried to tell Roland about what had happened, and he assumed I had smoked DMT or something while I was at the conference. I confided in Mary, ever the compassionate mother-figure. I told my assistant guide, Fred (Reinholdt), that maybe I would have to give up my job, and he just laughed. After so many years in community psychiatry, what was a little psychosis! He remarked, cryptically, "Look at you! You're glowing! You better get outta here before it's too late."

If Tucson was my wake-up call, the month after my sister's Earthly departure was my Hopkins death knell. One morning shortly after I came back from the funeral, I walked into the research building to find the security guard, Gloria, in tears, her face red as she tried to fake a smile. "What's the matter?" I asked. "Did something happen?" "It's Tony," she replied. "He's dead."

I was in shock. Tony had been the jovial gatekeeper of the Behavioral Pharmacology Research Unit for decades. He and Gloria kept the whole ship afloat, making sure all of the drugs stayed safely in the pharmacy and the drug-users felt safe showing up for our crazy studies. A few months before, we had celebrated Tony's retirement with a big cake. "Please don't say anything yet," Gloria pleaded. "I don't know when they're going to tell you all."

I swiped my card and walked up the back stairwell to my office. I was in a daze. I saw an email announcing a faculty meeting. As I sat down at the conference table, I could see tears in the eyes of a couple of the long-time staff members. The head of our unit broke the news without a hint of emotion, "Well, as some of you may have heard, Tony passed away last night. I guess he won't get to enjoy his retirement after all." Brief pause. "OK. Moving on to the rest of our agenda." I was stunned. Decades of steadfast protection and morning greetings and evening farewells. So this is how the higher-ups here respond when someone dies. Given my fresh outrage from my sister's nightmare experience in the ICU, I was proud of myself for leaving the room without throwing a punch.

A few of the staff members and postdocs arranged for flowers to be sent to the family, and we paid our respects at Tony's wake. But most of the senior faculty members couldn't seem to be bothered to make time to attend the actual funeral. I remember stopping by Roland's office and saying, "Are you planning to go on Friday?" And I saw the gears start turning, imagined him contemplating all of the deadlines and work he had to finish for the week. "You know it's the right thing to do, Roland. It really mattered to me who showed up when my sister died." He later told me that Tony's wife came up to him after the service and said, "Tony would be honored to know that a real doctor came to his funeral."

After that, it was just a matter of time and logistics for me to get out of there. I couldn't stand being in a place that seemed to care so little for human life; where the only point was working as hard as you could, bringing in as many research dollars as possible, until you croaked. I couldn't stomach giving people psilocybin and watching miracles happen against the backdrop of shooting deaths and abandoned buildings. I felt sad for my colleagues and even warned Roland, "I better not find out one day that you died sitting at your desk!"

It took me another six months to wrap up all my research obligations and convince Roland and the department to let me take a year of unpaid sabbatical. Luckily, I had already hand-picked my replacement, another brilliant postdoctoral student from UC Davis, like me. I handed over all my best ideas along with my preliminary research and prepared to leave for my adventure in Nepal. Walking out of the research building on my final day, I felt like I was getting out of prison. I remember turning around to get one last, good look at the place, and thinking, "After a few months, no one is even going to think about me."

CHAPTER 4

☾

Womb with a View

IT HADN'T OCCURRED TO ME until the day after my big experience in Freedom that perhaps the magic mushrooms had had a plan up their sleeve this whole time. That maybe Dartmouth and UC Davis and Hopkins were not rungs of an academic ladder, but rather spiritual stepping-stones on the way to a much bigger cosmic job assignment. In the whole scheme of things, the mushroom night in Freedom felt like I had finally graduated elementary school. I was ready for my mission!

As I entertained grandiose visions, sitting next to my guide Patrick in the little screened-in porch next to the room where we had completed the ceremony, I asked him, "Now that I've got my little girl back, what do I do next?" And his words brought me back down to Earth, "Take her out for ice cream. Make her feel special. Show her how awesome adults can be."

His advice was spot-on, and I often wonder, now, how much easier things could have been if I had just paused my life at that moment and allowed my body to start healing itself, slowly. But I had already planned two major international trips: one to South Africa to help run the mental-health support tent at a big psychedelic-fueled festival, and another back to Nepal. Thankfully, South Africa turned out to be amazing; supporting others while they navigated their own difficult trips reaffirmed everything I had learned with the mushroom altar. I even helped save a couple lives and held a woman's baby for a few hours while she tried to find her campmates.

But Nepal was a total crash and burn. I went back looking for answers, but what I uncovered was more trauma. The grief from Tsering's drowning accident was still palpable. I remember going to visit his mom, at her home, and she was in the same position on a small mattress on the floor, just as we had left her nearly seven months before. She was still begging to know if anyone had found her son's body. It was devastating and totally not what I had expected after all that time. Seeing his mom like that, I thought about my own mom and how she could never get over her brother's death by drowning from nearly forty years ago. How it just fucked her up, permanently. How now, on top of that, she had to somehow manage to cope with losing her daughter. Life was unfair. It was disgusting. I started to get sucked back into the whirlpool.

My traveling companion in Nepal was so worried about my mental health that she encouraged me to fly home early. I landed in New York City and went straight to Patrick's apartment to decompress. When I arrived, I curled up on the small creme-colored couch in his living room, below a wacky piece of art that I always thought evoked the mushroom space. Looking at those colorful threads traveling in all directions, connecting small bundles of knotted up, equally colorful little spheres, I doubted whether the mushrooms even cared about human suffering. All they see is connection; it doesn't matter what they're connecting.

Patrick handed me a cup of tea and I told him about how scared I was in Nepal, how I felt trapped in my own mind. I kept returning to the conclusion that suicide was the only compassionate solution to my unending horror show. "I just want it to stop!" I lamented. And he replied, "The real question you have to ask yourself is, are YOU finally ready to stop? Is this the last time?"

I silently fumed on the couch. Patrick waited for the full impact of his words to sink in. And then he said, "Have you ever wondered why it didn't work out for you at Hopkins?" And I gave him my usual song and dance about the patriarchy and capitalism and oppressive institutions, and he said, "No, no, no. I'm not talking about that." "Oh, you mean, like, my personality?" I joked. He didn't laugh. "It's deeper than that," he said. "You don't worship the same God as them."

His words reverberated throughout my body. I hadn't thought of myself as someone who had committed to a particular God, but I certainly couldn't deny my experience with my sister, or the altar. "Is this what it feels like to find religion?" I asked. "I thought it would be more joyful."

The next morning, John picked me up from Patrick's place and dutifully ferried me back to the peaceful normality of our life in the suburbs. A few months after my sister died, my dad had decided to buy his dream retirement house on a quiet lake in a beautiful, wooded neighborhood about an hour and a half north of New York City. And when John and I quit our jobs in DC and Baltimore, we moved up there to live with him and my brother. Well, John always joked that it was mostly him living with my dad while I traveled the world and my brother shuttled back and forth to his mom's house and high school. Considering the amount of trauma and grief we were all trying to hide from each other, we were a mostly happy family, on the surface.

That summer, I ate a lot of ice cream with my little girl. I sunbathed on the porch like my sister and I used to do during our high school years. I started waterskiing again, which helped me reconnect with my dad. I also developed a daily ritual to get my head straight and get into my body. Each morning, after my dad left for the office and John left for the organic veggie farm where he was working, I'd walk with my dad's dog down the wooded path to the lake. At that time of year, the lake water was still quite chilly, but I committed to swimming across the cove and back every day.

The first few mornings, all I could think about was Tsering and the whirlpool. I was an excellent swimmer and had never been uncomfortable in open water, but now I had a fear of the depths. It freaked me out that I couldn't see more than a foot below the surface. I kept thinking about all of the things that had settled to the bottom, never to be found. But after a couple of weeks, the water warmed, and I started swimming faster, so I didn't have time to be afraid. Twelve minutes, roundtrip. I would climb the peeling wooden ladder back onto the dock and lay in corpse pose for a few minutes, letting the sun beat down and fill my body with energy. Then I would run through the routine I had learned from my yoga teacher, Charlie, in Baltimore. I would smile when I remembered his perfect advice one anxiety-ridden night when I showed up to his yoga class all flustered. "Where are you?" he asked. And I said, "I don't know," thinking he was inquiring about my mind. And he laughed and stomped both feet on the ground and said, "Here!" This regimen of outdoor air, cold water, mindful exercise, and Vitamin D was the ticket. Back to life; back to reality.

That summer was also the first time I had been truly sober since high school; I even quit coffee. But I still felt like shit most days. The thing no one told me is that grief is physical. I felt like I had a hangover every morning, although I wasn't drinking. I had started feeling physically sick after I came back from South Africa, but then it got really bad in Nepal. Even after I came home and started taking care of myself, I couldn't shake this nagging feeling that something was wrong with me. I remember calling my trusted chaplain friend, Sarah. "Something got its hooks in me and won't let go."

During the quiet mornings by the lake, I kept thinking about a dream I had in Nepal, near the spot where Tsering had drowned. A small child is crying softly in the underbrush along the side of the trail, her black hair partially covering her face, and her dark brown eyes peering up at me through the leaves. I remembered that I had had a similar recurring dream as a child myself, of finding a baby crawling around lost, and picking her up and taking her home. It was such a special feeling: "my baby." I thought maybe this time the baby in the dream was actually Tsering, calling to me, choosing to try out his next life in America (he loved singing the classic Eagles' song *Hotel California* on the trail and told us he wanted to go to Harvard after he had saved up enough money). I told Prem, the trip leader, about my dream the next morning, and he said that the baby was probably an evil spirit, so I should banish her. "You know," he said, "The locals told me that Tsering died because we didn't sacrifice a chicken before entering their sacred valley. They said there's a Naga, like a snake goddess, who guards that river, and she grabbed that woman off the trail, and then pulled Tsering into the whirlpool. You don't want to mess with those spirits."

The month after I returned to America, my period was late, and I hoped that maybe I was pregnant after all. But on the 49th day after Tsering's death, the day that Buddhists believe marks the end of the death bardo, my period came heavy and painful, like a mini childbirth, and I sobbed and realized that he really wasn't coming back. My life seemed marked now by one tragedy after another, and I doubted whether I would ever have a baby to call my own.

I thought about the women at Hopkins who had managed to have children while balancing the insane workload. The head of the primate lab told me that back in the day, she just brought her infant into her office, closed the door, and no one even noticed! One of my fellow postdocs waited until well into her second trimester to tell the faculty, because she was afraid it would interfere with her job placement. I remember her mentor saying that she didn't think our research unit even had a maternity policy, and could she please continue to come in for weekly meetings? Thank God for FMLA. And the statistician I worked with on the Mystical Experience Questionnaire had to come back to work within days of giving birth because she feared she would lose her teaching gig, which covered half her salary. I learned more about the official Hopkins policies as I was preparing to take my unpaid sabbatical. At the time, faculty were granted only one week of paid maternity leave, unless you had already purchased short-term disability insurance. And in the case of the death of an immediate family member (parent, spouse or child), you were allowed to take three whole days of paid leave. If the death involved someone even slightly more distant from you, you only got one day off to attend the funeral. It started to really sink in what an inhumane place Hopkins was, and how maybe it was a really good thing I had left.

Of course, I couldn't fully appreciate my new life because I was still living at my dad's house and being constantly reminded of how terrible I felt in my own skin. I started to connect the dots between my own mushroom revelation and the experiences of some of the participants in our trials who had survived sexual abuse as children. Most of them, like me, had never told anyone before, but I guess there's something about high-dose psilocybin that inspires people to bare their souls. I remember the first person who told us during their final prep meeting that they had been abused by a family member. I was still in such denial of my own memories at the time that I just sat there, blushing from shame and embarrassment, having no clue what to say. I remember looking over at Mary and feeling this total calm emanating from her. "I'm so sorry that happened to you," she said. "It wasn't OK. It wasn't your fault." After the participant went home, I asked if I could talk to Mary for a minute. "I've never heard anyone say that before," I admitted. And she said, "Oh, it's so common."

Yet, I felt so alone. I felt like what had happened to me as a kid, and all the years of silence and shame, had left me permanently damaged. During my first year at Hopkins, as part of my genetic consultation for BRCA2, the doctors had advised me to stop hormonal birth control, which I'd been on since high school. After that, John and I had been trying to get pregnant (or, not NOT trying) for about four years. During the summer by the lake, I started to accept the depressing possibility that all the years of stress and alcohol and drugs meant I wasn't going to get to experience childbirth after all. Motherhood, like my career as a psychedelic researcher, would remain always out of reach.

And then, a magical fairy creature flew all the way across the ocean to heal me.

I didn't really know that that was why Eileen was coming to visit. I had fallen in love with this particular painting she had made, of a woman standing up in a tiny boat in the middle of a storm at sea, with her hands outstretched. It was the perfect artistic rendition of the impossible journey I had been on since my sister died. The scene was painted on a thick, heavy wooden board, and there was no way Eileen could send it from her home in Scotland. So I offered, "Why don't I pay for your plane ticket and that'll be the price of the painting?" And she agreed.

I first met Eileen at a psychedelic conference in London the previous summer, about six months after my sister died. I had no plans of attending, but then a good friend had to cancel her speaking engagement at the last minute and suggested to the event organizers that I speak instead. Remember, there were only like five women in psychedelic science at that time, so it was an easy sell. I was in a really bad place, mentally, when I got on that plane. But my trip was charmed from beginning to end. Everyone went out of their way to make me feel welcome, and even though it was still a boys' club, the psychedelic researchers in the UK were more fun and less pretentious than the ones Stateside. And my talk was a huge hit. It was the first time I had spoken about my sister's death in front of such a large audience.

But the attention was overwhelming. After being mobbed by young psychedelic enthusiasts, I retreated to a tiny alcove to try and collect myself. As I was sitting there attempting to disappear, this tiny woman with a perfect Scottish accent came up to me. I remember almost brushing her off because I was exhausted. But she quickly pulled out a pile of cards from her bag and said, "I want to show you my paintings." As it turned out, her dad had died of cancer too, and his death, like my sister's death, had opened up a mystical portal that she had been trying to understand ever since. She had never been into drugs before, but the psychedelic landscape was the only thing even remotely close to what she had experienced with her dad. And she painted her experiences because she didn't know how else to express them. These paintings spoke to me. She was a kindred spirit.

The next day was the hottest summer day on record, and I spent it galivanting around London with two of the psychedelic scientists I had met at the conference, Leor and Mendel. We found a totally trippy William Blake exhibit at the Tate Britain (a gorgeous marble museum that had been built atop an old prison in the late 1800s and was originally called the National Gallery of British Art). We contemplated taking a dip in the River Thames and ate mint chocolate chip ice cream in Hyde Park with actual white swans swimming by. It felt straight out of *Alice in Wonderland*. When I shared with them how messed up I was after my sister died, Leor admitted that he, too, was grieving his younger sister who had died in a freak accident. It felt like we were part of an extended cosmic family, finally rediscovering each other after so many eons. It seemed like London was courting me, showing off, inviting me not to give up hope for my psychedelic career.

But then Nepal happened, followed by my winter of despair. I didn't get to see Eileen or the psychedelic scientist guys again until Spring rolled around, when I was looking for any excuse to get away from my life. I flew into Heathrow and stayed with Leor in London for a few days, doing a bit of reconnaissance as I imagined what life would be like if I joined the Imperial College research team (not that anyone had invited me yet). I stayed in an actual castle outside of London, in the home of a woman who had become quite famous for taking loads of LSD and funding psychedelic research and also, for drilling a hole in her skull. (She even showed me her antique trepanning kit and asked if I wanted to add myself to the list of names for future procedures). Finally, I met up with Sarah, who was in the UK for a conference on hospice chaplaincy. On the train ride to Edinburgh, I remember Sarah asking, "So how do you know Eileen?" "I don't, really," I responded. Let's just say that the Scotland leg of the trip was a bit of a gamble.

And it was one of the best gambles I've ever made. I had never met a real artist before, and certainly not such a magical witchy one. Walking into Eileen's Edinburgh apartment felt like opening the door into a movie scene, with her cosmically inspired paintings covering every inch of spare space. Eileen was the quintessential hostess. She cooked us traditional Ecuadorean meals of *ceviche* and *patacones*. She showed us the town where John Muir was born and guided me through my first sober shamanic journey on the night of the Spring Equinox. On the last day of the trip, she brought us to Rosslyn Chapel, which is the alleged resting place of the holy grail in the myth about Mary Magdalene that was popularized in *The DaVinci Code*. The chapel itself was spectacular, but we discovered the real treasure in a grove of ancient yew trees by the creek that ran through the valley below the church. Walking through the glen alongside these great beings, softly touching their gnarled limbs and gazing up through their huge canopies, I said, "This is the holy grail! Nature herself, hiding in plain sight, far away from the holy temples built by men."

On our last evening in Edinburgh, I hung some Tibetan prayer flags from an old iron bridge and bought a lottery ticket. I stated, "If I win this lottery, I will name my daughter Rosslyn and build my research center." I did win, a total of forty euros. And that golden ticket was the beginning of the epic adventure that Eileen and I would consummate later that fall in New York City.

Eileen arrived in the United States in early October, as the leaves were turning gold and orange and red and the lake was getting really cold, and it was almost time for everyone to put away their boats and pull in their docks for the winter. We took the boat out one last time so she could see the lake that had taught me so much that summer. As we pulled into the narrow passage where a waterfall used to flow, back before the river had been dammed to create the lake, I snapped a quick photo of the sunlight glistening on the water. As we passed under the bridge named for two lovers who had met their demise going over the falls, I looked at the picture and noticed a bright purple arc over the water. I showed Eileen and she said, "Oh yeah, that's totally your sister."

We took the train into New York City the next day and got settled in the apartment that had been offered up to us for the next few days. I had been invited to be a keynote speaker at one of the most respected psychedelic conferences in the world, and the invitation came with free housing. But that wasn't really why we were there. We were there to see the altar.

Eileen and I arrived at Patrick's apartment shortly after lunch time. I had kind of prepared her for what the ceremony would be like, but she already had quite a bit of experience in shamanic realms. Just as before, we spent some time talking through our intentions. Eileen was very clear about hers: She wanted to learn more about death, and about the mushroom space. She also wanted to learn more about her dad's legacy, specifically a cave that her dad had spent his life obsessively exploring. I really wasn't sure about my intention, but I knew I was in a lot of pain and hated being sick all the time. Patrick offered, "When you aren't sure what you need or why you're here, it is perfectly fine to say to the altar, "I need help. Please help me." So this became my mantra.

We rested and fasted for the remainder of the afternoon, and then gathered in the small closet-like room off the entry way that Patrick had converted into the perfect miniature ceremonial space. There were African masks and animal-hide drums and actual wizard robes hanging on the walls, plus all manner of sacred talismans meticulously placed on a multi-level wooden shelf that filled the space of one of the walls, from floor and ceiling. There was just enough room for the three of us and that special square of blue fabric on the floor.

When Patrick first unrolled the mushroom altar, I half expected the glory of God to come spilling out. Nope. It was just the same old blue felt with grey markings. The initiatory ritual was the same as before: cleansing ourselves with sage, brushing ourselves down with the eagle feather, calling in the directions, tossing cornmeal over our shoulders, eating the mushrooms one by one, and sipping hot chocolate. I was still grossed out by the taste of the mushrooms, but it wasn't as terrible this time, partly because I had already spent the last several months feeling so sick.

The effects begin almost immediately. I feel the altar calling to me, pulling me in, like a black hole. It's so powerful. I have to actually put my hand on the ground next to the altar and say, "No. Not yet. I'm not ready."

Eileen is quietly sobbing next to me, immersed in her own process, but then my words catch her attention. As she looks up, I see a beautiful serpent emerge in the space between us, and I am suddenly very confused about whether we are actually in the middle of Manhattan and not some jungle ceremony in the Amazon. The serpent energy moves toward me, pulling me into the same vortex as the altar. It is overwhelming, and I finally have to surrender. I keep repeating my mantra, "Please help me."

The swirling serpent enters my stomach and starts spinning a spiral of energy within my womb space. It feels invasive at first, like I am being taken over. I start having flashbacks to some of the scenes with my dad. I keep focusing on the energy in my womb, swirling swirling swirling. I start crying and my hands start shaking, so Patrick hands me a rattle. As I let the energy inside me shake through the rattle, I start to feel more grounded in my body. I look at Eileen and say, "It's just so scary, Eileen. You don't know how scary it is. Patrick knows." And then I tell her about my dad.

It's worth mentioning at this point that the Mazatec mushroom ceremony is characterized by speaking and communication. Mushroom godmother María Sabina was especially skilled at expressing the will of the mushroom through prayer and song, adding "says" at the end of each statement to indicate that it was the mushroom speaking through her. Although I was aware of this historic fact, it didn't occur to me until much later in my own journey that the mushrooms had been speaking through me, too. It seems so simple, but they got me to verbalize the pain that I was trying to hold inside. My prayers didn't come out as chants or song. Just words. But with practice, I learned to verbally state exactly what I needed or wished for, and to say out loud what the mushrooms were showing me in my interior world. This process of verbalization seemed to move things along in terms of insight and healing. Now, I encourage others to do the same, but also to be careful what you say out loud, because it just might come true.

In response to my confession, Eileen shared that sexual abuse of girls and young women is rampant in her home country of Ecuador. She had known many women who suffered their entire adulthood from the after-effects. As difficult as it had been for her to leave her tropical, indigenous homeland for the grey, cold skies of the United Kingdom, she always believed that her mom had insisted on the move partly to protect her and her sister from the same fate. A big part of Eileen's vision for her work in Ecuador was teaching women about trauma and how healing was possible, through therapy and ceremony.

What transpired next is hard to describe. The mushrooms were much, much stronger this time.

We enter an alternate universe that only vaguely resembles Patrick's apartment. One memory is the clearest: I am laying on my back, nearly on top of the altar, with my knees spread wide open and one foot braced against the frame of the door. I hear Patrick in the kitchen, but he is actually an elderly female, a midwife preparing a bowl of hot water and folding clean, white sheets to receive a newborn baby. Eileen is my doula-sister, kneeling next to my body as I go through the contractions and expansions of childbirth. There is no pain, only the great joy and power of creation. I close my eyes and see a vast space opening up before me. My inhales and exhales feel minutes apart. I see how easy it would be to die, to simply follow my final exhale out into that great expanse of welcoming darkness. During the long pause at the bottom of my out-breath, I realize that when the breath simply flows out at the right time, death is not violent or painful. I hear Eileen crying, and think, "This is what it's like to be surrounded by grieving family members on your deathbed. Why can't they see there is nothing to cry about?" I choose to take the next inhale and open my eyes, and I know that a child is being born. Birth and death; "same, same," as the Nepali sherpas used to say.

As the ceremony is winding down, Eileen and I are lounging in Patrick's living room, chatting and giggling and enjoying the extra brightness of the colors and decorations, like the little fabric birds nesting in a woven lampshade. At one point, it is no longer Eileen but my sister across the room from me, laughing her characteristic, open-mouthed laugh. It feels so ordinary and lovely to be with her again. Then it's Eileen in her body again and she says, "Let me show you something" and she points her finger toward the lampshade and pretends to paint something in the air. The light of the lamp grows and glows like white-gold and I am shocked to find myself in the presence of Christ. The white light IS Christ, in his true, divine form. I crack up and remark, "Oh hi, Jesus, I didn't realize that's what you looked like." Let's just say that Catholic school would've been a lot more compelling if someone had shown me that first. The next day, Eileen told me that her dad had first showed her that divine light on his deathbed.

About an hour later, we decide to go up to the roof to see the full moon. The strangest sensation comes over me as I am about to walk out of the apartment into the hallway. I hesitate at the doorstep. "I just don't know if I can do this." Patrick responds, calmly, "You can do it. It's time." And as I step out into the hallway, I realize that I am also stepping out of my sister's hospital room. I had no idea I had been hanging out in an ICU room with her dead body for a year and a half now, unable to let go. Thanks to my new friends, and the mushrooms, I am finally ready to walk out.

Stepping over the threshold, I am overcome with relief and joy. My excitement builds as we take the elevator up to the top floor and walk the final flight of steps to the roof. The full moon can barely compete with the carnival of lights of midtown Manhattan. Even the Empire State Building is inexplicably glowing purple that night. I spin my glow poi and feel myself merging with the lights. Eileen whoops and exclaims, "Look at this amazing city you created for us, Katherine. You gave birth to a new world!"

☾

My favorite part of a psychedelic experience is actually the morning after; that deeply embodied feeling of aliveness and tranquility, plus the giddy optimism that anything is possible. At Hopkins we called it the afterglow. It seems to track with the strength of a mystical experience, and some participants come in the next morning simply glowing from the inside. Their happiness and peace is palpable.

Well, I woke up that next morning feeling reborn, but thankfully did not find any actual babies crawling around. I remember stepping in the shower and really feeling the water on my skin for the first time in nearly a year. I take my time. There is no rush. I let all of the amazing memories move across my mind like a film reel. I soap every single part of my body with total mindfulness. Each finger. Each ear lobe. Each ankle bone. All of the parts. They're all here. I'm back.

Over lunch, Eileen and I reminisced about our experiences from the night before. Without consciously planning it, our ceremony had occurred exactly six months since my first fateful encounter with the mushroom altar in Freedom. So now, whenever someone has a big psychedelic experience, I recommend that they wait at least six months before they undertake another one. "*Bistare, bistare* . . . Slowly, slowly" as the sherpas used to say.

I was still learning a lot about integration at the time—learning how to apply the grandiose lessons from my far-out psychedelic journeys into the tedium and challenge of everyday life—so I didn't fully understand how hard the process could be. Having done this many times now, I honestly don't know how people can go straight back into their lives—work and family and bank accounts and trying to put gasoline in your car. It's all too much. And the first week post-ceremony can be really turbulent. It's like a spaceship crash landing in the ocean after months orbiting the Earth. You feel like a hero and can't wait to tell everyone what you saw, but you also can barely stand up from the gravity and you're all dizzy and disoriented. Re-entry can be a real bitch.

I was so lucky to have Eileen with me, day and night, so I could reach out to her when the aftershocks hit me. The hardest waves came at night, when my heart would start racing and residual trauma memories would take over my body and flash through my mind. One night, I looked over at the mirror that was bolted to the closet door and suddenly found myself being pulled into a long, dark tunnel. I knew this tunnel and I knew where it went. I called out to Eileen and said, "I'm having a hard time. I feel like I'm getting pulled back into the bad memories." And Eileen spooned her body against mine, and reminded me where I was and reassured me that I was safe. Then she asked, "Did your dad come into your room at night?"

It was the first time anyone had asked me that question, and it felt invasive. Not even my therapist had pushed me to go there. I replied, "It wasn't like that. I mostly remember feeling soothed by his presence. He would always sing this one lullaby—"Lay down, my dear daughters. Lay down and take your rest . . ." and stroke my hair with his hand. Those memories are the good ones. But I would also get sick every night I stayed at his place. I would wake up suddenly in the middle of the night and have to frantically climb down from my top bunk and try to make it to the bathroom. I would never make it in time and would just vomit all over the carpet. There was a permanent stain on the spot just outside my bedroom door."

As I was describing this all to Eileen, I noticed that toward the end of the long tunnel I could see a little boy crouched on the floor next to a toilet, hiding, with a red light glowing all around him. He had brown hair cut close to his head, although from the position he was in, I couldn't see his face. The red light reminded me of the master bathroom at my grandparents' house. They had a fancy heat lamp that glowed red and made the bathroom look spooky at night. We weren't supposed to go in there, so it was always thrilling to try to sneak in when they weren't paying attention. I looked at this little boy and wondered, "Maybe that's my dad?" My dad had never offered up much about his memories growing up. He would only talk about his college years, hitchhiking across the country and camping in the wilderness of Canada and living on an organic farm one summer with my mom. Maybe the mushrooms were trying to show me something I hadn't considered before: My dad was once a little boy.

I was still having somatic flashbacks the day Eileen had to fly home. We had opened a truly powerful portal on that night of the full moon, and it hadn't closed yet. I didn't want her to leave. We kept getting lost on the subway on our way to airport. We got on one train going the wrong direction and didn't realize it for maybe thirty minutes, and when we hopped off, we couldn't even figure out how to reverse course. I thought (hoped) she would miss her flight. She didn't have a cell phone, so there was no way to communicate once she got on that final train. I remember jumping out just as the door was closing and looking at her through the glass. She tilted her head and made the same quizzical expression that Tsering had made right before he sunk beneath the water for the last time. Like, "Oh well. Here I go." What a terrible goodbye.

I wasn't able to vocalize my intention going into the mushroom ceremony with Eileen, but I sure knew what it was coming out: I was ready to have a baby. Had some greater power known my true intention all along? Or was it really my own inner power, some much wiser part of myself who knew what kind of life would make me truly happy? I thought back to the vision quest when the rattlesnake led me to a little girl curled up in a desert cave, and the haunting dream of the lost child in Nepal. I thought about my lotto ticket in Scotland; exclaiming out loud that I would name my daughter Rosslyn. And my first intention with the altar: I'm here for the little girl. Plus, this could explain all of the pain and illness of the summer; maybe my body was getting cleared out, detoxified, prepared to grow a new life.

Unfortunately, tensions were high when I returned to Connecticut. I tried to tell John about the magical, fantastical mushroom voyage with Eileen, but it was already losing its luster. To make matters worse, I was leaving for another conference, in Colorado, in a few days, and John wasn't able to come with me. "Well, I just had my period the night of the ceremony," I offered, "So I should be ovulating now . . . it's worth a shot, right?" We had sex, and I prayed that it would be enough; that this time, my little girl would decide to stay.

☾

Out in Colorado, I reconnected with the herbalist friend who had guided me through the soul retrieval experience a year earlier. She had found a new place, high up in the mountains, and invited me over to check out all the medicines she was wildcrafting and cooking up. I told her about the mushroom ceremonies and about my dad. She had a very different reaction from anyone else I had told: "That must be really hard for your dad, to have to live with that past. And feeling that hate from you all the time. You should really forgive him." I was so not ready to hear that. But she was always like that, pushing me beyond my comfort zone, challenging my narrative. "You're already the Buddha, so start acting like it," she'd say. Or, "You're the one creating all of this pain and suffering for yourself. Why don't you try creating something new?"

I thought I could weasel out of taking drugs that day. But I knew even before I stepped into her witchy abode that I didn't have a choice.

She asked, "When was the last time you smoked the changa I gave you?"

She had crafted a special blend of DMT and other herbs that she claimed could release both mental trauma and physical pain. When she gave it to me the year before, she had told me to smoke it every week.

And I gave some embarrassed, mumbling response, "I don't know, sometime last spring. It didn't do much. I don't think it's the medicine for me."

The truth was I had thrown the vial into the middle of the lake, mistaking the spirit of DMT as part of my problem.

"Well, I think you need to try again."

I continued to make excuses, but she insisted.

"OK, OK. Just this once."

My heart starts pounding, like I am strapped into a roller-coaster slowly clicking up to the peak of the first drop. I arrange a pillow and some blankets on the floor, and her saint of a dog lays down next to me. He was the one who had come to my rescue the night ayahuasca was busy telling me how fucked up I was and how I needed to stop drinking and take better care of myself. That dog had masterfully broken through ayahuasca's wall of judgement by just lying next to me and loving me. You know the saying, "All dogs are *bodhisattvas*?" Well, I would add that dogs are also great trip sitters. They have perfected unconditional love. And they keep their opinions to themselves.

"Remember," I tell her, "I'm dumb about smoking. I don't know how to do it right without coughing. You need to guide me through each inhale and exhale."

"Yeah, yeah, I know," she replies.

She holds the glass pipe up to my lips and starts heating the herbal concoction with a lighter. The process always feels mildly dangerous, like holding your nose over a bubbling vial in tenth grade chemistry class. The DMT smells like the grape syrup my mom used to give me when I couldn't fall asleep at night (wait a minute, DMT . . . Dimetapp . . . hmmmm). The first inhale isn't so bad, but by the second one, I lose my bearings. As I lay back, the fractal visuals erupt like broken glass across my vision: red, gold and green. I see Eileen's face float past, and then the serpent from our mushroom ceremony. I am now fully convinced that I have been in some days-long, delirious drug trance deep in the jungle this entire time, starting with my *Alice-in-Wonderland* tour of London. Then John's face floats past, "He's innocent in all of this," a voice says. In all of what? Confused and frightened, I reach out for something, anything, to hold onto, and find the dog's belly, which is soft and warm and momentarily reminds me of my research monkey from the Dartmouth days. I reach down with my other hand and feel my own belly. As I breathe, my belly moves up and down, and I feel like I am floating on a peaceful sea. As my breathing calms, a channel of energy comes surging from somewhere very high above my body and into my womb. If Rebecca's death channel was pure love, this new radio frequency is pure hope. The energy fills my body, like a little bliss-filled nuclear bomb going off and spreading its radioactive joy throughout every square inch of my body's ecosystem. And then, it collapses into a tiny dot, right in the center of my lower abdomen. I smile and start crying. "It's OK. I'm here," I say out loud.

☾

I felt like anything was possible in the wake of my daughter's miraculous arrival through the DMT portal. But I never expected to find myself in a very fancy London apartment having sushi and talking about the wonders of DMT with philanthropists, and then driving in a luxury sedan with electronic dance music blaring on our way to a gorgeous countryside estate where I would learn the ins and outs of MDMA-assisted therapy for post-traumatic stress disorder. Most of the team from Imperial College was there, plus a bunch of European clinicians and a handful of Americans from the non-profit organization that was hosting the training. The atmosphere was charged with optimism and excitement, and I'm pretty sure I was the only person in the castle asleep by 9 P.M. The biggest risk I took during the three-day training was soaking in the huge mirror-walled indoor jacuzzi.

The MDMA training was only a rest-stop on the way to our final destination. The philanthropists had invited me to visit a secretive island off the coast of Great Britain where they were in the beginning stages of complex negotiations with the medical board and local politicians to advance psychedelic therapy for terminally ill patients. The island had a state-of-the-art hospice, newly constructed, that was free to all residents. The philanthropists hoped to achieve an exception to the normally restrictive UK rules against the therapeutic use of Schedule A drugs (similar to our Schedule 1 drugs in the US). They thought that the results from the US studies of psilocybin for anxiety and depression in cancer patients would help convince the VIPs on the island to consider changing their territory's laws to allow similar clinical research to be conducted at the hospice. Even though I wasn't involved in the cancer study at Hopkins, my research on openness was well known, and I was a great spokesperson for the work. I wasn't the only person they had invited to meet with the island officials, but on that particular trip, it was just me.

The promise of a charitable psychedelic hospice played to my deepest wound and my greatest dream. After watching my sister's tortured death in an ICU to the tune of $10,000 per day, of course I wanted to help create a beautiful, spiritual, free alternative. Walking into that gorgeous building felt like a breath of fresh air after the stuffy, old Hopkins research unit. One of the doctors led us around to meet with a few of the residential patients and introduced us to the nurse who oversaw out-patient care. She reminded me of Mary.

I asked her, "Why are so many of the rooms empty?"

And she said, "Oh, you know, it's like everywhere, most people want to die at home. People usually only end up here if their families can't take care of them."

As we continued our tour, I noticed how the tile floors gleamed and our footsteps echoed quietly through the pristine hallways. Piano music floated past our ears. And then we arrived at a very special, separate corridor of the hospice: the children's wing. It hadn't occurred to me before that moment that children also needed hospice. I hadn't thought about what their special needs might be. The doctor was very proud of two rooms in particular: one was a play area for the patients themselves but more importantly, for their siblings when they came to visit. The other was basically a large refrigerator decorated like a living room.

"We designed this room so that parents could stay with their child for as long as they need to after death."

As we left, I noticed a big rainbow painted on the far wall and the name of the wing: Rebecca House.

The luncheon that followed was awkward and anxiety-ridden. I had never seen so much food piled onto a table before, with no one eating. Everyone was in suits, and I felt conspicuously underdressed. The philanthropists had prepped me a little bit for what to say and who the people were. I was encouraged to talk about psilocybin and openness and my sister, but not about my own psychedelic experiences and definitely not about how things sometimes went sideways in the Hopkins sessions. Whatever I shared about psilocybin had to fit with the ethos of the place, which was PEACE. Death is peaceful. Death is beautiful. Death isn't ugly, or scary. Death is definitely not a bad trip.

Toward the end of the meeting, I surprised everyone and myself when I went off-script. One of the very important people was talking about how they would need a point person to coordinate the research study, if it happened. They would need someone with experience in clinical trials, someone who knew how to manage high-dose psilocybin. Of course, I took this request very personally.

"I'd be happy to move here and be that person," I said.

I didn't catch exactly how upset the philanthropists were until we were walking out to the car.

"Well, Katherine. That was really something, what you pulled off in there," the woman said.

"What do you mean?" I asked. "Did I do something wrong?"

And then the man chimed in, "I think what you have failed to understand is that we are the ones doing the negotiations. Not you. We brought you here, and any decision about your involvement is up to us."

Oppressive silence filled the car as we drove the perimeter of the tiny island. I mostly felt like a teenager in trouble; *shit, Mom and Dad are so pissed*. Despite the cold, grey winter weather, we stopped for ice cream, which temporarily lifted the philanthropists' moods. The man started going on about a "bespoke clinic" he wanted to build on an outcropping by the ocean, in an old psychiatric hospital that had fallen into disrepair. He certainly had a grand vision for this particular overseas territory.

After an extremely turbulent plane ride back to the mainland that gave me flashbacks to Tucson, my day at the island hospice began to feel like a dream. I had taken the name of the children's wing—Rebecca House—as a sign that this was my next mission. Thank God! It was all finally starting to make sense again. I stayed up late that night planning out how I could split time between a new psilocybin-for-depression study at Imperial College and the hospice. I had already met with Robin (Carhart-Harris) and his mentor, David Nutt, and figured I was a shoo-in for the job. The next morning over breakfast, I pitched my idea to the philanthropists. The discussions were intense, but we managed to work out a salary and a strategy. I laughed to myself, "Maybe the Scottish lottery was right about the baby and the research center."

To my surprise, a dream job had also opened up for John while I was gone. Toward the end of the summer, my mom had seen a posting in the local newspaper about a town-owned farm that needed a new manager. The 100-year-old farm—including historic barns, a herd of beef cows, and nearly 90 acres of protected land—had been gifted to the town by an elderly farmer who was a local legend, born and raised. Sadly, the farmer died shortly after the transfer, and the town quickly learned that they had no idea how to take care of cows without blowing through the entire trust that the old farmer had left them. So they decided to find someone who could turn the farm into an actual business—and pay the town rent to boot. John had maniacally drafted a stunning fifteen-page proposal in a single weekend, but we all assumed they would end up choosing one of the local guys over him. Everyone was stunned when John and his business partner ended up earning the votes of more than half the town. We later learned that John was the only applicant who had offered more than $0 in monthly rent and who didn't expect the town to pay him a salary. As the saying goes, be careful what you wish for, because you just might get it.

John and I spent the final weeks of the year debating the

merits of our competing dreams. I was convinced that I could split time between the farm and London, or maybe John could get the farm up and running and then his business partner could take over for a year so that we could live our fairy tale life with our new baby in the British Isles. Plus, I believed that the mushrooms were on my side. "Remember John," I said, "they told me the farm is too big, it will destroy you." The mushrooms had even told my brother that John and I were supposed to live our life as nomads, always ready to go where we were most needed. But John was dead set on achieving his dream, and maybe there was a part of all of us that needed to believe his dream was possible, too.

The town graciously let us move into the empty farmhouse on Dec 31st, and I slept that first night on a mattress on the floor with my niece, Anya, while John and his best friend went to a local pub to celebrate. Anya and I ended up getting a terrible stomach bug the next day and I spent half of January eating only white rice, which my mom's long-time Greek doctor said was the best way to clear stomach bacteria if you couldn't take antibiotics.

All the way up to the 20-week anatomy scan, I kept worrying that something would be wrong with the baby; that I would be punished for playing with cosmic fire in the months leading up to her conception. But this was just my old Catholic upbringing trying to freak me out, as usual. After we made it safely past the dreaded half-way point in the pregnancy, my little girl's healing presence became unmistakable. I had never felt so happy, all the time. I loved my body; I loved the world. She spoke to me and explained how she wanted to be born at home. She told me it would be OK, and not to listen to anyone who told me something bad would happen. She told me she wanted to be named

Frances, which was her dad's secret first name marked only by an F. (Thankfully, she let me keep Rosslyn as her mystical middle name). She even helped me launch that psychedelic center the lottery had promised us, the first psychedelic education and integration center in New York City.

My final decision to give up my British psychedelic fantasy wasn't easy, but it did feel like destiny. I continued to work remotely for the philanthropist couple, helping them design the psychedelic hospice study they were trying to pitch, but the new opportunities emerging in New York were a more natural fit. I pulled tarot cards and sat at my altar in the room I had just painted purple and gold, my Muse Room. I did yoga every day and felt my daughter's growing presence in our life. I watched real magic happen as the ancient farm machinery refused to function until John and I walked the full perimeter of the farm and paid homage to a huge old, dead tree that looked like a horned owl. I imagined building a yurt in the far corner of the back pasture and calling it YIPPEE (the Yurt for Integrating Powerful Psychedelic Experiences). I witnessed the birth of our first baby cow—on Valentine's Day—and then our first baby goats. My mom had always told me that my birth was the thing that restored her faith in the world after her brother drowned and then her father died of a broken heart, all when she was only eighteen. I didn't understand what she meant until I was living through it myself. Creation is nature's antidote to death.

CHAPTER 5

((

Happy Happy

You can tell it was the right decision because it's the one that you made.

—GARY WEBER

W E WANTED SO BADLY for the farm to work that we managed to ignore the obvious, early signs that maybe the mushrooms were right. During the first week after we moved in, about six inches of snow fell overnight and the local guys refused to plow our driveway because we "weren't from around here." The driveway remained covered in snow—which we thought looked kind of pretty, so we posted a pic to social media—and then the First Selectman (the small-town equivalent of the mayor) threatened to evict us for preventing emergency services access to town property. This was the same guy who had posed, smiling, next to John and his business partner just a few weeks earlier as they signed a five-year lease. We began to suspect that the politician's friendliness had all been for show.

Even as I gave birth to our daughter in the farmhouse that summer, there were monsters lurking outside our window, literally. During the early morning hours before my water broke, we were awoken by the bright glare of the automatic driveway light and sounds of things being smashed in the barn. John ran outside to find some young guys from one of the neighboring farms fleeing the scene. They were the same guys who liked to hurl insults at us as they drove past the farm; the same guys who never wanted us to win the vote; the same guys who never wanted us to live in "their town." What we didn't fully appreciate at the time was that the town leaders felt the same way. They never wanted John to win the vote and were committed to making him as miserable as possible until he couldn't take it anymore and left. But they seriously underestimated how much John could take.

That first year, we focused our energy on community events that would hopefully garner us more support from the town. Local families would bring their kids to play with the baby goats and swing on our swings and eat farm-fresh burgers. Even the town leaders would make sure to show up for a photo op for the local paper. After we hosted a few hundred townspeople for our first chili cook-off (with a live band!), we convinced ourselves that maybe the town was finally getting comfortable with us. We might be liberal academics who had lived in . . . California! The horror! Still, we thought John had proved himself at least tolerable enough among the good ol' boys for them to let us live in relative peace.

But then things went south with John's business partner. To everyone's surprise, his girlfriend had become pregnant and decided to quit her lucrative job in the city. We tried living together for a few months, but they were quick to move out as soon as our newborn daughter's cries pierced the muggy noon-day air. We figured their move was going to give everyone the space they needed to create their little family nests, but in hind-sight, it was a pretty obvious indication of underlying tensions.

When the business partner's girlfriend had her baby, she began to share how she really felt about everything. She was pissed that she was "forced" to leave the farmhouse. She wasn't a big fan of my psychedelic work and was worried about what it would be like for her child to grow up around "that kind of person." A myriad of other bombs went off over the next month or so, including a major one between me and another couple who had moved in to help run the garden. Long story short, the business partner decided to leave and the other couple moved out and John was left with a big empty farmhouse, ninety cows to feed in the middle of winter, and, unsurprisingly, major depression.

As John marched through that second year, the underlying pattern of his prior physical symptoms became clear. He had been tolerating low energy, weight loss and anxiety during our entire first year on the farm, which he chalked up to the never-ending work and hassles from the town. Farm work, especially in the summertime, is so grueling and thrilling that you're basically too busy running to keep up with the abundance of Mother Nature to think too much about academic issues like, oh, your sanity, and whether your business partner's girlfriend actually can't stand you. Plus, our dear daughter was one of those special kinds of babies who really didn't like sleeping through the night, or by herself, and also liked to cry a lot. It was a perfect storm.

The real tidal wave hit when our town went for Trump in the national election, and our local leaders began to show their true, full colors. Of course, I had made it known that we did not vote for Trump, with a large sign in the front yard that proclaimed,

"Love Trumps Hate," which the head politician promptly stole. Things really went downhill from there.

After that, John's anguish was palpable. The only reprieve came during the few vacations we took to get away from the farm. Within a day or so of leaving, John's symptoms would lessen, and he'd feel like his old self. Then the anxiety and depression would hit him again as soon as he caught a glimpse of the big blue silo sticking up through the trees. "Happy Acres," it announced. Yeah, right.

Whenever the weather turned cold and rainy, we would retreat to the grand old hallway at the center of the farmhouse. The hallway was the home of a Baldwin upright piano that I found in an estate sale the first winter, and we took turns pretending we could play. Frances had all her toys strewn about and it was like a super large, child-proof playpen. One evening in late January, shortly after Trump was inaugurated, John was slumped in a bean bag chair in the middle of that hallway while Frances played around his feet. His body was there, but his soul seemed to be kind of slinking away, disappearing into some invisible void behind him. Frances, ever the optimist and natural healer even at eighteen months old, unexpectedly jumped on top of him and starting pounding at the center of his chest with her little fist saying, "Happy! Happy! Happy!" And John burst into sobs and said, "I just don't know what to do."

It was devastatingly obvious that John's depression could sink all of us, not just him. So the next day, I called my meditation teacher and asked if John could join the next week-long retreat he was leading. Usually, being in silence for seven days, alone with your thoughts, is not the ideal prescription for someone struggling to see the point of being alive. But I knew that John loved discipline and routine and healthy, vegetarian meals, and he really needed to be around someone other than his wife and

daughter and a bunch of cows. Plus, I could vouch for this particular meditation community. During my pregnancy with Frances,
I had participated in two, week-long retreats with them at their
center in northern Vermont, and I found them loving and funny
and supportive of a beginner's attempts at enlightenment. I
mean, they even let me cheat and eat PB&J sandwiches in my
room at night to quell my pregnancy hunger. This community
had helped me discover the confidence I needed to be a mom.
Maybe they could help John discover the confidence he needed
to survive the farm.

I was facing my own existential crisis of sorts about whether
or not I could stay in America with Trump as president, living
alongside the people who agreed with him. I had been joking
about immigrating to Canada, so I told John that while he was
on retreat, Frances and I were going to see what it was like in
Montreal that time of year. I should've remembered from my
college days, when we would drive up to Montreal and spend
the entire night dancing and then drive back the next morning; it was bitterly cold, grey, and flat. At least the people spoke
French.

I found myself going through the motions of what it would
be like to leave our homeland for good. I took pictures of every
room in the farmhouse, which I had painted brilliant, bold
colors while pregnant with Frances. I realized that the rooms
formed a full rainbow when I placed the photos next to each
other. We packed a normal amount of winter clothing, including our ski gear, but the most important bag I packed was a
small, green, retro Pan Am carry-on bag that I would always
bring with me on ceremonies. I wanted to see if I could fit
everything of real importance in that one bag. Passports, birth
certificates, photos, my journals, and my sister's ashes. It was
heavy, but it all fit.

We booked a room at a quaint bed and breakfast in a small, farming town in the Northeast Kingdom of Vermont. The roads were long and winding, with big, open fields between. The inn-keeper and her husband had raised many children and grand-children in that house and had collected lots of books and toys over the years. Frances immediately fell into playing with the fake kitchen set from 1973, and it felt like home. John and I were both nervous, but tried to enjoy this temporary reprieve from the catastrophe that was our life at the farm. Light snow had been falling all afternoon, and when we pulled back into the driveway after seeing some friends of friends at their farm nearby, our car tires formed an accidental heart in the snow.

The next day, Frances and I dropped John off at the medi-tation center around lunchtime. I saw a few familiar faces, but some of my favorite folks had moved on. John smiled for the first time in months and I said to him, "You're in good hands. Trust these people. They'll take care of you." And as Frances and I drove off, a feeling of lightness and possibility filled the center of my chest.

Even before we'd made it down the dirt road, I had lit a cig-arette. I know, I know, maybe you didn't see this coming, but I had been smoking since college. I distinctly remember my first cigarette, walking down the adorable main street of my college town while rolling on MDMA; I literally floated off the side-walk. There is nothing better than MDMA, and nothing more addictive than nicotine, so there was no way I wasn't going to become permanently hooked. Throughout college and graduate school, before I even had a concept of being responsible for lives other than my own, I smoked on and off, less when I was happy or training for a triathlon and more when I was writing my dis-sertation or getting jealous about John playing tennis with an ex-girlfriend. Cigarettes were my own personal island.

My dad had smoked throughout my childhood, while sitting next to me on the chairlift during our ski vacations and in the car while I was in the passenger's seat, so my body was already super familiar with all the sensations. The sharp sulfur smell of the lit match followed by the easy, wafting smoke from the cigarette, and then the slight light-headedness. I secretly enjoyed it when my dad would smoke, because it meant he was happier and calmer, and I got a bit of a second-hand kick. Plus, we always sang our favorite songs—mostly U2 and Paul Simon—against the backdrop of his smoke. I could ask him complicated questions, like how car engines worked, and he would puff away and regale me with his superior intellect.

But my sister hated—HATED—that my dad smoked. She even wrote an essay in high school English class called "In Love with an Addict," about what it was like to love her father while being disgusted and horrified by his lifelong habit. My dad had tried to quit so many times, the most elaborate method being some fancy hypnosis retreat in Northern California. Nothing worked. Until my sister's double mastectomy in 2010 when he finally managed to quit for good. I suppose he knew that if he didn't quit at that point, there was no hope of any further relationship with my sister, or her daughter.

When my dad first told me he had lung cancer, I felt like he deserved it. John and I had just moved into the farm, and I was riding high on pregnancy hormones and just could not be bothered. I wouldn't even drive him to his chemotherapy appointments. I wanted nothing to do with his treatment or cure. I was still furious with him about what had happened with my sister; I figured that if she could get cancer and die at twenty-nine because of some shitty genes she inherited from him, then he deserved whatever outcome followed forty years of non-stop smoking. It didn't matter that my sister had already forgiven him, which was one of the more shocking things she revealed to me in the hospital. "How can you forgive him?" I asked, disgusted. "His inability to deal with reality just cost you your life!" But like I said, she was a fucking saint

I never told my sister I smoked because I assumed she would never talk to me again. John was the only person in my immediate family who knew. But even John believed I had quit when Frances came into our lives. And I had. Until one night in New York, when Frances was about a year old. It was one of the first nights I was able to be away from her for a whole evening, since she was the kind of baby who wanted to nurse every two hours, 24/7, and hated drinking milk from a bottle. I was literally physically connected to her for fourteen straight months. But that one glorious summer evening, walking through the East Village with my best friend from college, I felt free again. He never used to smoke but he did now because it was the one thing that seemed to keep his own mental demons at bay, and I asked him for a cigarette. He was not happy about giving it to me, but I said, "Hey. I spend the rest of my life taking care of people. This is the one thing I can choose that has nothing to do with taking care of anyone, including myself."

And, as anyone who's tried to quit a million times knows, cigarettes don't care if it's been a couple days or a week or 9 + 12.5 months (which is how long I had been pregnant and nursing). They are just thrilled to get you back. I felt bad enough about the potential effects on Frances that it prompted me to wean her and get on with my life as an independent adult. I nursed her for the last time that fall and traveled to a tiny island in the Pacific Northwest to lead a sanctuary space in the middle of a big festival, and of course, smoked cigarettes the whole time. Nicotine had always been a great, focusing energy for me while having to stay up all night surrounded by other people losing their minds. And when I got back from the festival, Frances was happily drinking milk from a sippy cup and sleeping in her crib. I was able to wean myself down to about one or two cigarettes a day, and I thought: this is manageable. Maybe I can be a mom after all.

Each morning and afternoon, while Frances was with John or napping, I would put a single cigarette and a lighter in my coat pocket, and walk way out into the back section of the farm field, into the Sacred Grove as I called it, beneath tall, sweeping trees whose leaves formed perfect fractal shadows against the sky. Whenever someone who knew about trees and plants would visit the farm, they would always make sure to inform me that these trees were actually an invasive species—dun dun dun! But they were always the Tree of Heaven to me.

It took about ten minutes to trudge all the way back there, through the cow fence and around the big pond, dodging stinging nettle and piles of poop. Once you got beyond that final hill, you could no longer glimpse the farmhouse or the barns or even that stupid cell tower on top of the silo that was the source of so much of the strife with the politicians. You couldn't see or hear any neighbors or cars, and it felt like another world. The wild world, barely hanging on at the outskirts of everything else that had been mowed and landscaped and built up and paved and politicized. John and I always dreamed of setting up a bunch of tents and hosting some kind of bonfire, camping rave back there. I dreamed this dream as I sat on the grass and luxuriated in every single inhale, often holding the smoke in my lungs much longer than necessary to get an extra buzz.

Cigarettes really helped get me through that winter of John's depression. If the day was really hard, and the two forays to the Sacred Grove didn't cut it, I'd wait until John was putting Frances to bed, which always took at least half an hour, and sneak out onto the covered front porch and sit in the old rocking chair and furtively enjoy two and a half minutes of parenting-free perfection with my old friend. It was the only time I could just be myself.

So of COURSE I rolled down the window and lit a cigarette after dropping John off at that meditation center. I felt hopeful and free. Although I also admonished myself for smoking in the car while Frances was in the back. That yucky feeling of self-hatred and shame and judgement snuck in, as I remembered every time my dad had done the same thing and how my sister and I had judged him for fucking up our lungs along with his own. But this time I realized what it might have felt like from my dad's point of view, being a frustrated, exhausted parent who just needed a fucking break, and a cigarette. Maybe cigarettes were his best friend too.

As I drive, the sun starts setting and the snow starts falling. Ahhhh, snow falling in the hills of Vermont at twilight! It is quaint and beautiful at first. But twilight becomes darkness, and there are no street lights on Vermont country roads. The snow starts coming down harder by the minute and I feel the adrenaline begin coursing through my body, like during the first few bumps of turbulence on an airplane before the pilot tells the flight attendants to take their seats. The roads are windy and unpredictable, and then I lose my GPS connection, which is when I start to panic.

I check in the rearview mirror to see Frances sleeping peacefully in her car seat. She had been really struggling with a bad respiratory illness for the past few weeks but could usually breathe more freely while sleeping upright. I feel doubly guilty about the cigarette, now, and think maybe God—not mushroom-altar She-ra God, but that cranky dude from my Catholic upbringing—is punishing me for aggravating her little lungs. So I try the same strategy I had used on many a plane flight when the turbulence would get bad and my mind would start spinning on whether or not we were about to crash. When mindful deep belly breathing doesn't cut it, I start making pacts with God. In this case, I say, "If we get home safely, I'll stop smoking tomorrow."

Without knowing where I am turning, relying only on the compass directions, I manage to find my way to a tiny restaurant in the literal Middle of Nowhere. We eat pizza, and I slowly sip an IPA to calm my fried nerves. Somehow, despite the snow-covered roads, we make it the rest of the way back to the inn. Once Frances falls asleep, I sneak downstairs and out onto the snowy lawn to breathe in the fresh, cold air and remind myself of my new commitment. I think of John and the adventure of self-rediscovery that awaits him at the meditation center. The night feels like a fresh start for both of us.

The next morning, I packed up all our stuff and loaded the car and we headed to Burlington, which is a small city on the banks of Lake Champlain, about an hour south of the Canadian border. On our way, we swung through a local bookstore and bought a book about two hedgehogs who were best friends and wanted to turn into butterflies. We stopped for lunch at a tiny roadside diner and Frances ate a humongous bowl of mac n' cheese, which was unusual because she always had such a small appetite and had been eating even less since being chronically sick. We arrived in Burlington, satiated and excited for adventure, with the snow melting and the warmish winter sun beaming down as we walked around town. One of the former residents at the meditation center was going to be away for the weekend and had offered us her house. Her roommate was also gone, so we had the whole place to ourselves.

We let ourselves in and found it mostly clean but strangely decorated, with lots of weird shamanic accoutrements and herbs hanging to dry. Let's just say, the witchy vibes were intense. I had visited many similar abodes and generally found them welcoming. But this place felt different. It was a little bit like Hansel and Gretel stumbling into the witch's cottage, and I got a bit of a pit in my stomach. I tried to unpack quickly as Frances picked up every single drum and rattle and flute and ancient spellcaster, while also trying to put every tiny, choke-able thing in her mouth, including some of the dried herbs that had floated to the floor. I was quickly beginning to understand that the witchy places that had helped me through my own dark nights were not necessarily the best places for a kid.

That evening, we had dinner at the home of a woman I had met at a conference in New York. She made us yummy spaghetti and meatballs, and Frances played with her daughter, and I felt for the first time in a long time that I could just relax and not worry that something bad was going to happen to me or John or Frances. After dinner, we walked the short distance home, and it was starting to snow again. I tucked Frances into a little nest of pillows in the middle of the queen-sized mattress on the floor and snuck quietly out into the living room to have a small glass of wine and check Facebook and maybe think about meditating. But, instead, I found myself planning how I was going to wait until she was definitely asleep and then sneak out onto the porch for a cigarette. But wait! Hadn't I made that pact? With God? The nerve. And I did. I went out into the snow and had that cigarette and stated rather smugly, "Well, God, you're probably not real anyway and I'm in charge of my own life, so there."

When I return to the house, something feels off. I go up to the door of the bedroom and hear the normal pattern of Frances's intermittent coughing. Since getting sick, she would often have a short period of easy sleep followed by an hour or so of pretty intense hacking. The doctor had checked her out a few times, but the nagging cough would not go away. As a first-time mom, every little illness felt like the end of the world to me, and we had already had our fair share of trips to the ER. This was partly because we traveled so much—for my work and to see family and friends and escape from the farm—but also because I had terrible, lifelong anxiety. I always envisioned the worst things happening to people I loved, which had already come true with my sister. So I couldn't help but see Frances dying in my arms whenever she got even mildly sick. I had no barometer for assessing whether her coughs were run-of-the-mill snotty-nose kid stuff or life-threatening asthma. It was easier, if not slightly humiliating, to just take her to the hospital and have someone tell me definitively that she was not, in fact, dying, and she would be better in a few days, and here's some Tylenol for her fever and some Benadryl to help her sleep.

I go in the bedroom to see if I can prop Frances up with some pillows and turn her on her side, which often makes the coughing a little less bad. But she keeps coughing. So I pick her up and hold her in my lap, facing me with her legs wrapped around my hips, rocking her. I ask her if she's OK. And she says, "No. Dada." "Is Dada OK?" I ask. And she says, "No, no, no . . ." And then a new sound is coming out of her, but it's not coughing, and I can't figure it out and suddenly I realize she is choking. On what? I flip on the light and she has somehow vomited all over the bed. But because her nose is also congested, she can't breathe in-between the heaves, and she now has this panicked look in her eyes of someone who is drowning but not in water. I try to hit her back the way they teach you in child CPR and also comfort her at the same time, which would have been ludicrous if I didn't think she was about to die. Eventually, the vomiting subsides, and she is able to breathe.

My mind is racing now. The bed is covered in vomit. There's nowhere else to lay her down. The rest of the living room is just hard wood. It's snowing hard outside, so I start panicking that if something is really wrong, I won't be able to leave to get help. I am still holding Frances while I start frantically texting my friend whose house we just had dinner at, hoping in a slightly sadistic way that maybe she or her daughter also got sick and that it's some kind of stomach bug that's going around. Nope, they're fine. Frances projectile pukes again, all over the living room. Now I am really freaking out, because I don't have John there to balance out my usual catastrophic thinking. A voice in my head makes it super clear: "Frances is definitely going to die tonight, and it's all your fault, Katherine." I call the pediatrician's after-hours number and wait forever for a call back from the elderly doctor, who sounds like he's still dreaming when he admits that it's probably a stomach bug, but it also could be an allergic reaction to some new food she ate, and in which case, I need to take her to the hospital immediately. Fuck me.

I somehow manage to get Frances out of her vomit-soaked pajamas and dressed in her winter jacket and hat, throw on my boots, and run with her out to the car that is now half-buried in snow. It is freezing cold, and she is screaming as I shove her into her car seat. I can barely see through the ice-covered windshield as I navigate the maze-like roads across town to the hospital. We manage to park and get through the door of the ER without another vomiting episode, and of course, by then, Frances is awake and not crying and seems basically fine.

The lady at the desk is looking at me quizzically, "Can I help you?" I try to explain the seriousness of the situation, how we are from out of town and I'm solo parenting and my daughter is about to die, and instead I just feel like some tweaked-out, homeless lady who's looking to score a warm bed and some opiates for the night. They take pity on me and give us a private room. After about forty-five minutes, once Frances has fallen peacefully asleep on my chest, the doctor comes in to check her out and informs me that a particularly virulent stomach bug called norovirus has been going around and that's almost certainly what inspired the projectile vomiting. She leaves some anti-nausea medication on the bedside table that I remember from my sister's chemo days, and says, "It's a slow night. You can rest here for a bit before you venture home. If your daughter wakes up, you can give her these tablets to help her get through the rest of the night. They'll dissolve in her mouth."

When the doctor leaves, I immediately take the meds myself and pass out. After a few hours of fitful sleep, holding Frances in one arm as I lean against the metal railing of the hospital bed, I manage to get us back out to the car. The snow has stopped and daylight is beginning to break. Back at the house, I pull the vomit-covered sheets and blanket off the bed and throw them outside in a pile on the porch. I lay a bunch of our clothes on the bare mattress, and we fall asleep again for a couple hours before Frances wakes up, chattering, cheery, totally fine. And I feel absolutely wretched.

It's worth briefly mentioning at this point that most of the psychedelic plant medicines I had taken over the past few years had made it super clear that alcohol and cigarettes were not great for my health, or my temperament. On our first and only night together, ayahuasca had rather rudely told me that I needed to quit drinking or my life was over. Mushrooms didn't seem to care one way or the other, but they did keep telling me how much they wanted me to be a mom, which seemed inherently incompatible with drinking and smoking every day. And San Pedro, in a much more chill and cool manner than ayahuasca had basically told me that if I really wanted to be happy, I should think about putting as much energy into my marriage as I did into my love affair with cigarettes. So, the signs had all been pointing in one pretty obvious direction for a while now. But I am so, so stubborn. I just wait until either someone I love dies or is about to die until I get serious about turning my life around. Well, I guess this was one of those moments.

The main thing that is so hard about accepting a rock-bottom-type revelation, even when it's obvious, is it typically happens first thing in the morning when you feel like absolute shit from the night before. Exactly when you would most love to cover up that absolute shit feeling with something like alcohol or cigarettes. But lucky for me, I had an eighteen-month-old who remembered nothing from the night before and needed to be fed and there was nothing in the fridge. I briefly entertained a beautiful vision of me and Frances enjoying a picnic lunch at the local library, until I stood up and suddenly felt very, very ill. Oh, right. Norovirus. Now it was my turn. I had spent enough of my college years hungover, so I knew how to keep it together in public and just hang out in that super unpleasant liminal nausea space. We somehow made it through the grocery store and to the library, but I had zero plans for how to address nap time and my friend's vomit-covered apartment, let alone where we were going to sleep that night.

So, I called my mom. This is the thing about being a mom. Your kids will likely never thank you for the sleepless nights and panic-driven hospital visits, and you sure as hell won't get any credit for the million potential catastrophes that were narrowly averted only by your constant, exhausting vigilance. But you know for sure your adult child is still going to call you first when she's sick and stuck in a strange town with no plan. The second miracle of our trip—the first being Frances not choking to death on her own vomit—was learning that my mom's best friend's sister lived in Burlington, and we could stay with her for a night. Thank God (not sure which one).

It wasn't the best night, but it wasn't so terrible either. Frances managed to eat a few bites of plain penne and I managed not to puke, and we somehow felt good enough the next morning to head to Montreal. I had booked a sweet hotel at a super discount, so come hell or high water, I was going to cross that damn border. And as we drove north, things really began to look up. The weather had cleared and Frances wasn't screaming the way she normally does in the car and my nausea had lifted. I started to think about John on his retreat and wondered if maybe we were all more connected than we could imagine. Maybe the vomiting and panic and near-death experiences of the past two days were some cosmic reverberations of John's epic journey to save his own life. Maybe Frances and I had been purging all the nasty psychic shit along with him. And if this is what it would take to get our family back, it was totally worth it.

The hotel was indeed awesome, and our suite had a little living room and kitchen area, so I didn't have to worry about venturing out into the cold for every meal. And it was extremely fucking cold. But Montreal knows this, and so has designed a bunch of family-friendly indoor/underground entertainment options in the winter. We took the metro to the Olympic complex and meandered through the Biodome, which is this epic, indoor botanical garden and zoo. We checked out an art museum and even visited the spot where my favorite dance club used to be before they tore the whole building down. When we settled in for the night, I texted Patrick about the weirdness of the past couple days, and he came through with some killer advice, which is something that I suppose every real shaman knows: Always set up your altar while you're traveling. Create your ritual space; say the prayers of protection; repeat your intention. Life is psychedelic so you must always be prepared for the ceremony. And no, he didn't think it was weird that Frances was literally purging John's demons for him while he was on retreat. She was a natural-born mystic, after all.

After a couple more frigid days in Montreal, we started the drive back to Burlington. I had been in contact with the meditation teacher, so we were trying to plan the right time for a rendezvous to collect John. John was allegedly doing really well and might stay an extra night after the retreat was over. Great! The ceremony was almost complete. We're all going to be fine! Which I have definitely proclaimed, incorrectly, several times in the past after taking LSD. I say LSD because it just lasts so fucking long. It's been six hours and you've made it through this crazy wormhole and the world is coming back into form and you think, "Wow. I made it. It's almost over." And then it's another seven hours before things are even remotely over. So, that was the kind of naïveté with which I assumed that we would have a totally normal time waiting out the last day or so for John's return.

At least I was smarter about a few things on the return path. Rather than throw the dice with a stranger's apartment, I booked us into a modern hotel/conference center with a restaurant and bar, right across the street from an excellent kids science museum. Plus, there were two queen beds! And a TV! And Beyoncé was performing at the Grammys! We were totally going to just sail through this next 48 hours.

But God damn! Even Beyoncé was in on this unavoidable psychedelic ceremony. She was dripping with glittery gold,

absurdly beautiful and voluptuous and pregnant, and her performance was all about motherhood, and birth, and love, and
the pain of relationship, and healing, and starting again. "OK,
Universe, I'm paying attention. What is this all about?" And She
promises me (of course Her message was for me!): The curse will
be broken.

I wake up in the middle of the night with a sharp pain through
the middle of my stomach and run to the bathroom. Everything
is coming out of me from all directions. Oh. So, the purge isn't
over yet. The onslaught continues throughout the night until
Frances wakes up around 7 A.M. I am completely beat down and
worn out. I have no clue how I am going to take care of her feeling like this. I am dejected and pissed off and completely alone.
I have no one to call on. In an act of humiliating desperation, I
jump on Facebook and ask if anyone is in Burlington and could
come help take care of Frances for the day. No one offers. Not
one of my 1500 "friends." But someone steps up. My dad.

At this point I was still in the thick of it with my dad. During
my first trimester with Frances, I had thankfully reached a point
in therapy where I was no longer wishing torturous deaths upon
him. But once Frances was born, everything kind of blew up
again. I didn't trust him around her. Every time he held her or
played with her or talked to her, I felt like I was reliving my own
childhood with him. All the moments I felt like he was going
to drop me or laugh when I cried; it was just so painful to have
to relive that as an observer. I wanted to enjoy these moments
with my dad as a grandpa, not be constantly triggered back into
my own traumas. He was a better caretaker this time around,
but barely. I couldn't help but focus on every single sarcastic
comment, about Frances needing to nurse too much, or him
needing to make her tough, or my absolute favorite, "When are

your parents going to make you cry yourself to sleep like we did with your mom?"

So my dad calls and says, "I saw your post. I'm coming to Burlington." "But Dad, it's snowing! It's gonna take like six hours!" "No, it'll be fine. I have some meetings today, but I can leave right after work."

Shit. The last person on Earth I want to come take care of Frances while I'm too sick to even get out of bed. But I was helpless to turn him away. So I accepted this bizarre turn of events, offered Frances a sippy cup of milk and a bowl of oatmeal I made with hot water I boiled through the little hotel coffee maker, and turned on morning cartoons so I could pass out.

Whenever my dad would walk in a room, his deep, booming voice would project his tough-guy energy throughout every molecule of air. It was the voice I could never get out of my head. The voice that always told me what to do and corrected me and explained the world to me. It was unmistakable. It wasn't scary, it was just overpowering. My dad initially made his living as a trial lawyer, and then as general counsel for two health-food companies. His voice was his power, in the courtroom and at home. He made sure that everyone in the room knew he was the boss.

When he knocked on the hotel room door and entered, I braced myself for this voice. "Helloooooo, Frankie!" I was relieved but on edge. I desperately needed help, but I had never left Frances alone with him. I was caught between two of my biggest fears: being too sick to care for my kid and something terrible happening to her because of a bad choice I made (in this case, entrusting my dad with her care). He said, "Why don't I take Frankie to get breakfast downstairs and you can shower." What a totally normal and kind suggestion! I did my best to play it cool and not let every possible horrific scenario run through my head.

The next few hours were mostly uneventful. My dad had stayed in the room right across the hall, so he and Frances played and read books in his room while I recovered. The craziest thing about trauma is how much it can distort reality. The present moment showed a little girl, in love with her grandpa, having a joyful time. Laughing, joking, soaking up all the special attention. She totally trusts him! She loves him! But my mind turned it into a series of near-fatal disasters, like Frances choking on a piece of food or falling down the hotel stairs. Or the thing I had survived that felt worse than death: the constant, unpredictable threat of violation that my mind couldn't help but conjure every time my dad was near my daughter. While trying to block these nightmarish visions from my mind, I was also still trying to figure out the logistics of meeting up with John. Then, my dad suggested that we just drive back to Connecticut. He said, "I think you'll feel more comfortable at home. You don't want to be stuck here for days if John decides to stay longer."

During the drive, Frances and I dozed in the back seat and my nausea came and went, but mostly went. It was good to be back at our refuge by the lake, even with all its difficult memories. Most importantly, Teddy was there. Teddy, the humbly heroic golden retriever who had helped me through so much of my personal hell after returning from Nepal, running alongside me on the frozen lake and curling up next to me on the couch. Teddy, who had been by my dad's side through his addictions and anger and illness. Teddy, who had been like a bodyguard to my brother as he walked his own tortuous labyrinth. Nothing could go wrong now. Teddy was here. We were home.

And, because this is actually a romantic comedy, not a tragic one, it was also Valentine's Day. I watched Frances sitting on my dad's lap, drinking her milk as he read her a Dr. Seuss book. With his reading glasses and bald head, he looked like the quintessential, kind grandfather. And a single thought arced through my mind like a shooting star on a dark night: "My dad is the only person in the world who would drop everything to come save me." And I felt myself turn the slightest corner toward what psychologists and Beyoncé might call reconciliation.

CHAPTER 6

☾

Mama Bear

The essence of bravery is being without self-deception.

—Pema Chödrön

Y MEDITATION TEACHER used to joke that married couples do well on the spiritual path together because they can take turns going crazy. At any given time, there's at least one sane adult to take care of the house and kids and financial realities. Well, John's recovery was nothing short of miraculous. He returned home renewed, refreshed, energized and basically a version of himself that I hadn't seen in a very, very long time. He was able to sleep through the night and wake up without his heart pounding. He even stopped snoring! And he initiated some very difficult but necessary conversations with town officials to lay a path forward for the remainder of our lease. He was somehow able to treat them with kindness and compassion, and he found that he wasn't even angry with them anymore.

So, it was now my turn to lose it. I admitted to John that I was barely hanging on. I tried to share with him how scary it was that night in Burlington when Frances couldn't breathe, and how shitty it felt to be so sick and alone, and how humiliating it felt to have to let my dad take care of Frances. I was still dealing with so much bottled-up anger and constant thoughts about the distant past, and it was killing me. With all of that compressed rage, I felt like a caged monster, that if I let go of control, I would just lash out and destroy anything in my path. But the more I tried to explain it out loud, I realized that these were my issues. I needed to face them just the way John had faced his. No one else was going to understand the root of his depression or the root of my anger and anxiety. So I signed up for a week-long retreat with the same group.

The retreat I joined was going to be the first session the group held at their new retreat center, which was a gorgeous, dorm-style lodge surrounded by hundreds of acres of new growth forest on the slope of a small mountain. The views toward the north were epic; you could see all the way to Canada, and it felt like you were sitting on top of the world. There was a small, man-made pond just below the lodge, and plenty of hiking trails to explore. There was so much space that I even got my own room with a queen bed! What luxury. I figured this was going to be the perfect little self-care getaway to lovingly get in touch with my interior world and finally calm down my nervous system after nearly two straight years navigating the Mommy Hell Realms.

Because of my mushroom journeys with Patrick, I was no longer naive enough to waltz into a ceremony without an intention. My best sense of what psychedelics do is this: they amplify intention. If you don't have an intention, all sorts of shit in your mind will get amplified, some of it entertaining, some of it mystical, and some of it demonic. Back in my Hopkins days, we never suggested that our participants have a specific intention going into their sessions. We just encouraged them to Trust, Let

Go, and Be Open. And I believed that mantra for a long time. It certainly seemed to work for most of the folks in our studies. But for me, personally, I didn't start to heal until I started to use an intention to focus my mind during ceremony. If psychedelic healing can be compared to surgery, it's just better to use a laser to carve out those psychic tumors. Can you imagine a surgeon saying, "Hey, I don't really have a goal in mind today, I'm just gonna cut you open and hope for the best!"

In the spirit of preparing my mind in advance, I had a few phone calls with my teacher to discuss my intention. I recognized that most of my anxiety centered on safety: am I safe? Is Frances safe? And then anger flowed easily from that space of fear: what would I do to someone who hurt Frances? What would I do to myself if something happened to her? My anger seemed dangerous, violent, so my initial intention was to neutralize or tranquilize it. I had even said something similar to my therapist back when we were first dealing with my abuse: I just want to go into that part of my brain and zap it away. I don't want to remember it. I don't want to understand it. I don't even want to resolve it. I just want it gone.

My meditation teacher had also dealt with some pretty intense anger—actually, he called it rage—when he was a young man, and that anger was his primary motivation for dedicating his life to being a monk. He helped me see that wanting to tranquilize something was a form of violence too, thinking that zapping or turning off a part of you will save the rest of you. If you imagine a wild animal that has been tamed and trapped in a circus, like a huge rhino, breaking out of the gates and storming through a city, you would only tranquilize the rhino if you didn't know how else to handle it. It would be the last thing you tried before you just killed it. Better to spend some time with that animal and understand why it's trying to break free from its cage.

Darting the animal just to re-cage it won't resolve the destructive behavior itself.

The closest I had come to a wild animal was during the time I worked in that monkey lab at Dartmouth. We had all sorts of safety protocols in place, but I was still always afraid of the male monkeys. One time as I was putting one of the big boys back in his cage, he jumped free and just kind of clung to the side of the cage, looking at me. I had to decide in a split second what to do to avoid being attacked. I didn't stand a chance if he lunged at me, and these monkeys sometimes carried a virus that could be deadly to humans. So I froze. And I breathed. And I waited. I had to get super calm super quickly, or die. There was no choice. And after several infinitely long seconds, he decided to voluntarily climb into his cage.

Because of this experience, I knew that being calm was key to getting close to that kind of wild energy. If I wanted to understand my anger on retreat, I would need to do some pretty serious spiritual and psychological prep work to at least calm down the part of myself that was getting so angry all the time. So I returned to a tried-and-true healing medicine that I hadn't used in a long time: MDMA. It was kind of an accident, but a happy one. John and I had planned a date weekend in New York City while my mom stayed with Frances at the farm. It was inspired by a Valentine's Day card I had received from a friend that included what appeared to be two tabs of acid, with little cupids printed on them. John and I took this to be a good omen, and an invitation. We hadn't taken acid together since our first trip to Burning Man, over a decade ago and well before our lives got so serious and somber. Maybe this was the Universe giving us a ticket back into the amusement park. But the cosmic joke was on us, as the tabs were just art and contained zero illicit substances. I actually had a fairly strong come-up, because my psychedelic placebo response is so dialed in, but then John blurted out, "I think we got microdosed!" And all of the effects stopped, and we had a nice laugh about it all.

Not one to be sidetracked in the face of an entire weekend away from mommy duties, however, I announced that I had also brought a small amount of MDMA in case the acid trip took a sinister turn. John wasn't interested, as he was still riding high from his retreat, and MDMA had always given him wicked depression and malaise afterward. But he was happy to sit and hold space for me while I explored this territory. It was just enough of a dose for me to talk through some of the early childhood stuff and share about how Sarah and Patrick and my therapist were the only people who really believed and supported me. I was able to voice how I didn't want the abuse to be true, and how I was beating myself up about having these partial memories and not knowing the whole truth. Every day, sometimes several times a day, my mind would run through all of the scenarios, like pieces in a chess game, looking for the secret combination of moves that would finally rid me of the king. But I got stumped every single time. Every day I doubted whether any of it was true, while also knowing deep down that it definitely was. And because I didn't know exactly how it had happened in the first place, I didn't know how to protect Frances from something similar happening to her. "I mean, if someone did this to Frances, I would kill him," I told John. I was getting worried that this pattern of fear and rage was simply my life's curse. What if there was no way out?

Then the next day, we attended a short day-long retreat with an American woman who teaches her own form of a Tibetan-inspired somatic mindfulness practice that she developed during the process of healing herself from life-long gut problems. As I followed the guided meditation, I saw the core of my body as a broken down, dark, haunted mansion. As I traveled through the rooms, the place reeked of old fights and scared, crying children, and a whole bunch of creepy, unresolved ancestral energy. When the teacher invited us to imagine what it would take to restore life and vitality and warmth to this house, I immediately thought, "Burn it down and start over." This was what 30+ years of holding onto my trauma had done. My stomach and my lower abdomen, my womb and my sexual center, all of this haunted, forbidden space. Maybe this had something to do with why I was angry all the time. But how could I reignite the flame of my life without also accidentally burning the whole house down?

My final test before the retreat was a vacation with my dad, daughter and niece. We were going to one of my absolute favorite places in the world: Bermuda. And I loved being with my niece and daughter together, who were like sisters. But my dad was always the wild card. He could be really fun on vacations, but also, his normal temperament didn't change, which meant he had his usual anger outbursts and cranky moods. I was worried that all my background fears about safety would be exaggerated since I didn't have John or my brother around to help take care of the kids. But I was happily surprised to discover that I couldn't find my old anger anywhere. It was gone (at least temporarily)! I know, very hard to believe, after a single dose of MDMA and a quick tour of a haunted body-house. I enjoyed so many moments of joyful intimacy with Frances, really appreciating the reality that she was growing up and wouldn't be this little and dependent on me forever. I wasn't even frustrated that she still needed to sleep on my body for nap time, because I found that the weight of her body helped me stay connected with my own body and stay out of my mind's recurrent machinations. My niece and I had a lot of fun together, and I was even able to trust my dad with Frances so that Anya and I could go on some excursions just the two of us. Most amazingly, I never got mad at my dad once.

After Bermuda, I was pretty sure that I had cured like 80% of my anger issues. "I've successfully tranquilized my anger!" I proudly announced to my teacher during our final phone call before the retreat. "Well," he said, rather unfazed, "Let's see what we can do to ignite it again."

☾

I was surprised by how much grief emerged on the six-hour drive up to the retreat center. The flood gates really opened while I was listening to a song my dad used to play, by Shawn Colvin, called *Cry Like an Angel*. I never registered the lyrics as a kid, but all sorts of deep, non-verbal emotions came up along with my new-found adult grief. In the song, the woman talks about going back to her hometown, perhaps as an adult who had moved away, and kind of dealing with her past and giving herself freedom to stop running, and not be so tough. Yeah, that was it. I needed a refuge, a safe zone where I could put down all my shit and just cry. Surviving abuse was hard. Being a mom while re-living all that trauma every day was even harder. Why was it all So. Fucking. Hard? But, perhaps more importantly, why was I trying to walk around pretending it was so easy?

When I started the retreat, I was really out of practice. I had to get used to the discomfort of the various sitting postures and re-train my body to breathe naturally and deeply without forcing it. The teacher had suggested I use the technique I was most comfortable and familiar with, which was mindfulness of breathing. Simple, right? Just breathe and pay attention to the sensations of breathing. What a relief. This week is gonna be a breeze! And he added one thing: instead of focusing on the sensations of breath moving in and out of my nostrils—which is how I had originally learned the practice—focus on the breath sensations in the lower abdomen, an energy center called the *tanden* or *hara*. I imagined this place like a hearth, a glowing place of nourishment and togetherness. Luckily, this was also the location of my womb, and the center of that haunted house that was my body, so I could now practice breathing life back into it. I commented to the teacher, "I remember when I was pregnant with Frances, that *hara* space in my body was so full of love and aliveness. It was easy to keep my awareness there." And he replied, "Well, let's see if you can learn to do it without relying on another living being."

I diligently showed up to every meditation session, enjoyed the healthy meals, did my chores, and spent every free moment outside walking the property. I didn't feel a strong sense of belonging, not simply because I was the only non-resident, but because I was the only woman and one of maybe three adults, including the teacher. It was comedic, actually—like how did Mom wind up on Pirate Island with all the lost boys? But they were kind and helpful and sweet. During the teacher's dharma talks, I learned that the purchase of this retreat center marked not only a new beginning for the community, but also a huge responsibility. The teacher used his daily talks to challenge and inspire these boys, most of them in their twenties and without any real responsibilities, to step up and become adults. So, maybe it wasn't coincidence that I was there as the archetypal mother figure. During one of the talks, as the teacher was sharing about once having to take care of an entire orphanage of little boys in India, he kind of laughed and said, "I mean, if I can do that, or Katherine can be a mom, any of you can do it."

During one of the initial interviews, the teacher and I were exploring more deeply what my anger was all about. And I said something to the effect of, "I have a bone to pick with God."

The teacher said, "You really don't want to start that fight."

And I said, "No, I absolutely do. I'm done playing around. Someone has to answer for all of this. He's the one who's ultimately responsible, right?"

The teacher probed further, "What will God be able to give you?"

"I just want to know what's going on," I stated firmly,.

Something about my fear of terrible things happening to myself and those I loved, my anger when things didn't go the way I wanted, my hatred of what had already transpired in my life that I couldn't even remember correctly, the fact that my trauma and my sister's death could never ever be repaired . . . all of this was fueling my anxiety about what might happen in the future. And the answer to that entire mess of fear and anger boiled down to Knowing. My working assumption was that if I knew the Truth, including what was going to happen in the future, I would no longer be angry or fearful.

The teacher said, "Well, if you keep pushing forward, into the future, you will become more and more deluded. But if you allow yourself to move backward, into the past, that is the space of Knowing."

My therapist had once said something similar, but in psychological terms.

When I stated my desire to zap the part of my brain that was holding the terrible memories and just get on with my life, she said, "Well, you know, it *is* possible to do that. But the process isn't easy. You would need to go back as far as you can remember, through your infancy and your birth and your conception, until you finally remember what happened before you were born."

Whoa.

Between that mysterious pearl of a *koan* and my prescribed task of keeping my awareness on the sensations of breath moving in and out of my lower abdomen, I certainly had enough to keep me busy for the first few days. The daily routine was always the same, but the Katherine who sat down each day kept changing. I felt myself cycling back through the periods of my life. For the first day or so, I was just an agitated, stressed-out mom in need of about twenty naps. Then I felt some of the energy and confidence and mental discipline of my twenties come back. Then the stubbornness and invincibility and self-righteousness of my teen years. And then the glorious, open-minded, exploratory space of my late childhood. Those were my golden years, when I spent as much time as possible by myself, exploring the woods, letting my mind wander, imagining entire worlds that only I knew about.

This is how I spent a lot of my free time on the retreat as well. Hiking through the woods. Walking in slow circles around the pond. I noticed every little living thing on that property. I watched how the salamanders and tadpoles and fish congregated in miniature ecosystems along the bank. I even found myself using a stick to poke at them to see how they would respond, and feeling simultaneously like a little kid, unaware of how that stick could harm such a tender, fragile being, and also like a wise adult, noting: ahhhh, this too is one of the seeds of violence.

The honest truth is I spent a lot of time by myself outdoors growing up because I didn't feel safe inside. The manufactured world of man was threatening and had already proven itself to be uninterested in protecting me from harm. As the retreat went on, I found myself becoming hyper-vigilant for potential threats. The "Exit" sign that illuminated the hallway at night in an eerie red glow made me feel I was actually a patient trapped in a psych ward. I was clearly re-entering the trauma landscape of my early childhood. And like the mind of a young child, my Mind-on-Meditation had become so fluid that it could no longer recognize the difference between interior and exterior. The real fears and traumas contained in my deep memory banks flooded into the space around me. These sweet, kind young men were suddenly untrustworthy and dangerous, not because they were evil but because they just weren't paying attention. Everywhere I looked, I saw men and boys inflicting incidental harm and threatening safety, simply because they didn't know what they were doing, or didn't care. I even took offense when one of the residents picked some flowers and placed them in a vase on the altar at the front of the small meditation hall. Who are you to rip these flowers out of the ground? Just because it's something you like, something you want to have? It's not up to you to decide to kill this beautiful living thing just to satisfy some temporary desire. It doesn't belong to you! Just leave it alone. Leave HER alone. Don't touch her.

Our days began very early in the morning. We had to be sitting on our meditation cushions by 4 A.M., ready to chant the morning prayers. I only barely managed to survive these first few hours of each day, usually via some form of dissociation. I would chant the words and participate but not with any deep awareness of my body or mind. I would mostly think about how delicious breakfast was going to be. But this one morning, probably around day four or five, I was just super agitated. For the life of me, I couldn't shake this feeling of wanting to escape. Several times I had to resist the physical urge of my legs pushing me upward out of a sitting position, like they were already running me out the door. Of course, the easiest target in the room for my agitation was the teacher, because obviously he was the one who was requiring me to be here.

By the time chanting was over and we had reached the personal interview portion of the morning, I was in a rage. When the bell rang for my turn, I walked deliberately down the narrow hallway to the small room where the teacher was sitting, ready to give him a piece of my mind. And when I turned the corner, I noticed that he had the window open, which made the room unnecessarily cold. And this whole charade just seemed designed to put us through hell, like let's figure out how to make everything as unpleasant as possible. Was that the path to enlightenment? It just seemed cruel and pointless. I took my seat on the meditation cushion in front of him, and instead of speaking, I started breathing. I breathed in a way I never had before. Well, *I* didn't breathe. I was being breathed. My body was pushing each breath in and out of my lower belly, like a huge bellows was blowing air on a dying fire in a desperate, insistent attempt to rekindle it. All of the energy of my agitation and frustration and hyper-vigilance of the past two days was now transmuting into the most powerful sensations of breathing I had ever experienced outside of running track. After about a minute or so of this, the teacher, clearly also surprised and happy at this unexpected turn of events, exclaimed, "Finally we have a real relationship! Keep going . . ." In other words, I had shown up without my mask. I wasn't trying to perform my highly cultivated theatrical role of Katherine. And I was starting to get familiar with my anger, not as a concept, or a problem out there in the world, but as a direct experience in my body.

In psychology, we talk about insight as a cognitive event marked by an "Aha!" moment. When you suddenly see things in a totally new, enlightened way. It is not a gradual shift in understanding but a sudden awareness of a new perspective, a new reality. Like Einstein discovering $E=mc^2$. Eureka! That's it! Well, that morning, I learned that you can have exactly the same type of insight with your body. It was like a new day. I no longer felt like a stranger in a strange land, an alien trapped in a bizarre and uncomfortable human body, surrounded by potential dangers at every turn. This was MY body. This was my home. And I could just live in it. I wasn't even responsible for keeping it going! It was so intelligent, this infinitely complex, living machine, that it could breathe and move energy and digest food and meditate all on its own! It felt amazing.

This shift in somatic or energetic awareness was the key that opened the door to my earliest memories, the ones that formed when I didn't even know I was a self separate from the world. My meditations during that period are hard to describe. Perhaps they were truly ineffable, which is a classic marker of mystical experiences. You simply can't explain them in words. But I'll try my best, because I have a hunch that these direct, non-verbal, embodied memories were critical to restoring my belief that the world was actually not such an evil, unpredictable place after all.

During one meditation, with my eyes closed, I remember seeing the impossibly large foot and leg of an elephant and understanding that this elephant was critical for my survival. I wanted, needed, to show it how much I loved it, but I couldn't speak. And I couldn't even move. It was the most foreign thing, to have a seemingly totally coherent and articulated intention, an aim, a desire formed in my mind, but with no agency over my limbs or my head or my mouth to bring that intention into action. So my body as a whole took on the vibration, or energetic signature of love, and this is what I beamed at the elephant's leg. I felt myself psychically hugging this elephant's leg, but without moving my arms into the position of an actual hug; saying "I love you" without verbalizing any words; and trying with my whole body to bridge this barrier between human and animal, between mental and physical. "Thank you. I love you. I'm sorry. I forgive you." I felt these words with the entirety of my being.

I had first learned this prayer, called *Ho`oponopono*, from a Hawaiian teacher at a science and spirituality conference in Italy right after I got my Ph.D. This was back when I was still quite skeptical of most spiritual practices. I even believed that meditation was just a formal mental practice designed for improving attention and emotion regulation. Certainly nothing supernatural going on here! So, I latched onto this Hawaiian mantra because it was simple, and the aspirational meaning was clear. The *metta* prayer in Buddhism—wishing happiness and lovingkindness for yourself and others—works in a similar way. You can say the words to someone you've harmed, or you can say them to yourself, and their power is to restore right relationship, to restore love as the foundation of that relationship. Actually, the original Hawaiian prayer says, "Please forgive me," not, "I forgive you." But since I was dealing with all this anger toward my dad, I had changed the last phrase.

"Thank you. I love you. I'm sorry. I forgive you." I had repeated these words so many times before, hoping for some kind of breakthrough. I kept saying them, but I didn't believe them. And I remembered one female resident who had been part of the community when I attended my first two retreats while pregnant with Frances. She had been in a terrible accident that left her walking with a severe limp and in unbearable pain. I was always so inspired watching her sit through our long meditation sessions. Most of the time, she even had a smile on her face. But one day during her interview with the teacher, I remember her letting loose this primal scream that we could hear all the way down the hall. It was the kind of unadulterated expression of pain and hatred that I had never allowed myself to utter. But boy, did I know that feeling. And then, during the Q&A period that evening, she asked for some advice in front of the group. She said, "I've been working with the mantra, 'I love you.' But I don't believe it. I've been saying it for years now. And I just want to know, how many times do I have to say it for it to be true?" And our teacher smiled, tenderly, and said, "As many times as you have told yourself, "I hate you."

And as I say the *Ho`oponopono* prayer for the millionth time, I find my body growing smaller and smaller, until I am just a tiny creature floating in a vast, salty, warm ocean. I feel my body curving inward, like a half-moon, and my hands curving into the shape of little fish flippers as my fingers melted together. Even my head becomes curved and smooth. I feel my eye lids seal against the skin of my face, and my lips seal together. Although this might sound terrifying, it was the most safe and perfect and whole I have ever felt. I float in the ethereal ocean for so long that I forget about the world; I am just existing, being. I don't even remember hearing any sounds in the meditation room. I am in my own bubble, literally, and it is so huge that nothing can reach me. Then, after an eon or so, I feel an ever so subtle nudge, like a signal, "OK, it's time to move." Time begins speeding forward again and I am growing into my human body, and then I am exiting my beautiful ocean and suddenly, I am completely embraced by a love that is a hundred times more powerful than the heavenly love I encountered when I died on 5-MeO. It is more powerful because it is personal. It is all for me. As I recall this embrace, I realize that the love is my mom. This is my birth. "Oh my God. I remember!"

As an adult, fear and anger had dominated so much of my interior world that I doubted whether I had ever felt real love in the first place. But this direct experience totally contradicted the story I had been telling myself, about how my life was mostly about pain and betrayal and loss. How could the entire world be callous and dangerous if this big love was also true? It was literally the force that kept me alive as an infant, when I had no ability to care for or defend myself. The traumatic events of my early childhood had succeeded in blocking out these earliest, loving, amazing memories. But that day on the meditation cushion, I remembered. I really remembered. No one could take this from me.

❨

On Sunday morning, one of the young men broke silence to wish me "Happy Mother's Day," and the wheels of my mind started turning my thoughts toward home and seeing Frances again. I had achieved so much already, I felt maybe the retreat was over for me. I could breathe again, joyfully, and with my whole body. And I remembered being born! What more could a girl ask for? On top of all that, my usual waterfall of thoughts had slowed to a trickle, and I was able to sit for extended periods of time without fidgeting or getting distracted by sounds in the room. My longest uninterrupted sit was about two hours, and it was the closest I had ever come to what my first meditation teacher called *shamatha*, or calm abiding. I used to think *shamatha* was some kind of mystical, enlightened state of being. But during that two-hour sit, I experienced it as refreshingly ordinary. Just sitting. Calmly. Clear mind. Totally aware of everything inside and outside of me, but not pulled or pushed by any of it. No need to do anything at all. What a breakthrough.

Regarding my anger, I had come to a very practical realization that I needed to take a vow of non-violence. Too many of my thoughts, toward myself, my dad, and the world (specifically, people who might one day harm my daughter) were so hateful and vindictive that it was like throwing gasoline on a fire and expecting the fire to stop burning. I still wasn't sure what to do about my angry feelings, but I could at least change my relationship with my thoughts. I felt like this vow of non-violence was a very practical tool that I could use in my everyday life. I was grateful. And I was ready to go home.

After lunch, I decided to do a little ritual of gratitude out in the woods, similar to thanking the altar at the end of a mushroom ceremony. I hiked up the path behind the lodge and kept following some instinct to go deeper and deeper, tracking along the ridge of an outcropping of granite. Just as I reached the end of this outcropping, I noticed a little pillow of moss that looked like the perfect seat. And as I bent down to sit, I saw a single, white, star-shaped flower, with the faintest rose-colored center, peeking up through the green moss. I can't explain it, but I knew it was my sister. "Oh, hi Rebecca!" I sat down and scattered her ashes around the flower and sang the *metta* prayer I had learned on my first retreat in Santa Fe. And as I stood up, the world took on an ever so subtle wobble. I looked around the forest and the light looked different, like there was extra light within the light. I looked at my hands, and they seemed to shine and wobble too.

I got back to the lodge with about twenty minutes left before we had to congregate in the meditation room. I was feeling good about myself, and it was Mother's Day after all, so my mind started to bend toward a celebratory cocktail of sorts. Obviously, there was no alcohol on the premises, but maybe I'd treat myself to a little hot cocoa. I filled my white ceramic mug with already boiled water and added a packet of what I thought was cocoa but also seemed to have some coffee in it. Hmmmm. Well, a little caffeine boost might be just the rocket fuel I need to power through the evening session. I also heard Patrick in my head explaining how the spirits like chocolate, which is why we always consume hot chocolate along with the mushrooms.

Before I explain what happened next, I feel like I need to take a moment to break it down for those of you who may not be following exactly how all this works. Most of the time, I can't even remember how it all works either until it's already happening. But basically, I had just opened the gate for the spirits and ancestors to enter my reality. By the ritual I did in the woods, and my sister's ashes, and the prayer, and the hot cocoa. Yes, of course, all these things can be viewed simply as cognitive associations, things that primed my mind by reminding me of past psychedelic ceremonies. And, also, many, many spiritual traditions believe that there are realms of reality beyond the physical one that our modern culture seems so obsessed with. And when you are in a space of ceremony, whether it's a tipi or a hospital room or a meditation lodge, you can open yourself up to communication and engagement with those other realms and the beings that reside there. So, you might ask, if I was feeling so ready to go home, why would I open the gate? Well, let's just say that my rational mind might have been ready to call the game, but my creative, irrational, intuitive mind was ready for another round. I was signaling to the other realms that I was finally ready to go to That Place that I had been carefully avoiding during the whole retreat up until that point.

We sit down on our respective cushions and wait quietly for the teacher to enter. The room is brimming with excitement, as everyone has their own Very Important Questions prepared, and the retreat is drawing to a close.

The teacher comes in, sits down, and looks straight at me, "Could you come to my cabin?" My heart starts racing. My cheeks fill with heat. I am so embarrassed. Why would the teacher ask me to come to his cabin, alone, after dark? I immediately remember all those stories of women who were sexually abused by their seemingly kind and ethical Buddhist teachers, and I think, "Oh no, this is totally how it happens. How can this be happening?? Right now! After I've made so much progress and am finally feeling safe in my body!" Embarrassment shifts quickly to anger. But before I can say anything, one of the extremely eager young residents blurts out, "I can come! When? After Q&A?" And we all laugh, and the teacher says, "No, no. I was asking Katherine if she had come by my cabin earlier, because I saw footprints in the snow and thought maybe she needed something."

But my heart is still racing, and now my mind is racing too. I recognize that I am having paranoid thoughts, and possibly a panic attack. Yes, probably from consuming caffeine late in the day. But also, it feels like I have been strapped into a new kind of rollercoaster at the amusement park, and I have no idea where it's going. I keep trying to breathe through my stomach while the boys asked their Very Important Questions about sutras and what the Buddha said when, and finally when there is an appropriate opening I say, "Ummmm, I feel like I'm having a panic attack. What should I do?" Confusingly, the teacher responds by leading me through an intellectual puzzle, which actually works to replace my paranoid, racing thoughts with neutral content. Next, he guides me in moving the energy of my thoughts, which I experience to be "high up, in my head" down lower and lower until the same energy is circulating in my lower abdomen instead. He says, "You can't stop your thoughts, but you can redirect their energy." Ah yes, this made sense. It's like what happened during that interview, when I was so angry, but the anger shifted into amazing breathing. It's all the same energy.

Then, the teacher throws the final gauntlet. He says to all of us, "You know, I can keep answering your questions and giving pep talks, but honestly, it's Sunday evening. The retreat will be over in two days. And it feels like we're wasting our time. It just seems like none of you are taking things that seriously." One of the students pipes up, "But there's still time!" And the teacher continues, "Yes, but why would you assume that you can achieve in two days what you couldn't even start in five? Imagine if we were all lined up for lunch, and we started singing the lunch prayer, and one of the cooks realized he hadn't made the rice. It takes at least an hour to cook. There's just not enough time to cook the rice before everyone serves themselves. It's literally impossible. So, let me ask you. What would you do in that situation?" And the student exclaims, with totally misplaced confidence, "I would still try to cook that rice." And we all laugh, and the teacher says, "Well, the clock is ticking. There's no time left. Let's see what kind of rice you can make."

I could hardly sleep that night. My mind kept mulling over what happened between the ritual in the woods and the Rice Challenge. I kept replaying the cabin question in my head. I KNEW the teacher had said, "Could you come to my cabin" not "Did you come to my cabin." He was always so particular about his speech that he wouldn't have just made a casual mistake like that. But why had he said that? What was going on?? Reality was really starting to warp and bend. I knew something important was happening, but I couldn't figure out what. I thought about my sister, and how she had languished in the hospital for two weeks and then suddenly, on a Saturday night, with panic in her eyes and realizing there was no way out, she made the choice to go all in. And she died in two days. So I said to myself, "OK, Zen Master, I've tried it your way. I've done the technique and made some progress. But now I'm going to do it my way. I'm going to ask my sister for some divine intervention. I want to show you the kind of rice we make."

The next morning, my body is buzzing with physical energy, like I could run a marathon. When it's my turn for the interview, I walk into the room and sit down, and that same intense breathing takes over. And then suddenly my hands are in the shape of claws, like a muscle spasm, and they start shaking, like a tremor. I briefly remember that this is one of the weird side effects of holotropic breathing, which is a cyclic breathing method for inducing an alternate state of consciousness. But it doesn't matter that there's a scientific explanation for this; I am starting to freak out. I look at the teacher and say, "What is going on? Why are my hands shaking?" And he says, "You might be afraid." And then I demand, "Then why won't you hold me?" I am shocked to hear these words come out of my mouth. I place my head on the floor in front of me, with my hands clasped over my head, almost like I am praying, and then my whole body is shaking and the energy just pushes itself out of me and I am screaming, screaming, screaming. I have never heard myself scream this way. You know how horror stories always talk about "blood curdling" screams? Well, that morning I learned that they are a real thing. This is the kind scream that only comes out of you when you think you're about to be murdered. I had no control over it. And then he says, "You're safe here. Just stay with the sensations in your body." And I scream, "No! I'm not safe. They're just little boys! If they don't get this, you'll just be another institution that rapes people!" As I say this, some bizarre light bulb turns on in my mind. I see my dad as a little boy, and I see him as an angry adult man who can't grow up. And I remember earlier in the retreat, walking around the pond and poking that salamander with the stick just to see what would happen. And I see these men doing the same thing, poking their sticks at whatever they want, just because they can, because they want to see what will happen. And all of this violence, these men who keep hurting people, not because they're evil but because they just can't grow up. They are just little boys. It's all so obscenely innocuous and horrific. "Oh no! They're just little boys!" I gasp and bring my hand to my mouth in shock at what I have just seen, and I look at the teacher straight in the eyes to see if he, too, has made the connection. And then I run.

This is definitely out of protocol. No one ever just leaves the interview without the teacher dismissing you. But I am running for my life. I can't even see where I'm going. I am lurching down the hallway, past the meditation room. I frantically pull on my puffy down jacket and hat and boots and shove my body into the thick metal bar at the center of the heavy fire door marked by the red Exit sign. I burst out into the cold morning air. It is raining and mucky. At first, I think maybe I'm going to get in my car and just leave this fucked-up place, but I don't have my keys. Then I briefly consider actually running away, down the dirt-gravel road, but I realize I won't get far and who knows what weirdos live up this way, in the middle of nowhere. I start to walk toward the pond out of habit and then just collapse on the ground. I lie down on my back on the cold, wet grass, and I breathe and cry and scream into the clouds swirling above me, hoping that some portal will open and I will be removed from Earth for good. No portal opens. But soon, I can actually feel the rain drops lightly hitting my cheeks and mixing with my tears. My hand reaches up to touch my cheek, and I am back in my body. My current, adult body. The wave has subsided. The fear is gone. I walk back into the lodge, remove my damp jacket and hat and boots, calmly walk down the hallway, and take my seat again in the meditation room. To everyone else's credit, they are still sitting there, quiet, unfazed. No one even indicates that they have noticed I'm back. The bell rings. It's time for breakfast.

The rest of the day is rather uneventful, at least in comparison to the bizarre out-of-body nightmare of the morning session. I am grateful that these so-called little boys are actually mature enough to take it all in stride. I don't have to explain myself or hide what happened. I can just keep showing up and following the routine. Which is why meditation retreats have such a predictable schedule; when you really start losing your grip on reality, the routine and the community carries you along. Not only do you not have to account for what happened two hours earlier, you don't even have to remember it. Just do your chores, show up for lunch, clean the kitchen, take a walk, sit again. During the evening interview, the teacher encourages me to resist trying to analyze my earlier experience, but just to let the method keep working. Keep breathing; stay with the sensations in my body; keep the energy low in my abdomen. And he also says I can skip the Q&A that night.

So, I head upstairs to my room and get ready for bed. Just as I'm about turn off the light, I look in the mirror and realize I'm not alone in the room. A chill runs up the back of my neck. I see someone else looking back at me through the mirror. I mean, she looks like me. She's a very good Katherine imposter. But she also has this kind of psychopath look in her eyes. And I feel like I'm suddenly stuck in a very small room with a very charismatic axe murderer. Now, maybe most people would be so freaked out by this that they would just turn off the light and bury their head under the covers and go to bed. But not me. Why? Well, first, because I knew she wasn't going to go away just because I stopped looking in the mirror. And second, I was curious. I had taken enough drugs and looked into enough mirrors on drugs to know that there was always something very special to be discovered there. Who was this supremely evil twin looking back at me? Could she tell me something about my anger? I remembered my first encounter with a monster on retreat, nearly ten years ago. During one of the evening sits, a kind of trollish, hunchbacked, tiny man in orange monk robes popped up in the corner of my vision and kind of lunged and snarled at me. He kept showing up every evening and I kept trying to ignore him. I finally told the woman who was in charge of the center about it. And she said, "Well, he's been hanging out in your mind for a long time, so why don't you invite him to sit down with you and have a cup of tea?"

Well, this lady in the mirror was not the kind of person you'd want to invite over for tea. Still, here I was. So I figured, what the hell. She's already in the room with me, and I can't weasel my way out of this, so maybe I should get to know her. I spent the next hour or so talking to this woman in the mirror, always keeping in mind that while she looked a whole lot like me, she was really a serial killer and could not be trusted. I had to be extra kind to her so that she wouldn't kill me. I just kept making the conversation all about her, to keep her focused on the only thing she cared about, while also keeping my eye on the door, ready to bolt. It was a wild experience. I'm sure some of you will read this and perhaps finally give up on this book for good, because I'm clearly just some crazy bitch who's taken way too many drugs. That's OK with me. But maybe some psychologist will read this and decide this is actually a fantastic way for people to get in touch with their shadow selves, their inner monster. But I was just winging it. I found that I could empathize with evil Katherine while also being wise, compassionate Katherine. I could be both. And I could see how the survival instinct that told me, "Run away! She can't be trusted. She's a monster" had really been getting in the way of a real relationship.

I made it through the night with minimal further hallucinations. Honestly, I had to give in and listen to some of the music from the days in the hospital with my sister. There's only so much insanity that is healthy for one night. I found myself really appreciating the care and attention we gave to our participants in the psilocybin trials while they were navigating their own nightmare trips. And how much the music helped. In my experience, it's a whole lot easier to face your biggest fears, your own personal monsters, when you have a bit of support. And sometimes, music is even better than having someone there to hold your hand.

So, now, it's the last day of the retreat. The first thing I notice during my morning meditation is that my hands are freezing cold, like I've dunked them in a vat of ice water. I was assigned to help with lunch prep that day, so I spend most of the morning in the kitchen. I'm going through the motions, chopping vegetables and putting dishes away. And I'm holding this totally ordinary spoon in my ice-cold hand. And suddenly it's like I'm staring straight into the mushroom altar. This is the most exquisitely beautiful spoon I've ever seen. But not only that, I love this spoon as much as I love my sister, as much as I loved her as she was dying. This spoon and my sister: same same.

I keep trying to get the lunch ready, but everything is just Too Much. I am in a bejeweled castle where every single stupid item is hand-wrought by God. No, not wrought. IS God. I try my best to keep my shit together as I load up my bowl with rice and beans and veggies, and stand behind my chair, ready to sit down. And I keep trying to keep my shit together as I slowly eat, one spoonful, then another. Then a single thought breaks my non-dual revery: I wonder what Frances is doing today? Suddenly, the dream collapses and I am trapped in a funhouse of mirrors. What was only moments before a dazzling, fractal world of beauty and light is now a prison. Everywhere I see reflected the maniacal signature of the Devil himself. He has just been masquerading as God. The beauty was only there to seduce me. It's all been a trap. And I look across the table at the resident whose job it is to make sure everyone is doing OK, mental health-wise. And I see that he is totally not paying any attention. I look for the door to assess how fast I can sprint there before someone comes after me and drags me back to the table. And I remember one of the most important things we tell every single participant in the psilocybin trials: If you need help, ask for help. If you are scared, say it out loud.

So I slowly put my spoon down and I bend my head down toward my chest and let out an animal-like groan. And as my head comes up, I say, "Guys. Uhhhhhhh. I don't know what's going on. I need help."

Slowly, ten separate heads rise and look up from their meals. This is very unexpected. Definitely against protocol. The looks of neutral confusion are nearly uniform. No one is responding or saying anything. I repeat, more emphatically now, "I need help. I'm freaking out. Please someone help me." And the teacher slowly puts his own spoon down, pushes his chair back from the table, and walks ever so calmly over to my chair.

As he stands behind me, he places two fingers of each of his hands on each of my shoulders, and kind of rocks my body back and forth. If there was ever a way to touch someone without any confusion about whether this touch meant something more, well, this was the way. It was the most robotic form of human comfort I have ever received. And as he does this, he says, "You're falling." "Uh huh," I say. "And why don't you want to fall?" he asks. I say, "It's violent." And I suddenly find myself standing on a very high bridge, over water, and my hands are ice cold as I'm hanging onto the railing. I let go, and I'm falling, but it's not at all what I hoped it would be. It's all happening too fast. I just want it to stop. This is all my fault. And then the teacher says, "So, instead of falling, just float." Suddenly, I am back in my body and my mind is clear and JOY is coursing through my veins. I start laughing a little and close my eyes, and I see myself again, but as a baby on a changing table, rolling off and falling through the air. My mom reaches for me, as a swirling vortex opens in the space between us and she sees me falling into it, never to return. But she catches me just in time, and the vortex closes. Somehow, in this moment at the lunch table, all of this falling makes ultimate sense and I say silently, "It's OK. I forgive you."

The robotic rocking method has worked so well that as soon as I snap back to reality and become aware of the touch of his hands on my body I say, "OK, OK. That's enough. Thank you. Please stop." And he stops, and I kind of stumble to say, "I just . . . I need . . . I need to know if Frances is OK. I have this feeling that something terrible has happened to her and you already know about it but you're waiting for the end of the retreat to tell me." And the teacher says, rather simply, "I've been in touch with John, and everything is fine. Everything is fine."

I make it through the rest of lunch with a big smile on my face, not even sure what I'm smiling about, but knowing that I have truly forgiven myself for making stupid, life-threatening decisions in the past. And I know that I have forgiven my mom for all of things she did or thought she did that might have threatened my life. And I know with every fiber of my being that none of these harms were intentional, and that it was no one's fault.

After lunch concluded, the teacher asked if he could speak with me outside for a moment, to make sure I was OK. I asked the head resident—the only resident I considered an adult—to join us, because I was still paranoid about being the only female and alone with the teacher. We walked outside and I found myself saying very matter-of-factly, "You know, my father abused me when I was little." And the resident said, "I was abused as a kid, too. It's not your fault."

The conversation was so simple and normal, without any strong emotions or rationalizations. I said, "It's just weird because I've only told a handful of people, other than John. I've never said it out loud like this, in the daylight." And the teacher said, "Well, you can say it anytime you want."

And just like that, this overpowering, confusing, embarrassing, terrible thing that I had been wrestling with for over thirty years lost its death grip. I could still see it as a part of me, a part of my history, but it was no longer all of me. I could relate to it rather than be consumed by it. The secret was out in the open and it was so much better. I didn't have to carry it.

At Hopkins, we used to joke that the best indicator of a full-blown mystical experience was the desire to call your mom the next morning and thank her and tell her you love her. And that's what I did. When my mom picked up the phone, her voice sounded totally different, sweet and light, like I was hearing it for the first time. I wasn't hearing her through the filter of what she could do for me, or how annoying I found the same old stories she always told (mostly about terrible things happening to her or me or my sister), or how her anxiety makes me so uncomfortable and how I hate myself for also being that anxious. I could just hear her. It was like I was finally talking to the woman my mom really was, not My Mom.

I am not reactive, not triggered, not judgmental. I am just receiving what she's saying and have so much love for her and everything she's been through. I share a bit about how I've been trying to deal with my anxiety, about whether Frances is safe when I'm not with her, and how I can't imagine doing it without John. In return, she shares how hard it was to be worried all the time when we were little, about whether me and my sister were safe, with my dad being so reckless and inattentive and unpredictable. She tells me how she would get physically sick when we would go stay with our dad for the weekend, which she never wanted to agree to but was required to by the divorce court. And I say, "Wow, mom, that must have been really, really hard." And I mean it. I'm not putting on a nice-daughter show, not trying to think of what to say to get through the phone call and on to the rest of my life. At least in that moment, I no longer hate her for not stepping in or doing something different to protect me from my dad.

Right when I think the conversation is over, she says, "Oh! I have to tell you about a dream I had Sunday night."

Hoo, boy! I'm not sure I'm ready for this. This has always been one of my biggest triggers with her! These terrible nightmares she always has and the stories that are so long and convoluted and she doesn't even seem to enjoy telling them. The nightmares often have the same theme, about huge bears threatening her, or her losing my sister or my sister's daughter in a crowd. Her dreams are like the most epic examples of the world being a mean, dangerous place. Which makes sense, because she clearly has untreated, complex PTSD. And I'm always asking her about what she thinks the bears mean and begging her to go see a therapist or at least a dream analyst or something. So, anyway, this is a big test for me, and I kind of brace myself to listen and keep breathing into my lower abdomen.

And she says, "I was in a high tower with a small bear cub. And I'm fighting with the bear, and I don't want to do it, but suddenly, I shove the bear out of the window." And I laugh and think to myself, "I'm that bear. I got out."

Then I video-call Frances and John. They are walking through the upper pasture at the farm and John says, "We can't talk for long, but Frances has something she really wants to say." And in this sweet little toddler voice, she slowly says, "Ma-ma Baaa-yer." John has been calling me this since Frances was born, because of my fierceness and protectiveness. And yes, because of my anger. This is the first time Frances has ever said it. *Mama Bear.* Yep. That's me.

((

Before I conclude this portion of the story, I do want to clarify a few things about trauma. I don't think it's a great idea for a woman to go on a retreat in a strange place in the middle of nowhere with a group of men. Even if the setting is objectively safe, it's just not worth the risk of being harmed. Women being sexually abused in spiritual or therapeutic settings is unfortunately quite common. I met a therapist once who spent a good chunk of her professional life supporting women who had been abused by spiritual teachers. This therapist stated that of the five or so women who contacted her EACH week over many years, more than 95% of the abusers were men.

That being said, I do think that this particular retreat was the medicine I needed to confront my own deep trauma, to literally call it to the surface. After years of therapy and mushroom ceremonies and personal MDMA sessions, I needed this particular week for my subconscious stuff to play itself out. I needed the reminders of potential threats in my physical environment to help conjure up the emotions and bodily sensations that I worked so hard to suppress the rest of the time. It was a risky move, but I think it worked. I did have to wrestle with pretty intense residual anxiety and nightmares for a couple weeks after I went home. I had a lot of support from John, and I wasn't working at the time, so I could recover at my own pace. I remember the same thing happening after my mushroom ceremonies, needing at least a few weeks to let myself integrate and return to some normal functioning mode.

It was a teachable moment for the meditation community, too. The teacher and the residents asked me to spend some time the day after the retreat ended debriefing with them about how they could make the retreat center a safer place for people with histories of abuse and trauma. The teacher admitted that other women, like me, had a hard time during their silent retreats, and the community was even considering only allowing males to attend, or not allowing guests. I didn't think it was necessary to make it so restrictive. We came up with a few simple changes that could help women and other guests with trauma histories feel safer, like using more comforting lighting in the hallways at night. We also talked through the protocol for dealing with major mental health events, like my panic attack at the lunch table. The teacher asked if anyone had noticed anything before I asked for help, and no one had. He said, "I thought something might be amiss when Katherine put down her spoon in a particular way, and dropped her head. If you're the person whose job it is to watch for these kinds of issues coming up, you should be able to tell me which eye the first tear came out of." We even joked about having a wise, loving mother figure living just beyond the boundary of the property, who could chat with people who were having a tough time in the middle of retreat. The teacher said that that model had already been used in monastic environments in Asia. It was always the elderly women living at the edge of the monastery who knew the most about human nature and could teach you more about your own mind over a cup of tea than a meditation master ever could.

This retreat also got me thinking about trauma more academically. If trauma, and the violence that erupts from trauma, is passed down from generation to generation, how do we interrupt the cycle? So many people—1 in 4 individuals assigned female at birth, and 1 in 6 individuals assigned male at birth—have been sexually abused as children, and about one third of these children are abused by a family member (as reported by the National Sexual Violence Resource Center). Yet hardly anyone feels OK talking about it. And physical abuse is even more common. According to the American Psychological Association, up to two thirds of Americans still approve of spanking, even though physical discipline often perpetuates violent behaviors when a child grows up. If violence toward children is so common, it's hard to know where to begin. I think one solution starts with education, helping people see the situation for what it is. I knew a meditation teacher who was also a mom and a pediatrician, and who was often called to testify in court cases regarding child abuse. During one of her dharma talks, she said, "If you were abused as a child, and you grow up to not abuse your own children, you have already done something truly remarkable." In other words, the power of violence and trauma is so great, that it is a heroic act to overcome it in even the smallest way. Of course, we all want to be perfect, peaceful parents, but we have to start with a much lower bar. We should help parents see that they are doing a phenomenal job even when all they are doing is not repeating the worst things that happened to them. Obviously, progress will be slow, but it will happen. Clearly, I think another big part of the solution is removing the pressure of secrecy, and helping people say out loud the things that our culture and families have told us are unspeakable.

This meditation retreat helped me see the entire scope of the problem I was facing, from what I believe was the last memory from my previous incarnation—hurtling toward my intentional, if totally misguided, suicide—to the amazing womb space that is all of our beginnings, followed by my physical birth as baby

Katherine and my mother's great love that received me, and yes, through the worst of my childhood. I was finally able to see it all from a bird's eye view and appreciate how the endless cycle of violence and suffering, what Buddhists call samsara, will continue as long as we think it's fate, or divine punishment, or something other people are doing to us. We can no longer get away with categorizing people or ways of living as inherently good or bad. Instead, we can choose to compassionately apprehend the iterative impact of actions and conditions over thousands of generations—what Buddhists call karma—in producing humans that appear, from the outside, to be "abusive" or "violent." Looking in the mirror that hallucinatory night, I remember remarking, "I am the same as my father. I am the same as Trump." Since that retreat, I understand what Buddhist teachers mean when they say that, if you consider all of your past lives, you have been your own mother, you have been your own child, and you have even been your own abuser.

During my final interview before leaving the retreat center, the teacher confirmed that I had actually achieved something important, meditation-wise, though he wouldn't say what. He said, "You can feel good about what you've accomplished. Don't try to analyze it. Just go slowly and keep using the technique." And then he added, "Maybe one day you'll share with me more about what happened when you were a child." And as he said this, I thought about what my dad might have gone through as a child, and his dad, and his dad before that, and how people who hurt others are not evil monsters, for the most part. They are mostly children who were hurt who never got a chance to heal; children who were so filled with hate for what happened to them that it spills out in all manner of harm and violence as adults. I don't believe that trauma excuses violence toward others. But I also don't believe we will make much progress by simply trying to tranquilize the monsters.

CHAPTER 7

(

The Pain is Important

FOR MOST OF MY DAUGHTER'S LIFE, I was convinced that I could only survive mothering one child. Making it through the first two years with Frances took everything I had; I often said that it felt like I was running a marathon every day. By the time she could eat and sleep (at least half of the night) and stay alive mostly independent of me and my body, I was finally able to pause and catch my breath. Considering my own exhaustion, combined with John's depression, I didn't think it was worth taking a chance on a second child. Plus, we had big dreams to focus on, like a farm retreat center and psychedelic hospice. It felt like we had to choose between those dreams and another child.

But I also knew there was a part of me that was born to be a mother: a primal part of me that knew how to protect and defend and love and nurture and teach. Mama Bear. Embracing this identity reminded me of the natural power that is bestowed upon us by the great mother, Mother Nature. In the natural world, having only one cub would be rare, even dangerous. The cubs learn from each other and teach each other how to play and fight and survive. Luckily, the decision ultimately wasn't up to me. Just as she did with her own Earthly incarnation, Frances made the right choice for us.

Just before Frances turned two, one of my sister's best friends lost her brother to a brain aneurysm. We had all gone to high school together, and this young woman was one of the few friends who had been able to visit my sister in the hospital before she died. There was no question in my mind that I would attend her brother's wake and show our support, after everything she had done for my sister and our family. And I decided to bring Frances.

I know that some people purposely avoid exposing young children to death. This was simply not an option for our family, starting with my brother, who was just a baby crawling around my dad's feet as he gave the eulogy at my grandfather's funeral, and then my niece, who sat in the front row of the church for her mom's funeral when she was only four years old. Because of our lineage of cancer, and especially because of my sister, we talked a lot about death. When Frances was only six weeks old, I brought her to meet a dear friend who was in hospice. Before she was a year old, she helped me guide another friend through a spiritual journey only a week before he died. It was important to me that Frances not grow up fearing death the way so many of us do. And since we were living on a farm, death was all around her anyway. It was a natural part of our life.

As I parked the car at the funeral home and got out, I picked up Frances and held her close to my body and spoke to her about what she would see when we walked in. I told her that a young man had died and his family and friends were very sad. I told her it was important to be quiet, but that she didn't have to feel sad, too. I told her that she would see his body, and he would not be breathing. She was amazingly composed and calm as we stood in line, waiting to approach the casket. As we got up to the front, I hugged my sister's friend and shared well wishes with her parents and family. We stood briefly in front of her brother's body and said a prayer for his safe and easy transition and walked out. We stopped for ice cream on the way home. When we got back to the farm, my friend Cassi was waiting for us.

Cassi had a way of showing up at important junctures along my spiritual path. She lived thousands of miles away but happened to be nearby for a professional meeting. I always viewed her as an exemplar of contentment and accomplishment in the academic world, so I was surprised to learn that she had just been through an extremely difficult period in her life. She was relieved to be able to take a break from the world of achievements and responsibilities, and just enjoy an evening of simple moments with me and Frances. We took a walk up to the highest point on the farm, a huge granite outcropping that we called Pride Rock. The sunset was epic, and Frances relished in Cassi's special, magical energy and attention.

When she felt comfortable, Frances said very matter-of-factly to Cassi, "You know. Kid died in ocean." First of all, yes, Frances could speak this well even before she turned two. And second, this was not at all what happened to the young man whose funeral we had just returned from. Cassi looked at me, curious, and asked Frances, "Are you sure?" And Frances said, "Yes. Died in ocean. Very sad." We asked her a few more questions about the child and the situation, and she was insistent that a boy went into the ocean and got lost and everyone was very, very sad.

For the next few weeks, all Frances could talk about was this little boy, and how his family missed him. It was sometimes confusing whether she was talking about someone and someplace else, or her own memory, because the biographical details were so specific. One time she looked at me and cupped her little hands around my cheeks and said, "I so sorry go in ocean, mom." And another time she asked me where her "real mom" was. Then finally, one day, she stopped talking about the little boy and the ocean and started talking about her brother "in town." His name was Akul, and she usually found him hanging out at the playground. He had blue hair. She asked when her brother could come to the farm.

I'm sure there are many of you who choose to remain agnostic about what happens before we are born or after we die. Christians certainly don't believe in multiple lives. And while reincarnation is a necessary element of both Hindu and Buddhist belief systems, many American practitioners do not accept reincarnation as a physical fact. They prefer to interpret it metaphorically, or in terms of some kind of nebulous energy that moves from Nature into a growing embryo and then explodes back out into the cosmos again when we die. But hearing Frances speak so clearly and specifically about this boy and the ocean and his original family forced me beyond my own skepticism. The fact that Cassi was there to receive the first instance of this past-life transmission made the whole situation even more humorous and strange, because the organization that Cassi led was responsible for funding and studying some of the more out-there ideas in the science of spirituality. One long-standing project was focused on documenting hundreds of extremely detailed past-life stories told by children. For Frances, it seemed that something about attending the funeral—maybe seeing all those sad people or the dead body—had reminded her of this past/other-life. The question that remained for me was not, "Is her story true?" but, "Am I ready to let this little boy into our life?"

I hadn't taken mushrooms since the ceremony that preceded Frances's conception. And while John and I had taken mushrooms together before, he had never experienced the altar. So I invited him to do a ceremony with me that fall. I felt like it was important for our marriage, to take this sacrament together, and for John to understand this new religious practice of mine. We were still unsure about whether we would stay on the farm or start a new adventure, so we hoped that the mushrooms would help us navigate whatever was coming next. Reflecting back, it's pretty obvious that I also wanted the mushrooms to help me decide whether or not to have a second child. But strangely, that wasn't my verbalized intention for the experience. I never wrote it down and don't remember it now. Let's just say that this particular ceremony took care of itself.

When John and I arrived at Patrick's place on a sparkly autumn afternoon, we discovered the newest addition to his shamanic lair: a Grizzly bear skull. Patrick had received the skull from a Native friend in the Pacific Northwest and had spent most of the previous month sitting with and welcoming in this powerful new guide. Patrick shared with me that among the various empowerments he had received from indigenous elders, Bear Medicine was the main one. I began to wonder whether the ceremony he had been offering was really about mushrooms, or whether the mushrooms were just another gateway to something much more mysterious.

The mushrooms shared many important visions with me and John that night, including the incarnation of our son and the looming death of John's dad. And they also revealed to me my soul identity. I didn't really know this was a thing, although John and Frances and the meditation retreats had been steadily pointing me toward it. Patrick had also sensed it in me, but being respectful of my own pace and path, was waiting for me to discover it.

Toward the middle of the ceremony, following the now-expected entry of pain and shaking energetic spasms and vomiting and fear, I find myself in similar territory as the vortex with Eileen, when I felt like I was giving birth while also on the edge of death. I remembered what I had thought last time at this stage, "It's so easy to die." I close my eyes and the same vast space opens up before me. But I see it with a new understanding. Whereas before I had associated this space with the immensity and tranquility of death, I now see that it isn't death at all, but the physical representation of safety and protection. I had only connected safety with death before because I was still in a very early stage of recovering from trauma and was convinced that death was the only thing that could ultimately protect me from being hurt again.

But this space! It is huge! It is safety beyond measure. Words come through. "I am safe in this body, and I am not my body." And suddenly, I am no longer relating to this space as other-than-me. I am the space. I am the protector. I am vast. I am a guardian of the eternal womb, the space of both creation and destruction. More words pass through my lips, like an ancient lullaby, "I am what you call Death and what is really Life." (Note: I looked up these words later and they led me to a poem called "Thunder, Perfect Mind," which was found in upper Egypt in 1945 among a collection of ancient texts now referred to as the Gnostic Gospels. These texts were thought to have been destroyed during the early Christian struggle to define orthodoxy, and they included alternative gospels, including the Gospel of Mary and the Gospel of Truth).

I open my eyes and say to John and Patrick, "I know who I am." And then I dive back into my internal world to relish in the grandeur and immensity of it all. A few minutes go by until they both say, "But you haven't told us yet!"

"What?" I ask.

"Your name!!"

"Oh right," I reply, laughing, "I have to say it out loud." And in that moment before speaking, I understand that I already know the name of this space. I proclaim, in a rather scientific manner, as if I am pointing at the night sky and naming a new constellation: "Mama Bear!"

Patrick hands me the Grizzly bear's lower jaw. I pick it up and feel a fierce power come into my body. I kneel and bow my head toward the altar and place the jawbone across my shoulder blade, so that the teeth are nearly piercing the skin along my neck and back and upper arm. Then I raise my head and hold the jaw to my chest. I can feel an eternal connection with this powerful protector. So, this is the line between monster and mother. A line that humans have drawn, straight through the natural world. In that moment, I reject the split and reclaim my eternal, ferocious guardianship.

When we return home to the farm the next day, Frances is thrilled to tell me that her brother is now at the farm. "Dada's little boy is here!" she squeals as we swing on the big tree swing together. Unsurprisingly, I am pregnant within the month.

So now the mushrooms had helped escort two souls through the portal to Earth. But perhaps it was really Frances, not the mushrooms, orchestrating our new family arrangement, by calling in her brother. Which made me think about my mom and her brother, who were born seventeen months apart when my gram was already in her forties. And I wondered about how I got here, followed by my sister two years later. I had joked with Rebecca once, in a dream, that life on Earth was so miserable there was no way I was coming back. And she said, "What if I asked you to?" And I replied, "Well, for you? Sure. I'd come back for you." And maybe this is how second and third and fourth children really come about. It's just so hard being an only child, being the first, that you have to call in reinforcements. The mundane and unceasing distress of being a vulnerable child in an insane adult world is made survivable by having a partner in crime. And only a true friend would come back to do this dance on Earth a million times, just for you.

☾

In the New Age world, there's a popular view that we are all born with birth trauma. According to this theory, a deep psychic-somatic wound is created during the process of being kicked out of Paradise (the womb). The baby endures, first, confusion and discomfort as the pressure and frequency of contractions increases; next, is sent along a hellish journey through an impossibly narrow birth canal, leading to feelings of intense claustrophobia and fears of annihilation; and finally, emerges into a cold, bright, harsh world characterized by gravity and adults who haven't learned how to regulate their emotions. As we grow up, especially during early childhood, other moments of fear and pain get wrapped up with this original traumatic memory. If our caregivers happen to be enlightened *bodhisattvas*, then we can naturally resolve this trauma as our millions of moments of fear and pain are each met with trust and loving kindness and compassion. But for 99.99% of the rest of humans, by the time we're adults, we are walking around with these incredibly complex and knotted masses of trauma that seem like a much bigger deal than any of the individual traumas on their own. In some psychedelic therapy circles, it's believed that one way to unwind these twisted knots is to revisit your own birth experience during a psychedelic session and release the original trauma, which, like glue holding the rest of the traumas together, allows the others to be released too.

Early on in my first pregnancy, one of the most experienced psychedelic therapists in America gifted me a book called *Birth without Violence*, by Frédérick Leboyer. In the book, Leboyer describes how physical factors like ambient temperature and sound and light, plus the presence of supportive humans could influence the baby's perception of safety and comfort during birth. It laid out methods for mitigating potential harm and suffering to both the baby and the mother during natural childbirth. While the author admitted that a "birth without violence" could be achieved in a hospital, he cautioned that it was often difficult to find doctors and nurses who were willing to accommodate things like lowered lighting and soft music or allowing the mom to have sips and small bites of nourishment throughout labor. Most concerningly, it was often required that women labor in the worst possible position for natural birth: laying on their backs. The author's best advice for a trauma-free labor was to birth at home, if possible.

LeBoyer's approach must have seemed quite radical when it was first published in the 1970s, when most hospitals had only recently given up the common practice of strapping women onto hospital beds and knocking them out with a drug called scopolamine during labor—a fascinating and terrifying technique euphemistically called "twilight birth." Thankfully, the birthing world has advanced quite a bit since then. Now there are natural birthing centers and birthing tubs and birthing doulas and all manner of adaptations that mark a return to the natural, supportive methods that were used by families and midwives for the rest of human history before medical institutions decided to claim "labor and delivery" as a hospital event. But even with these additions and alterations, the modern hospital birth is still not that different from the one LeBoyer was advocating against. His book was my entry point into learning how things often go terribly wrong during hospital births, and how it was actually possible to make birth amazing.

In preparation for Frances's arrival, John and I spent months reading books on mindful birth and intentional birth and even orgasmic birth and watching natural-birthing videos. All of this education and training, along with Frances's own telepathic transmissions, helped convince me to birth at home where I would feel the safest and where the environment would be the most comforting for Frances once she was born. Throughout my final trimester, we diligently prepared ourselves and the home environment to give me and Frances the best chance at a trauma-free birth.

The most common reaction I heard when I would reveal that I was planning a home birth was: what if something happens? In case I missed the meaning behind the question, one woman even followed this up with, "Well, you're still young. I guess if the baby dies you can always have another one." To this day, this comment shocks me, because maternal fatality rates are extremely high in America precisely because the chemical and surgical interventions that are common in hospitals end up being so dangerous for so many women. Because of my vivid memories of my sister's death in a hospital, I don't think my body would have relaxed enough in that environment to allow Frances to navigate her way safely through. Nevertheless, I didn't tell my parents I was planning a home birth. I knew that they would be just as scared as everyone else, worried that "something" would happen.

My own birth story was a tutorial in the exact kind of trauma that psychedelic therapists and breathwork coaches specialize in. My mom's labor progressed very quickly until she was admitted to the hospital, when things inexplicably stalled. She hadn't had anything to eat since breakfast and had no more energy. The only thing the nurses would offer her was ice chips. She was given Pitocin (a synthetic version of the natural contraction hormone, oxytocin) to speed things up, and she eventually became so exhausted from three hours of artificial pushing contractions that labor stalled again. Finally, when she demanded, "Somebody do something!" she was offered the lovely ultimatum of forced extraction or emergency C-section. As it turns out, this is a very common chain of events—ineffective chemical induction that often goes on for many hours until an emergency surgery is required because the mother's or baby's health is in danger— and is one of the reasons that both the C-section rate and the maternal fatality rate in America are higher than in any other developed country. Anticipating that the extraction wouldn't work, they gave her spinal anesthesia, which left her temporarily paralyzed from the waist down. Then my dad, the lawyer, was told to leave the room and they gripped my little baby head with forceps and forcibly yanked me out. As if this wasn't enough trauma for one day, I was whisked away to spend the entire night alone in the nursery with a bunch of other traumatized babies, while my mom slept off a terrible hangover from all the chemicals they had pumped into her, and my dad went home.

Mine was a pretty typical American birth circa 1981. And this was the story that was hanging in the back of my mind leading up to Frances's birth. But I was determined that my experience would be different. My first contractions began at four in the morning and John guided me through the first few hours of labor, in our bedroom, before the doula arrived. Through a combination of the doula's expert counter-pressure on my lower back and transitioning in and out of a warm birthing tub, I managed to navigate most of the physical challenges of early labor without much distress. By the time the midwives arrived around 11 A.M., however, the pain was getting much more intense. They didn't believe I could be that far along, because first-time moms often labor for more than twelve hours. I insisted that they check to see how dilated I was and to everyone's surprise, I was fully dilated and ready to push.

I remember holding onto the edge of the birthing tub in a deep squatting position, trying to will my body to push and relax at the same time. It's such a bizarre combination of sensations, and it did not come naturally to me, but the warm water and my midwife's instructions to use each vocalization to move the energy down through my body helped. I couldn't imagine trying to push and relax that way while laying on my back in a sterile hospital room. I could see how easy it would be to get stuck at this stage and feel trapped and panic. I was thankful that everyone in the room was calm; there was no pressure and no concern about me or the baby. I was so tuned in to Frances that I knew exactly where she was in my body and could even guide the assistant's fetal monitor to the exact spot on my lower abdomen where she could hear the baby's heartbeat.

The pain of each contraction obliterated any other thought or intention; all I could do was breathe and endure it. But during the time between contractions, I experienced such total pain relief that I entered a deep, peaceful trance. I'm sure these breaks lasted only a couple minutes or so, but it felt much longer. I focused my gaze on a photo of my sister I had hung right above the birthing tub. She was dressed up for a Hollywood screening party of *Green Lantern,* and we always referred to it as her Superhero persona. John said it reminded him to be brave, because my sister was always so tough and could seemingly withstand any amount of pain and suffering. Following the birth of her daughter, my sister had confidently declared that childbirth was "easier than running a 400," which was the race I had specialized in in high school and that we had run together as State champions in the 4x400 relay. She said, "You can do anything for one minute," which by that I guess she meant how long she pushed during the final contraction. But this was way harder than a 400. I felt duped.

I appealed to her, "Can't you make the pain stop?"

She laughed and said, "No. That's part of it. That's the deal."

After she said that, I knew the only way to end the pain was by giving birth. "In and through," as one of my mentors used to say about psychedelic trips.

Midwives describe a phenomenon where birthing mothers will sometimes try to run out of the room, or even out of the house, during the final stages of labor. It's like some animal instinct kicks in. They say that this is often the moment when first-time home-birthing moms will demand to go to the hospital, and then their babies are born minutes later. Well, that instinct propelled me out of the tub, and I started to pace frantically around the room. I tried laying on the bed. I tried standing. I tried leaning against the wall. Nothing was right. And then I remembered a trick I had learned from Patrick about how to conclude a mushroom ceremony that has been going on for too long. At the beginning of labor, I had set up a little altar space, with sacred objects and a candle burning. I had also created a psychedelic-inspired soundtrack that had been playing the whole time. I went over to the altar and brought my hands up to my forehead in a sign of prayer and gratitude and said to myself and Frances, "This has all been very lovely, but the ceremony is over now. It's time to be born." I bowed toward the altar, turned off the music, and blew out the candle. Then I went straight to the bathroom.

I vaguely remembered the midwives saying that sometimes women labor over the toilet because it's the only position that is even remotely like labor: pushing and relaxing at the same time. For many women, their own bathroom is also a very safe space. The bathroom had certainly become a refuge for me, especially during the last trimester when the only comfortable position I could find was floating in water. But I didn't go into the bathroom thinking all of that, my body just propelled me.

I sit down on the toilet and say to John, "Can you just stay next to me. I don't know why I'm in here, I feel like I have to go to the bathroom or something." The assistant-in-training is standing calmly near the doorway and asks if she could just feel between my legs to see if the baby's head is near the opening. Then suddenly and quite unprofessionally she screams down the hallway, "The baby's coming out!" I frantically push her away and stand up and tell John to put his arms under my armpits. As John lifts me up, holding all of my body weight, I let go, completely. And with the help of gravity and one perfectly relaxed push, Frances is out. Somehow, like a superwoman, the lead midwife dives through the room just in time to catch her.

☾

Let's just say that my second pregnancy and labor were not nearly so smooth. My son, Ray, arrived at a time when I was trying my damnedest to restart my full-time career. I was traveling internationally and leading mushroom retreats and training to be a therapist on a clinical trial of MDMA for PTSD. Ray's incarnation, mushroom miracle that it was, was simply inconvenient. With Frances, I was totally focused on nesting at home and taking care of my body and developing my intentions for a safe, spiritual birth. With Ray, I spent most of the pregnancy focused on being out in the world and ignoring my body's need for rest and focusing on what other people needed from me. It was a recipe for disaster.

Luckily, a wise force that some would call Spirit intervened at two pivotal moments. The first was during a women's mushroom retreat in Jamaica. I was nearing the end of my second trimester and was simply huge, way bigger than I had been at the same point during my pregnancy with Frances. It's worth pointing out that in the Mazatec tradition, each ceremony is focused on the healing of one, maybe two, individuals at a time. And on top of that, pregnant women are barred from leading or even attending mushroom ceremonies. Any *curandera* worth her salt would simply laugh, and then maybe weep, at my attempt to bear the responsibility of twenty women at once, while pregnant. So foolish.

In addition to the size of the group, a good number of the women had never taken mushrooms before, and quite a few were attending the retreat to address sexual or reproductive trauma. It was a heavy load to bear. But I had chosen excellent co-facilitators, including Eileen, and I felt up to the task. That is, until the middle of the first ceremony.

About an hour in, I was holding the hand of one woman who had been suffering from intense monthly pain due to endometriosis when my contractions began. At first, they felt like menstrual cramps, which was certainly strange given that I was so far along in the pregnancy, but then they started to feel more rhythmic and intense. I remembered that my first contractions with Frances had felt like this, so I started to get a little nervous. I also remembered that Braxton–Hicks (so-called "practice contractions") can begin much earlier in pregnancy the second time around. And I knew for sure that I was tired from standing and moving so much over the past few days. So, I motioned to my co-facilitators to take over so that I could have a short break.

The retreat center was a somewhat primitive set-up, and the small number of comfortable, reclining chairs were already in use, so I had to lay down straight on the cold cement floor. The waves of pain started to take on a more psychic-spiritual dimension, as my mind and body became yoked to the journey the women were undertaking. This used to happen to me at Hopkins, too, when I would feel like I was on psilocybin during a participant's session, even though I hadn't ingested anything. I rubbed my belly and focused my mind on the baby in my womb and tried hard not to let my thoughts spin out on how I would lose him if I gave birth at that point, far from a modern hospital. Finally, the pain got so bad that I told my co-facilitators I could no longer lead the ceremony, and we collectively decided to wrap things up a bit early. Being the first of three ceremonies, the dose was relatively low, and it wouldn't be the end of the world if the women had to wait until the second night to continue.

I woke up the following morning feeling pretty worn out. I managed to make it to breakfast and lead the group integration session before handing the reins over to my co-facilitators. I went back to the house to crash. By the time I woke up again, I had a high fever and harsh cough and pain in my lungs. I remembered this same constellation of symptoms from one of my hardest sessions at Hopkins, when I had gotten very physically sick after attending to a young man who had worked through and released a lot of difficult traumatic material. I've often wondered if this is a form of natural empathy gone awry. By resonating with the participant's energy, I had a much better sense of what they were going through, but to my own detriment. This time around, because I was pregnant and working with a whole group of women, it was way more intense. The gates were open, so to speak, and I was automatically (and unskillfully) absorbing the psychic and somatic energy from the space the women were navigating.

What had I gotten myself into? I was really regretting pushing myself so hard and thinking I could just gut it out. I started googling how far I was from the nearest hospital, and then how far I was from the States if I needed an emergency evacuation. My mind started to spin out. Later that day, Eileen guided me through a visioning session where we could connect with the baby and see how he was feeling about everything. She didn't get the sense that he was in any danger, but he definitely was not happy about being here, so far from home. She said his energy felt much more introverted than Frances's. She felt that the contractions were him pushing against the retreat experience, resisting it, and basically forcing me to rest.

I made it safely through the remainder of the retreat, but by the time I got home, I knew I had to take a break. I stopped drinking caffeine and started drinking a gallon of water a day. I spent about half of each day laying on my side and resting. The contractions subsided and would only come back if I pushed myself too hard or had to travel into the city for meetings. The start of the MDMA clinical trial had been delayed, as well, and I realized it was too dangerous for me and unfair to the new participant to start their sessions so close to my baby's birth. I was worried that this meant I would miss my one opportunity to become a certified psychedelic therapist, but obviously, I didn't have a choice. Thankfully, my bosses were also my friends, and they promised me that my job would be waiting for me once the baby was born, and I was healthy enough to return.

((

The second nudge from Spirit had to do with a bunch of goats. One of the oldest women on the Jamaica retreat had decided to take mushrooms for the first time to address her lifelong and unrequited spiritual longing to "see the face of God," and also to process her mother's death. She found the mushroom ceremonies confusing and unpleasant and had pretty much given up on her hopes of both spiritual transcendence and grief resolution. But one day, she encountered a mama goat and her baby along the dirt path that led from the lodge to the ceremony space. She became totally transfixed by the beauty of this pairing, and she relayed her experience to some of the other women over breakfast.

At the end of her story, I sat down and one of the women said, "She's been telling us all about the ghosts she saw on the path!"

And the storyteller said, "No, goats!"

Then, the other women said, "Right, ghosts."

And no matter how many times they went back and forth, everyone kept hearing her say ghosts instead of goats. After we all went home, I received a card from the woman, saying that she had come to realize that the goat/ghost encounter on the path was her mother, and that God had indeed shown up, not as the heavenly Father in the Sky she was looking for, but as a huge pregnant lady (me). She helped me remember my soul identity and divine mission, which was way more important than any missed career opportunity.

Which brings me to my own goats. That same glorious summer before Frances was conceived, when I swam in the lake and sunbathed and water-skied, I also got a pair of twin baby goats from the farm my husband was working at. I named them Genevieve (Gen) and Freda (Fritz), after my grandmothers, and called them the Granny Goats. They were the babies and wise elders in my life who paved the way for Frances. Once we got to the farm and the goats were old enough, we bred them for milk and the herd multiplied. Those baby goats were one of the more endearing and joyful aspects of our farm life, and every spring we would have an open-farm day where community members could hold and play with them too.

Sadly, Gen was not a natural mother. She struggled through her second pregnancy, like me. John's general approach with the farm animals was to let the mamas birth the way they wanted, which was informed by several botched attempts early on at trying to "help" the cows give birth in the barn by pulling the babies out with chains looped around their hooves, as the old farmers had told John he "had to do." After trying this barbaric and ineffectual method a few times, John decided that these animals knew way more about birthing than we did, and he just stayed out of their way during labor. Which is also why we mostly left the goats alone during labor, too. But that year, Gen needed help. She had been in labor for a few hours when I noticed that she was in distress and asked John if I could intervene.

"What do you think you're going to do?" he demanded.

"I don't know," I said, "but I have to do something. If this were me, I would want someone to step in and help."

Remember, I was still hugely pregnant myself, and on partial bed rest. This was a big exertion for me. I squatted next to Gen in the hay and rubbed her swollen side as she endured each contraction. Things were clearly not progressing, and she was exhausted. Even while she was pushing, there was no sign that the baby goat was getting any closer to coming out. Normally, goats, like cows, are born with their front hooves first, but all I could see was the baby goat's head. Realizing that I was the only hope for this poor mama goat and her babies, I reached past my own discomfort and managed to get both of my hands inside Gen to maneuver the baby into a better position. In two more strained pushes, the baby was out.

Gen was exhausted and hardly noticed the baby. But I whooped in delight. She's alive! She's warm! She can move! I wrapped the baby up in my jacket and laid back against the old barn wall, basking in the relief of a narrowly averted disaster. But then I saw exactly why Gen hadn't taken time to clean the first one. She was still in labor! The second baby came out easily but was already on death's doorstep. I tried to wrap her up and rub the life back into her, but it was only a few minutes before her body was cold and lifeless.

In a daze over the sudden swing from birth to death, I carried the healthy baby goat in my jacket back toward the house to tell John what had happened. "You better go check on Gen, she's not paying any attention to this one, and the second one is dead already." By the time we returned to the barn, we were shocked to find a third baby lying in the hay! We were thrilled that maybe two would survive, but the third also died a few hours later. John later told me that burying those tiny bodies in the Sacred Grove was one of the hardest things he had had to do on the farm. Unsurprisingly, Gen never really bonded with or even nursed the only surviving kid, but luckily, her sister Fritz was willing to take over. It all hit way too close to home. I felt like I was witnessing the animal version of birth trauma and postpartum depression.

The experience really shook me. I started to question what this trajectory of motherhood was all about. I thought about my mom's experience toward the end of her labor with me, screaming for someone to do something, and how the memory of that desperate terror was planted somewhere deep in my consciousness. I remembered the moments of my sister's death journey right before we started the palliative sedation, when she was simply delirious, frantic with pain. She was yanking off her oxygen mask to cough up blood and pulling desperately at the hospital sheets, trying to climb out of bed. As her husband and I held her and tried to reassure her, she said, "I just want it to be easy. Why aren't I dead yet?" In a flurry of confusion, the whole nursing team piled into her room and tried to get her comfortable and fix the bed sheets while waiting for the palliative care doctor to arrive to start the high-dose morphine. I kept my gaze locked on my sister's panicked eyes and rubbed her legs, saying to the nurses, "Please stay calm, she's dying. Don't frighten her." And in the middle of this storm of energy, my sister pulled her legs up close to her chest, in a birthing position, and said, "It's unbearable! I've gotta push the pain out." Her amazing lead nurse didn't even miss a beat when he said, "You go ahead, girl! Do your thing!" Once everyone had left the room and the morphine was starting to kick in, just before my sister lost consciousness, she tried to explain, "The pain is important, but everyone's like, 'It's not me. It's not me. It's not me.'" She pointed with her finger to emphasize each phrase. No one wants to be responsible for this pain; no one wants to admit it's their fault.

☾

After I had surrendered to bed rest and gallons of water and quitting work and travel, I also started a course in hypnobirthing. Given how much discomfort I'd been in, I figured I could use an extra coping strategy. For the final four weeks of my pregnancy, I visited my teacher every week, at her home. She was a retired doula and a grandma, living alone in a beautiful cottage at the edge of the town where I had gone to high school. The course, developed by Marie Mongan, involved various self-hypnosis techniques targeted at relaxation and pain relief, as well as a soundtrack that you were supposed to listen to every night before bed while you practiced. The theory behind hypnobirthing is that childbirth takes care of itself, and your only job as the mom is to stay as relaxed and calm as possible. The cognitive structure of the course is designed to reframe the narrative that birth is painful. For example, your water doesn't "break," it "releases;" and contractions are called waves or surges. Since many women don't have examples of painless, easy labors to draw on, there were also a few DVDs you could watch that showed seemingly normal women just happily birthing their babies into water while their other children played around the birthing tub. There was even a video that showed an intentional birthing community of Russian women who timed their pregnancies so that they could give birth in the Black Sea during the warmest weeks of the summer. The hypnosis techniques themselves were most effective for helping me fall asleep at night, when the pain and discomfort would often keep me awake and agitated. I latched onto the fantasy that I, too, would have a quick, painless, easy labor.

On the night of the summer solstice, following an epic purple-orange sunset, my water broke—sorry, RELEASED—right at midnight, and I alerted John that I was going to move into the extra bedroom where I had decided to labor. At the time, Frances was still sleeping with us most nights, so she stayed with John. The early contractions—sorry, WAVES—were very similar to the ones I had had in Jamaica. It was a familiar sensation, and I was mostly able to doze and rest in between each one. My doula and midwife arrived around 2 A.M., and John started filling the birthing tub.

Just like all those videos I had watched, I was convinced that I was going to have a beautiful water birth this time around. Also, everyone and their mother (literally) had informed me that second labors "always" go faster than the first, so I was pretty sure we'd be holding our son before sunrise. Shortly before the sun came up, I hopped in the tub and started practicing the hypnosis technique that is designed to move energy downward during active labor. After maybe half an hour, my midwife came in to check on me and said in a kind of annoyed and shocked tone, "You're already in the tub??"

"Sure, why not," I said. "It's where I feel the most relaxed."

"Well, the heat is going to dehydrate you and sap your energy," she replied, "so you should probably try a different position until you're much further along."

And if my hypnobirthing fantasy was one big, sparkly, morphine-filled balloon, those words were a pin.

Downstairs, I heard my mom arrive to scoop up Frances. We had given Frances the option of staying for the birth, but she ultimately decided that a special day with her Meema was much more enjoyable. (My mom later told me that she saw a huge rainbow over the valley as she was driving to the farm that morning, which was one of the things that inspired us to choose Ray as our son's name). As soon as my mom and Frances had left the farm, whatever remained of my magical pain-relief balloon just popped. That was when my real labor began.

Suddenly, my pain jumped from maybe a 4 to a 7. I hopped back in the tub, which definitely helped reduce the pain, but for some reason, my midwife was still fixated on me needing to limit my time in the water. I had heard women talk about "back labor" before, but I never knew what they meant until that morning. The pain in my back was excruciating. Each contraction felt like my lower back was being broken. It was pain for pain's sake, not a beautiful wave of energy gently coaxing my baby down the birth canal.

I started sobbing and when I closed my eyes, all I could see was vision upon vision of women in pain. Sexual abuse, assault, domestic violence, miscarriage, childbirth, torturous deaths. It was never-ending and had been going on since the dawn of humanity. This burden of pain was the female legacy. I wailed, "Why is pain our common experience? It's the only thing that ties us together."

I got out of the tub and tried walking up and down the big farmhouse staircase. I tried laboring on the toilet, like last time. Nothing was working. I had vocalized several times that I couldn't take the pain anymore, but no one seemed to be hearing me. Finally, with John and the midwife and the doula all circled around me in the bathroom I said very clearly, "This is torture. I can't do it anymore. I need to go to the hospital."

What transpired next reminded me of the protocol we would sometimes have to implement at Hopkins when someone would say they needed to leave a session. From the participant's perspective, they believed we were contacting the attending physician and calling their pick-up person and getting their shoes and phone, etc. And we were; we were just doing it really, really slowly. It's almost never a good idea for someone to leave halfway through a psychedelic session. So we would intentionally drag out the process and eventually the participant would forget their initial request or give up on their desire to leave. Most times it worked, but one time, it really didn't. It was one of the more tragic outcomes I have ever witnessed in psychedelic therapy. This one participant was so disappointed with how the session was going that he demanded to leave and kept demanding to leave up until the point that his pick-up person actually arrived and the clinician had to discharge him. He went home and refused to participate in further assessments or sessions, and then he killed himself less than two weeks later. The FDA determined that the death was not due to participation in the study trial, but it didn't change how sad and tragic the whole thing was.

So, my midwife promised me that she was calling the hospital and getting my records prepared for the transfer. And the doula kept telling me it could be a very long time, maybe even two hours, between leaving the house and getting an epidural, which I suppose was intended to encourage me to stay and give birth at home. But all I heard was, "This torture will end in less than two hours if you leave now." It was all taking way too long. I was confused about whether they were intentionally trying to keep me at the house or that maybe the hospital wasn't accepting the transfer because I hadn't registered for a hospital birth. I started to get paranoid.

I found myself back upstairs in the tub, with John, when I said, "Wait, why am I still here? Do you guys not understand how serious this is? I'm leaving. Right now."

And somehow, I threw on clothes and charged straight downstairs and through the outside door toward the car. The blast of fresh summer air and bright sunlight momentarily erased the pain and confusion I was in, and with that extra dose of lucidity, I knew for sure I needed to get to the hospital immediately.

John ran after me, calling back to the midwife and doula, "We'll see you there."

If anything could have been worse than hours of back labor, it was that half-hour car ride. The only position I could physically tolerate was kneeling in the backseat while holding onto the headrest, facing the rear windshield. John turned on the hypnobirthing soundtrack in a desperate attempt to provide me some grounding stimulus, but the only method that seemed to help counteract the pain was me literally biting my own forearm. The pain of the bite was at least somewhat distracting from the agonizing contractions. Once we parked, John ran ahead to try to get a wheelchair, and I followed behind like some wounded zombie, lurching and limping and bleeding through the parking garage toward the hospital entrance.

I could barely tolerate sitting in the wheelchair for the short elevator ride up to the maternity ward. I stood up as soon as we got to the registration desk and insisted on walking myself to the delivery room, dropping splatters of blood on the white tile with each step. I remember a very sweet nurse handing me a robe and me throwing it back at her, thinking that it was the stupidest thing in the world because of course I didn't care about being naked at that point. What I cared about was getting a fucking epidural.

I started to have the same sensation as I did at the very end of labor with Frances, of intense pressure and needing to go to the bathroom. But when I sat down on the toilet, I couldn't even pee. I had now stumbled into a totally new region of the Land of Pain, where there was no more relief between contractions.

I somehow managed to lie still on my back so that the doctor could check to see how far along I was, and she surprised no one when she stated, "You know, you're fully dilated, you could just push."

"I didn't come here to push. I came here for the drugs," I (probably) snarled back at her.

Normally, I suppose, they wouldn't give you an epidural at that stage, but someone must have done the quick calculus of me tearing the room apart or threatening someone's life, and they gave it to me.

During the endless minute between the needle going into my spine and the first sweet taste of opiate pain relief, all I could focus on was the green of the trees that were visible just beyond the hospital parking lot, subtly waving and dancing in the wind. I could barely keep my eyes open, and I felt my life force follow the movement of those waves—up, up, up—as my soul quietly and softly whispered, "It's OK. I'm leaving now." And then, just before I departed Earth, the drugs kicked in. I was back. I looked around the room. There was John and my midwife and my doula. I felt completely, totally, utterly, comically, normal. The pain had been obliterated. My mind was clear. The room sparkled. I was myself again.

I smiled and laughed, "Hey guys! Oh my God, I feel great. What a relief!" I started chatting about some nonsense and you could tell everyone else in the room was still reeling in shock from the insanity of the past two hours.

Finally, my midwife said, "You're still having a baby, you know."

I looked at the clock on the wall and knew Ray would be born right before noon, just like his sister. "Well, I'm for sure gonna enjoy this half hour, then," I said. And to this day, I maintain that that was one of the best thirty minutes of motherhood, and possibly my life. Total contentment. No pain, no discomfort, no anxiety. Just joy and pleasant anticipation. Real happiness. I even remarked in a professional interview later on that that single experience showed me how totally reasonable it is that people become addicted to heroin. It was perfection.

I was still having intense contractions but couldn't feel any of them, so I was completely dependent on my birth team to tell me what to do when. My doula placed a large exercise ball between my legs to help keep my pelvis wide as little Ray moved down the birth canal. Eventually, my midwife noticed that the baby's head was crowning, and the doctor and doctors-in-training quickly piled in. John had a front row seat, right next to the assistant. I bore down with all my might when they told me to, and in just a few pushes, Ray was born and on my chest. "You made it!" I said to him, "You're here!"

And just like that, our ray of sunshine chose his birth without violence. Not at home in a birthing tub to a mother who was trying really hard to hypnotize away the fear and pain while actually being slowly tortured to death. But in a modern hospital with the best drugs and a pain-free reception. This was the gift of Ray's incarnation: he showed me that there was another way, a peaceful alternative to my familiar path of self-violence and frustration and exhaustion and grief. He reminded me of the vow I took on that meditation retreat: "I promise not to hurt myself or anyone else on purpose." He showed me that it was OK to admit I couldn't do it on my own. I didn't have to force myself to endure pain just to prove how tough I was. I could give up, and it could be glorious.

CHAPTER 8

☾

Immunity

THE FIRST MONTH with baby Ray was a beautiful, precious honeymoon. We slept together every night in the
gorgeous guest bedroom in the front of the farmhouse
that had been painted a kind of bright blue that really belonged
in Tahiti. It was the same room I had tried so hard to labor
in, but the energy was different once Ray was there with me.
It was a surreal time, as one new mother put it, "reintegrating
into the matrix." One of my and John's favorite musicians, who
always reminded us of our glory days in California and who also
inspired Ray's name, had just put out a new album, and I would
put that on in the evenings and just walk around the room, dancing and singing and nursing my sweet sunshine child. He was
the medicine I didn't even know I had needed.

The medicine of his spirit was so strong that I didn't realize how much pain I was still in. I was only sleeping a couple
hours at a time while nursing Ray throughout the night, and
often holding him while he slept, which I remembered as par

for the course with a newborn. Good friends came and went, helping with Frances and cooking and cleaning. We even managed to pull off an epic mariachi birthday party for Frances and my brother, on my brother's birthday, which is also the Feast of Mary Magdalene and the day that María Sabina's birth is celebrated. But right around the time the last visitor left, when Ray was about six weeks old, I realized that my back and right hip were in constant agony.

Each night started to feel exactly the same, like a hellish version of *Groundhog Day*: lying in bed crying, exhausted, held prisoner by the pain. I was so sleep-deprived but unable to sleep. I endured endless dark hours, waiting for Ray's final night feeding around 4 A.M. so I could hand him off to John, pop some ibuprofen, and get a couple hours to myself. My mind kept spinning back to the feeling of no-exit during Ray's birth. It felt like the torment of my labor—which had been temporarily suppressed by the amazing cocktail of epidural-plus-natural-adrenaline-and-oxytocin—was still trapped in my body and needed to get out. And I was pissed.

I was angry because I had convinced myself John wasn't doing enough to help with Ray (he was actually doing everything else) and hadn't come to my rescue during labor (misguidedly thinking that somehow, he should have known the right thing to do to keep us from winding up at the hospital). I was angry that I could barely walk and that I didn't get to play with Frances anymore. I kept snapping at our housemates until one of them moved out. I was like a wrecking ball, seeking out every possible target.

On top of my internal struggles, the situation at the farm was looking bleak. We had worked hard to help elect a new town leader, thinking he would be on our side. He was a Democrat and a teacher at a local college and played guitar (sometimes at our community events). He went out of his way to express his support for us during debates with the other selectmen. But as soon as he took power, everything changed. He was just as bad, if not worse, than the guy before him. One day, I received a text from him that said that folks in town were asking the resident state trooper about my mushroom work. I replied that I'd be happy to have an in-depth conversation about drug abuse and harm reduction and please, could he send the state trooper over right away? He didn't show up, but the message was clear: we're watching you, we think you're a drug dealer, and you're not welcome here.

And the psychedelic scene was even bleaker. During my third trimester, a courageous young woman of color came forward with allegations of sexual misconduct by a well-known therapist in the New York psychedelic community. Her report prompted a legal investigation by the psychedelic organization where the therapist was a board member, and they ended up uncovering multiple, credible reports of sexual misconduct. Ultimately, the organization decided to remove the therapist from his position on the board (Note: The organization made only one public statement about the matter, on their Facebook page, but otherwise, very little was ever reported about the incident. To this day, only a handful of people know the names of the women who put their own safety on the line to share their stories). I was one of the few people who had heard reports directly from some of the women who were harmed, and it was painful to see people rally around the therapist to defend him. One of the most powerful men in psychedelia even traveled all the way across the country to make sure the therapist felt supported in the weeks following his firing! I wanted so many things for the survivors: protection, justice, reparations, healing. But they got very little from the larger community. So few people said, publicly, "I stand with these women," or "I stand against sexual abuse in the psychedelic community." Some of my colleagues reached out and expressed sympathy for the victims, but others demanded to know exactly what had happened so that they could decide for themselves if the therapist's actions were bad enough to warrant dismissal. Most people simply didn't seem to care.

At the same time, complex ethical issues were emerging within the larger psychedelic research world. One of my colleagues told me that the philanthropist couple I had worked with on the hospice project had scrapped their original plans and pivoted to studying psilocybin for depression. But theirs was no longer a charitable endeavor; they were now backed by some of the wealthiest investors in the world and were poised to launch one of the first for-profit pharmaceutical companies to study psychedelic medicines. When I heard the news, I immediately called Roland (my former mentor from Hopkins). "I can't believe we shared our IRB protocols with them! I never would have helped them if I knew they were in it for the money!"

Then we got the worst possible news from John's parents. We had been hoping they would be able to visit to meet Ray, but they kept coming up with different excuses for why they couldn't make the trip, mostly having to do with John's dad's health. Finally, John's mom revealed the real reason: John's dad was dying. He had suffered with multiple sclerosis (MS) for nearly twenty years, the entire time I had known John. He often struggled to walk and was in constant pain, which he often managed to conceal from everyone around him. He was not a very emotionally open guy, and the rest of the family always joked that he was usually off in his own world. But he was brilliant and tuned into human nature and the world in a way that I had only encountered maybe once or twice in the halls of academia.

I always felt like he knew me and could see me in a way that most men of his generation could not. Having endured his own share of family trauma and loss, he naturally intuited how hard it was for me just getting through each day without my sister. Suffice to say, he had reached the end of his rope and decided to withdraw from all nourishment. He would die naturally, but on purpose. The decision fit his personality, but the timing was awful. I couldn't have imagined a crueler thing to happen at this joyful moment in our life.

There was no time to waste. John flew with Frances to Colorado the next day, and I stayed home with Ray. I was worried about flying with him so young and I didn't know if I could physically handle the travel either. The only place I felt safe was at the farm.

Resisting my own intuition but knowing how important it was for John's dad to meet Ray before he died, Ray and I somehow got on a plane a few days later and met the family out in Boulder. I don't remember much about the trip except that it was hard and weird, and I felt like I shouldn't be there. The family was doing their best to support John's dad and make the most of his final days, but it was clear that no one was ready for this to happen. It's like we had all known it was coming, for so long—and no one begrudged the man for finally saying "enough" to the pain and suffering—but we weren't ready to say goodbye. During our final conversation, I joked kind of half-heartedly, "I'm sure I'll see you again, Big John!", because he was a die-hard atheist. I was a recovering atheist, so I really wanted to believe that he would come back, but deep down I knew he wouldn't, at least not in human form. I guess I believe that people get what they think is coming, and with all his being, he expected nothing. Maybe he was one of the lucky ones. This was it. The end of the road.

I came home dejected and depressed. But like, depressed in the colloquial way, I thought, not actually depressed. Shortly after we returned, my midwife came over for the final check-up, which had been delayed because of our travels. I explained to her how much pain I had been in, and how I couldn't really sleep and didn't have the energy to play with Frances or socialize.

And my midwife replied, "Would you be open to answering a few questions about postpartum depression?" And I said, "Oh, you don't understand. I'm in physical pain." And she said, "Well, sometimes postpartum depression can present as physical symptoms." I filled out each item and because I had developed psychological scales myself, I knew my score before I had even finished. I was definitely depressed. It was kind of a relief to have a concrete thing to point to, to explain why I was feeling so terrible every day. And we came up with a plan: walking outside for thirty minutes every day even if my hip hurt, going to see a chiropractor to address the physical problem, and re-starting therapy.

It was a challenge even getting to that first appointment with Dana. I felt guilty that I had let my mental health slide so much since the last time I had seen her when Frances was a newborn. It was very, very hard to relax in her office without worrying about Ray. I remember her saying, "Frances is with John, and she's safe. Nothing bad will happen to her while you're here. Ray is with your mom, and he's safe. Nothing bad will happen to him while you're here. You are here with me. Nothing bad will happen to you while you're here." We talked for a few minutes, just so she could get up to speed on the family events, and then she offered that we spend the rest of the session doing "table work." We hadn't done this in years, but I remembered from our early sessions that she would often discourage talking and instead have people lie on the massage table for the first several sessions if they were dealing with acute trauma. A large part of her somatic healing work involved helping people relax and feel safe in their bodies. For many people with unresolved or complex trauma, even telling the story about it can put the body into such an agitated state that no healing can happen.

So I lie down on my back, and she begins by placing her hands gently on the bottoms of my feet. Then, after a minute or so, my lower legs. "It's OK. You can be here." And as she calmly, patiently, dwells in this seemingly neutral territory of my body, the tears start flowing. My sister. Her pain at the end. "It's unbearable. Somebody do something. I've gotta push the pain out." Me rubbing her legs and trying to get everyone in the room to stay calm. "Argh!" I say out loud, "Why is this still all about HER?" And the tears come harder. I'm sobbing and just missing her so, so much. And then Dana moves her hands to my right hip, the epicenter of the pain. All I hear in my mind is "I'm sorry. I'm sorry. I'm sorry." Then she shifts her hands underneath my body to my lower back. Things get a bit psychedelic at that point. I feel like I am laying in a canoe, a sacred funeral boat, floating down a lazy, silty river in the Amazon toward some new land, the land beyond life, the mystical world between worlds. I remember that this is my birth right. I know at some deep level that all of this pain and loss has been a portal to a deeper, spiritual knowing. I can trust this process as much as I can trust this canoe, and this river. I don't have to do anything. I laugh a bit, remembering an old psychedelic hippie adage: when in doubt, float downstream.

As Dana shifts over to my left side, my mental landscape shifts dramatically. I am suddenly defensive, on edge. I know I can trust Dana, but I don't in that moment. The character of that left hip is sly, sinister, callous. Very much like the monster in the mirror that I encountered during my Zen retreat. I don't feel safe with that monster in the room. Dana ends the session with her hands gently cupping the back of my skull. I let these two sides—the emotional, wounded side and the calculating, predator side—swirl next to each other. I share a bit about the different feelings and visions that came up, but she encourages me to just stay in my body and let the process lead the way. As I walk out of her office, I can actually feel the heat from the sun on my skin. I can smell the heavy, humid summer air. The drab parking lot is vibrant and sparkly. I had totally forgotten what it felt like to be present in my body.

I kept seeing Dana every week for the next month. And the chiropractic adjustments made a world of difference. As my chiropractor said, "Giving birth is like getting hit by a bus. And we still expect women to just get back to their normal life within a couple weeks. It's absurd."

With the help of Dana and my chiropractor, I eventually felt good enough, and safe enough, to allow John to go back, alone, to be with his dad one more time. Big John ended up living quite a bit longer than anyone thought he would: nearly two months from the day we got the call from John's mom. He had voluntarily given up all curative treatments, as well as eating and drinking, so everyone was quite amazed he made it two months. We were all back at the farm when John's mom texted that he had died. It was a stormy night, and Ray was sick and crying, and Frances was running all over the house whacking things with her purple wand. The energy was wild.

I went to see Dana the next day, as planned. My physical symptoms were getting better but I was still dealing with a lot of anxiety and anger; same old story. I realized that it would have been much better to restart somatic therapy during my pregnancy rather than try to clean up the mess after the fact. After I finished the session, I was sitting with my mom on the bench outside Dana's office, nursing Ray, when she told me about her vortex. She said, "Kath, I'm really sorry, but I can't go to John's dad's funeral."

I knew she was not a fan of funerals, and in this case, I knew for sure Big John wouldn't care, so I said, "Mom, it's not a big deal, it's OK."

"It's just that I get this spinning sensation," she continued, "it's like I'm falling into a pit, and I lose track of time and space."

And now, I am really, really paying attention. This sounds like the vortex! The one I stumbled into while meditating by the side of a waterfall in Tucson, Arizona. The one that precipitated my year of extremely uncomfortable and terrifying enlightenment, just before my sister died.

My mom is softly crying as she explains further, "It happened the first time when I walked into the funeral parlor for my dad's funeral. It was only two and a half months after my brother drowned, and I couldn't figure out whether it was his funeral or my dad's funeral, and I just lost myself. It's happened to me ever since. Even at funerals for people I don't know."

And in this simple, non-academic manner, my mom basically schooled me on what complex PTSD is actually like: an embodied, immersive, eternally recurring and looping nightmare, not a theoretical construct. She also, incidentally, schooled me on intergenerational trauma. It's quite a surreal and comical thing to suddenly realize that one's vortex has been inherited, like the pattern of freckles on your cheek or the color of your eyes. And while sitting outside your therapist's office, no less! In that moment, I felt closer to my mom than I had in my entire adult life. We both have anxiety! We both have the vortex! Same, same!

Then, I was pleasantly surprised by the thought that followed, "Maybe MDMA can help."

What unraveled next is literally unbelievable. I still can't quite accept the series of dominos that fell after John's dad's death. I still don't want to believe them. But the best thing I can say about it all, in hindsight, is that pain and depression do have a functional purpose: they expose reality for what it is. No sugar coating. In the state I was in, I could see the truth of what was happening, while others couldn't. And maybe the other functional purpose of pain and depression is to get you to stop living the life you don't actually want to be living.

I received the call about my dad having brain cancer while enjoying a drink with friends in the hotel lobby the night before John's dad's memorial. No, you can't make this shit up. Only real life is this fucked. My brother, who was only twenty-one at the time, had just come home in the middle of his Fall semester as a sophomore in college to find that my dad could barely speak. The extra fucked-up thing about this is that only my brother knew my dad well enough to immediately recognize what my dad had been trying to conceal from everyone else for months.

My brother called me from the bathroom of the restaurant that he and my dad would always go together, sobbing, "I think something's really wrong with dad. We were just having dinner, and he can barely talk. Have you noticed that he's forgetting words?"

I scanned back through the last few months and was embarrassed when I admitted, "I just thought he was being grumpy and reclusive." My brother said that our dad, ever the linguistic genius, was forgetting even simple words and hanging at the end of sentences, not finishing them.

By the time my dad arrived at work the next morning, it had gotten so bad that his assistant and boss, both very close family friends who had known him for a long time, insisted he go to the hospital to make sure he wasn't having a stroke. The scans revealed what my dad must have feared was coming: his lung cancer had finally metastasized, to his brain. When my brother called me again to update me, he said, "Honestly, Kath, I was more scared that it was early-onset dementia or something. Can you imagine Dad with Alzheimer's? I can't think of a worse form of hell, for him or us." My dad was given steroids to help reduce the swelling in his brain and was immediately scheduled for brain surgery the following week.

After that news, I numbly floated through the next day's events, unable to feel much of anything. Only one moment yanked me out of my disconnected stupor: a brief snow squall kicked up in the middle of a bright, sunny day, just after John's tribute to his dad, and I knew that it was Big John showing us that he had discovered Something, not Nothing, after death. By the time we got home, I was in a state of near total dissociation. I started to experience a new form of anxiety, like a big, empty hole opening up in front of me. This wasn't the vortex; it wasn't full of energy. It was just . . . empty. Standing at the edge of this chasm, I wasn't afraid of falling in, but I was sad. So, so sad. For me and John and the fact that our life together had become a continual series of unfolding tragedies. For John's dad and his lifetime of pain, concluded in such a torturous fashion. And for my dad, who definitely wasn't going to get a couple more decades to resolve things with me or my brother, or see his grandkids grow up.

And I was sad for me. I always desperately hoped for some final conversation between me and my dad. That maybe some-day I would finally have the courage to tell him my version of history, tell him what I remembered, tell him why I hated him so much and also, in spite of everything, really, really loved him. In my fantasy, he would accept it all and apologize.

I definitely wasn't ready to have that conversation yet. And if he didn't regain his cognitive abilities or speech after the surgery, then I would never get the apology I was looking for. The whole thing was pure delusion; I knew this conversation wasn't going to happen. It was just too theatrical, and not in keeping with our personalities. But the thought of never hearing the words I had always needed to hear from my dad, that was a sadness beyond death. I even remember my mom saying, after she learned of the new diagnosis, "You know, your brother is never going to get what he really needs from your dad. And neither are you."

The morning of my dad's surgery, I opened up a book of poems by Allen Ginsberg right to the one called "Father Death Blues." I read it out loud and knew the writing was on the wall. Maybe not today, but soon. On the way to the hospital, we tried to keep the mood light as we sang my dad's favorite songs, the ones he used to sing while playing the guitar for me and my sister when we were kids. As we sang, I thought, "My dad is easier to love at a distance," and I was thankful that even after his death, I would still have these songs. Maybe their medicine would be stronger than the residue of pain or anger. And maybe these songs could take the place of all the conversations we would never get to have.

As we drove, we passed the restaurant where we had had our last meal together, after my dad's prep before surgery. At one point during lunch, my brother had gone to the bathroom and John was walking around the restaurant with Ray, when my dad suddenly seemed totally normal and had no trouble finding the words he wanted. He said, "You know, your brother's having a really tough time."

"Yeah, no shit," I responded.

"But you're fine," he continued.

"No, Dad, I'm not fine," I continued. "I haven't been fine since Rebecca died. But I've made my peace with God."

And he replied, "I'm not God."

I've replayed that conversation so many times since he died. Somehow, when he said that, I knew that he knew exactly what I was going through. I knew that he knew what he had done, and I guess he was trying to say he was sorry, that it wasn't his fault, that things beyond his control had made him do what he did. I knew that he recognized the fight I had been fighting, when I said I had a bone to pick with God. And I knew that he knew that I was lying. My fight with God was far from over; there was no peace, no truce. I might have reached a semblance of a truce with some far-off idea of God, but not the God right in front of me.

When I hear my dad's words echoing in my mind—"I'm not God"—I also think of a woman who once shared about her ayahuasca experience at one of my integration circles in the city. She had a thick accent, and it was hard for her to describe in English what the experience had been like. She mostly focused on the pain and confusion, how it seemed like the whole thing was a waste of time. No visions, no insights, no divine plant spirits. And then she woke up the next morning and, in her exact words, "My memory cracked. Everything started flooding in. And I realized that I had been on an altar fighting with God." I've never heard a closer description of what Life has felt like for me. I had been fighting with the God that I was taught, through Catholic school and church and my upbringing: God the Father. The one who was kind of an asshole and seemed to enjoy inflicting punishments and being right all the time; the one who was willing to sacrifice his own child and leave him bleeding on a cross just to prove a point. And in my little kid mind, my dad was the closest thing to this terrible God. He seemed all-powerful. I wanted him to take responsibility for everything that had happened and fix it! But I had forgotten he was also human.

My dad really lucked out that first round. The largest tumor was in a part of his brain that was easy to access during surgery, and he was shockingly almost normal within a few days of getting out of the hospital. We even dressed up and celebrated Halloween with him the following weekend. There was one hilarious photo of him putting Frances's Goldilocks wig on over his head bandage, posing with us as the three bears. The following week, he went back in for targeted radiation of a few smaller tumors and was basically good to go.

☾

Just when things were momentarily looking up, the final hammer dropped. Over the course of the summer, I had been in touch with the guys running the MDMA trial in the city, and I thought we were still on track for me to come back early in the new year, at the end of my maternity leave. So much had transpired in the psychedelic world since I had retreated to the farm—including the sexual misconduct case and the ongoing debate about the role of for-profit companies in psychedelic therapy. I was one of a handful of people who had been very vocal about keeping profits out of psychedelic medicine and about not tolerating unethical behavior, and I imagine it made my bosses nervous. On top of that, they knew I was struggling with postpartum depression. They knew that John's dad had just died. They knew that my own dad had just undergone brain surgery. Yet, through all of this, they had said how much they valued me as a colleague. That my skills as a psychedelic guide were unmatched. And more importantly, we were friends. So I was wholly unprepared for what came next.

They asked for the call to be just them and me, not my co-therapist, which should have been my first clue. During the first five or so minutes, we were chatting and catching up and it was all lovely and normal. I tried to make a joke. "Well, it's been a hell of a few months, but Allen Ginsberg's poetry is really helping me navigate the 'father-death blues.'"

"At this point," I continue, "my only goal between now and January 1ˢᵗ is to grow out my hair so that it's long enough for a professional environment." And they both laugh, but in a nervous, sheepish way, and I know something is up.

"Unfortunately, it's not going to work for you to come back in January," my boss/friend says. "You know, with the timing of the study."

Confused, I reply, "But we always agreed on January. The study coordinator approved my leave. The entire clinical leadership said it was fine. You all said I could take up to six months, that there was no rush to come back."

No dice. I try bargaining, "Well, maybe I could come back a bit sooner. Why didn't you just tell me you needed me back?"

My boss/friend, who now also seems a bit like a robot, replies, "It's not only that, it's just with everything you're going through, we thought it would be better for you to be with your family . . . take care of your health."

Then the other one chimes in, "I feel badly that this is how things are happening. I really hate to punish you for being postpartum, but . . ." And he stops himself. Those really aren't the words you want to be saying to a woman during her maternity leave when you are her boss.

I can't let it go. "Well, who's going to take my place? You always said the woman who stepped in for me was temporary.

You know the other site is gonna be pissed when you tell them that she has to keep splitting her time."

And my dear friend, my close collaborator, is now clearly annoyed. His authority is being questioned. All emotional softness evaporates from his face. He states, simply and definitively, "That's already been worked out."

It's over. I'm being fired. Have already been fired, actually. The tears start welling up in my eyes and a big lump forms just behind my rib cage. But I quickly stuff all those emotions down and set my face to Serious Mode to mimic the faces across from me.

"OK," I say. "I'm gonna make this easy on everyone. I resign."

The call ends and the tears start flowing. I am furious. I storm through the house to find John and say, "Something really weird just happened. I think I quit a job I didn't want to quit. I should have made those fuckers fire me."

Over the next few months, I did everything I could to hold onto some remnant of hope for my career. I arranged a meeting with the female leaders of the organization, desperately wanting to believe they were still on my side. I reached out to an old therapist friend, and we put together an application for an "expanded access site," thinking the organization would just let me run my own MDMA clinic. We were *this close* to arranging the funding we needed to get things going when I discovered the truth.

I always thought that receiving intel from a real-life whistleblower would have been more cinematic, like meeting in a dimly lit parking garage in some broken down city and getting handed a worn briefcase with secret documents inside. But, in my case, it was just a phone call and some screenshots.

The person cuts right to the chase, "I recently heard that you

resigned from the clinical trial. But it was always my understanding that you were fired."

"Well, how would you know about that?" I say, defensively.

"I received a weird email last Fall," they say. "I don't even
know why I was included. I'll send you the screenshots so you
can see for yourself."

There it was, plain as day. My study coordinator was letting
everyone know that I was about to be let go. The email was sent
nearly ten days before the call with my boss/friends. And I wasn't
just being let go from that one study site; the email clarified
that I would no longer be working with the organization in any
capacity. The email mentioned that I was going through some
difficult life circumstances and to please let anyone who might
be friends with me know that this decision was coming, and *not*
to alert me. The second screenshot was the nail in my coffin, an
email from my boss back to the study coordinator, following the
call where he got me to resign. He declared triumphantly, "It
went smooth as butter."

I felt disgusted. These people were my friends! I had trusted
them when they said I could take as long as I needed for my
maternity leave. I had trusted them when I shared the details of
what was going on in my life. They knew how much this meant
to me. How much I had already given up since my sister died.
It wasn't just a single lost job opportunity; it was the rest of my
career. Now it was obvious that there was never any intention to
let me back into the fold. It was their MDMA, after all, and the
fortress gates had just been slammed in my face.

Of course, this all felt deeply personal and cruel. Over the
years, I have felt shocked, horrified, furious; ranting my story to
anyone who would listen. Many, many times I wondered, "How
could this happen to me?", as if what happened was exceptional.
But now I know that it was just typical. What happened to

me—quitting a job I didn't want to quit because I was presented with no other option—happens all the time, to millions of women, and is what one union-organizer friend called "a successful fire." This is simply how the patriarchy works. This is how they show their appreciation for people when they are at their most vulnerable. My friends were just following the script.

☾

Ever since my sister died, I thought I had gotten to know the underworld pretty well. All those dark places in your mind where monsters and ghouls and rotten things hang out. I thought I was well-traveled in that space. Kind of like how a tourist who visits their favorite foreign country once a year claims they really know the place. And the locals just kind of chuckle. Well, the denizens of Hell were really yucking it up, now. "Oh, my dear, dear child," they'd say. "You thought you knew what Hell was like! The last few years were just an introduction! Please, come and see what pain and suffering are really about."

With all sorts of new time on my hands, now that I was definitely career-less, I learned that the yawning chasm that had opened up alongside my dad's brain cancer was actually not empty; it was full of all manner of dark, monstrous things, including my biggest fears and all sorts of childhood anxieties that I thought I had successfully resolved in somatic therapy. But it was full of my dad's fears and boogeymen too. It was truly our shared pit of Hell. Obviously, I must have known at some level that my dad and I were yoked to each other, psychologically and spiritually. There's a phenomenon where empathic kids get really good at resonating with their parents' moods and patterns so that they can predict what's coming next, either to enjoy rewards or avoid punishments. And when you're an empathic kid with a rage-filled, emotionally-dysregulated dad, you can't help but grow a nervous system that includes all sorts of shitty, dangerous patterns. There's another phenomenon where empathic kids will do everything they can to try to regulate their parents' emotions for them, to avoid triggering some of the worst kinds of outbursts and painful expressions, like yelling, crying, lashing out. I knew all of this. I could remember a hundred times as a young child when I had tried to butter-up my dad to prevent an angry temper tantrum (his, not mine). I often felt like the adult in the relationship, even when I was a child. But I had no idea I would one day have to do battle with his biggest fears, directly. Weren't my own fears enough?

The nightmares started shortly after I left the clinical trial. I kept waking up in a cold sweat, heart pounding, convinced there was some kind of demon lurking in my bedroom. I would take nearly half an hour to calm down, convinced the demon was real. It was like a brief taste of psychotic terror, every night. I had had anxiety attacks before, but this was different. It felt "other," like it wasn't mine. I even tried to banish the demon during my somatic therapy sessions, but it kept coming back. I knew that my dad had always had trouble sleeping, and often needed to take things like Ambien or Benadryl to get a full night's sleep. He was an anxious person, but he masked it by being tough and smart and in control. I started to wonder if maybe my nighttime monster had something to do with my dad's unresolved fears, and his impending death.

Around this time, my dad invited my brother and me to Bermuda. It was clear that the mortal clock was ticking for him. The rest of my dad's friends and family were enjoying the delusion that my dad might fully recover and have another good ten, maybe fifteen years. But the three of us knew the truth. We read the research papers. We learned the statistics. Luckily, my dad had the courage to say it out loud before me or my brother had to tell him: "By my calculations," he said, "I've got one good year left."

Maybe it was the pressure of so little time and knowing how much had gone unsaid with my sister. But during that trip, my dad was actually able to open up a bit. He mostly wanted to talk about his favorite topic—finances—and outline all the complex legal structures he had set up to ensure that my brother, my niece, my kids, and I would be financially secure when he died. But he even opened up about some pretty heavy family stuff.

There was a big family secret that had been revealed around the time my grandma died, when I was in college. Apparently, many years prior, one of my aunts had been rummaging around in the basement and happened upon a birth certificate for my grandpa that had a different last name than the one we all grew up with. Eventually, the story came out that it was because my grandpa had been adopted. His birth father was allegedly an abusive asshole who abandoned him and his mom when he was only a baby. The man who stepped in and adopted my grandpa, the one who gave us all our last name, was also "not a very nice guy," according to my dad. Throughout all of this, my grandpa's mother suffered from serious mental illness, maybe bipolar disorder or some kind of psychotic depression. She had been institutionalized when my dad was a child and kept a journal while she lived at the insane asylum (yes, that's what they called it in the 1950s). When my grandparents' house was being cleared out after my grandma died, I was gifted some of those journals.

So, one afternoon during the Bermuda vacation, while Ray was napping, I took a chance and asked my dad about all of this. "Hey Dad, did Grandpa ever talk to you about what it was like for him, growing up?" And my dad said that he only ever talked about his childhood once, when he first told my dad and his siblings that he had been adopted. During that one conversation, my grandpa said he never wanted to talk about it again. But my dad also said that every Sunday, when my grandma would take my dad and his sisters to church, my grandpa would take the youngest sibling, my dad's brother, to visit "Beebop Grannie" at the asylum. After they visited her, they would park the car near the airport to watch the planes touch down. "You know, Grandpa was a fighter pilot. He flew at D-Day. He was a war hero. So I guess this was his version of church." And, of course, I had to ask, "Did he have any trauma from the war? Like when you guys were little, was he angry?" And my dad said, "No. Not at all. It was a great source of pride. He was always telling stories about flying that fighter jet. He came home from the war with the intention of creating the perfect family life for us."

You see, I was trying to play detective with what might have come before me and my dad. I was still looking for a reason, why it had all happened the way it did, with us. I guess it would have been too easy for my grandpa to have been abused as a kid and have PTSD from the war and be a raging monster at home while my dad was little, and for my dad to just pass that rage on to me. But grandpa was a kind man, very loving. Because of his shitty upbringing, he did everything he could to be the best dad he could be. And he was heroic in other ways. My mom once told me that he was the only person she could reach out to when we were little and my dad announced he was in love with another woman and he was leaving. My mom called my grandpa, confused and in tears, and he immediately drove the hour and a half to our house and listened to everything she was going through. Because he was normally so even tempered, she was shocked by how furious he was with my dad's behavior. His parting advice was, "Go to California and let that son-of-a-bitch feel what it's like to live without his kids."

So, here were the family patterns: abuse, betrayal, mental illness, anger. But there was also the cancer. My grandpa and his mom, my dad and his brother, and my sister—all tied together through this one fucked-up genetic mutation. I thought about the demon who kept waking me up at night, and the ones who had been visiting me, on and off, since college, in the form of sleep paralysis and anxiety attacks, hallucinatory meditation sessions and paranoid acid trips. These shadowy gremlins, lurking, waiting, ready to pounce. Maybe they were the manifestations of family trauma, our epigenetic curses. I could only imagine how much worse it got as you went back a few hundred generations. Like in royal families. Incest was how many of these genetic mutations started in the first place.

On the plane ride back from Bermuda, I had such a bad panic episode that I thought it was a heart attack. I felt like my heart was going explode out of my chest, and this thought kept running through my head: "It's all happening too fast. Make it stop."

Because I didn't really know what else to do, I planned a solo ceremony. It was the full moon in December, the Cold Moon. I mixed together a mini dose of mushrooms and a mini dose of San Pedro cactus and what I actually got was a whopping dose of confusion and unpleasantness. My mind was swirling, lost, as it tried to navigate this labyrinth of cancer and trauma and family secrets. I felt sick to my stomach the whole time. All my normal anxieties were just amplified. And the only real message that came through loud and clear: just be a mom. "But I can't be a mom! It's too hard!"

Then I tried again, the following month, again on the full moon, but with only a tiny amount of mushrooms this time, and the message was even more clear: "We have nothing more for you. We have given you everything you asked for. It's time for a break."

I was devastated. My dad had brain cancer. My sister was never coming back. My poor brother was really struggling, mental health-wise. I was permanently kicked out of my dream career. And it was our last year on the farm. We had absolutely no plan for how to make a living. Being a mom was apparently the only thing left for me to do but it was so hard and not getting any easier. And now, even the mushrooms were done with me. I thought my Dark Night had ended when I got pregnant with Frances, but maybe that was just the prelude. Every single thing I had come to rely upon for comfort and happiness was being stripped away. In the words of an elder shaman, I was being flattened.

Then one night, I awoke, not to a demon or a heart attack or a sick child or a phone call with terrible news about one of my family members, but to a lovely, sweet lullaby. I laughed, because it was so obvious:

emmmmmmmmm deeeeeeeeeeeeeeee emmmmmmmmmm aaaaaaaaaa
aaaaaaaaaaaaaaaaaaaaaaaaaa

The cosmic joke got funnier and funnier the more I let this mantra weave its way into my heart and bones. MDMA had been my original medicine. The medicine that broke my heart open and helped me feel my whole body for the first time. The medicine that gave me the courage to dance in a crowd and walk through graveyards alone in the dark. The medicine that showed me how easy it was to love, myself included. This was all back in college, and the effects were only temporary. I had only tried a full dose once since then, at Burning Man, and the darkness that followed was enough to scare me off for good. I had convinced myself that MDMA therapy was now something for other people, you know, THOSE people, with unresolved, complex PTSD. But I was one of THOSE people. I had complex PTSD! I needed this medicine. I was trying so hard to be the therapist but what I really needed was that therapy.

The punchline was the best part, because I remembered that I already had access to an amazing supply of high-quality MDMA. When my dad lost his speech and had to undergo brain surgery and I thought maybe he was about to die, I had asked a friend to give me enough for my dad and brother and me to have one or two sessions together. This was going to be my Christmas present to them. But then my dad got better, and I chickened out after the Bermuda trip and just stuffed it all away in the closet.

I walked into my altar room and gingerly took out the MDMA, kind of embarrassed that I had kept a deity imprisoned in a closet for months. I carefully placed the capsules on the altar: 80 mg for the first dose and 40 mg for the booster dose, just like the protocol says (and yes, the joke kept getting better and better, because this protocol was developed and published online by the organization that had just fired me). I opened up my well-worn copy of "Be Here Now" — the illustrated enlightenment guide written by Ram Dass back in the '60s, that I think I actually took from the Hopkins session room before I quit—and the words that stared back at me were like reading the words on my own tombstone: "I and the Father are One."

A shiver went through my whole body. I hated those words. "No! We are NOT one. I'm not like that monster!" God, the Father; my Father. No!

I immediately started to bargain my way out of it. Maybe I shouldn't take the MDMA, after all, it's bound to make me even more depressed afterward. Maybe I'll wait until Ray

is older and not nursing anymore. Maybe, maybe, maybe . . .
But in the same way that I knew my sister was going to die,
and I had no choice but to be there with her, I knew that this
MDMA ceremony had already happened, was happening,
and that I had no choice but to take the plunge. I knew in
that moment that this was the beginning of the end, the final
chapter. When I would finally be able to forgive my dad. And
not just forgive him as some monster outside of me or someone who had done monstrous things that we could finally forget about, but forgive him in totality. Forgive him by melding
with him, by fully understanding him, by finally accepting all
the ways we were the same. Forgive him by coming face to face
with the monster that was in him, and also in me. No more
hiding.

☾

When it finally came time for the ceremony, I was terrified. I
sent Frances to my mom's house for the night and managed to
pump enough milk so that John could feed and take care of Ray.
My friend Eileen had been working with a talented musician in
preparation for an immersive journey they were taking to the
cave later that summer. She had been using his songs to seed
really beautiful, luscious playlists to support her female friends
in their shamanic journeys. At least a few of these women had
been abused or were trauma survivors, like me, and she had been
sharing with me how the music was proving to be the perfect
companion. Even having someone in the room was too anxi-
ety-producing for some of these women, but having the music
plus virtual support from afar was just perfect. She sent me the
latest version of the playlist: Mother Magic. And it was the night
of the new moon.

By early evening, everything was ready, and yet, I kept coming up with excuses. I texted a friend, who was also a mother of young children and knew a lot about psychedelic medicines. I asked her about the half-life of MDMA and whether I should cancel the session because I didn't have enough breastmilk stored for Ray to take a bottle the next day. And she basically told me everything was going to be fine, to trust the way everything was lining up to support me in this amazing, courageous act. I called another friend, who was also a psychedelic researcher, and tried to cryptically explain what I was going to do without mentioning drugs on the phone. It didn't matter what she said; simply hearing her voice put me at ease. Even though I was facing this abyss alone, I knew I was supported by all of these amazing, psychedelic women in exile, what I liked to refer to as the Mothership.

Once Ray was asleep, around 8 P.M., I took the first capsule. I had never done psychedelics in front of my own altar before, in a room I had designed specifically for spiritual practice. It felt like a christening. I laid down on the bed and turned on the music, expecting the gorgeous melodies to simply carry me away. But the first song was wrong. It was creepy. It sounded like the rattle of a snake and reminded me of the snake that had slithered into the cave to show me that tormented little girl all those years ago, and the serpent energy that had manifested in the mushroom ceremony before France was conceived. I almost turned it off, but I kept repeating the mantra: "I and the Father are One." Soon, I was sick to my stomach and ran downstairs to the bathroom to purge. It only got worse. Every song was just wrong, wrong, wrong. There were lyrics about mothers and fathers, and I felt like I was being taunted. "Haha, look at your childhood! Your trauma! It's never going away! You can't even enjoy MDMA anymore!" I felt so gross, so ashamed, but I had nowhere to hide. I wanted to bail. But I still took the booster dose.

As the physiological effects of the MDMA got stronger, I was able to forget the music and focus inward. I started replaying a conversation I had had with my therapist when I got back from the trip to Bermuda. She had shared with me this very sweet children's book about a soul who wanted to travel to Earth so that she could experience forgiveness. And one of the other souls had agreed to go with her. I remember the companion saying something like, "I can't let you go alone. I can't let someone hurt you. But because I love you, I will go with you, and I will be the one to hurt you. If you remember who I am, and remember how much I love you, then you will be able to forgive me. But if you forget, then you will hate me, and we will both be lost."

I was so annoyed that she gave me that stupid book, because I was just not ready to see my dad that way. And yet, a deep part of me knew the book was right. Anyway, in that therapy session, I was telling Dana that I just wasn't ready to talk to my dad about what happened when I was a kid, and I had accepted that I wasn't going to be able to forgive him before he died.

She replied, "Instead of deciding that you will or won't forgive him, maybe you could consider what your terms are. What would it take for you to be able to forgive your dad?"

I started crying and said, "My sister would have to come back. And we all know that's not going to happen."

As those little magical MDMA molecules are coursing through my veins, I'm hearing this conversation with my therapist in my head and I'm just sobbing, missing my sister so much. Then I am replaying what Frances said the other day, when I was preparing a talk that I was going to give at an upcoming conference. I was planning to share my vision for a psychedelic future, a future that included legal protection for everyone to practice their own personal, psychedelic religion. I wanted to talk about psychedelics and God, but I realized I didn't know how to do that. So I asked my mystical daughter. "Can you tell me about God?" She looked down at her feet and got very sad and quiet, and said, "God left a long time ago. I don't think She's ever coming back."

Now I am really sobbing. I start saying out loud, "Please come back." It starts as a soft prayer, like the way you would pray as a kid at night to a god you suspect isn't really listening. One who left a long time ago, or was kicked out, and isn't coming back. As I keep saying this prayer, "Please come back" in between sobs, these two memories—of God and my sister—start merging. I keep repeating it, louder this time, "Please come back, please come back, please come back."

I can't tell if the music is coming from outside of me or inside of me, but to my great surprise, I hear the answer. "You've answered my prayer. You said we'd always be fine. You said you'd never stop coming 'round in the dead of night." Holy shit. It's Her. It's Rebecca. She came back.

I sit up in bed and it feels like I am waking up into a totally new body: a super-powered, brilliantly intelligent alien body like in that movie *Avatar*. It feels like the entire top of my skull has blown open, and my brain is wiring up with some cosmic matrix overlaid on the night sky. I look at my phone to try to figure out where these words are coming from, and I see the image of a human body being lifted up into the sky and it says, "Immunity." Oh! My God! She's here. She came back.

I look out the window across the farm fields and through the leafless branches of the huge trees on the hillside, the same trees I saw flowering for the first time when Frances was being born, and up, up, up into the moonless night sky. I see one brilliantly twinkling, oscillating star. It seems much larger than it should be, and I don't feel alone. It is looking back at me, with intelligent awareness, regarding me as I am regarding it. And somehow, I know many, many things all at once: that I was born of this star, and that I existed before I was Katherine, and that my sister is definitely not dead, and that God is real.

((

That night was both the ending and the beginning of everything. The end of my lifelong horror show. The end of my journey through Hell. The prelude to my new life. A life defined by creation, not destruction. One of the first things I did after that night was start painting the storybook that had come to me in a vision the same month Frances was conceived. It was about a little girl who lost her mom and traveled the universe to find her. The book was inspired by my niece losing her mom at such a young age. It was a mystical story of death and rebirth, told in a way that children would understand (and maybe some adults would understand, too). I had been holding onto this vision for years, trying to bring it to life but always getting caught up in the details. "I'm not an artist." "I can't paint!" "I need to find an illustrator." So many excuses. But after that night, it was easy. I decided to paint each scene alongside Frances, who was nearly the same age as my niece was when her mom died. As we painted the first scene together, Frances said, "Oh Mom! I've been waiting for this moment my whole life!"

A couple months after the MDMA ceremony, I took my last road trip to Vermont with my dad. I thought it would be fun, like old times, but my dad and I basically argued the whole time. He kept challenging me to tell him how I was going to re-establish myself, career-wise. He made half-hearted promises about helping with funding, but there were always conditions. Like I would have to agree to pay back the loan or prove to him it was a profitable business idea. He was really sick with some cold or flu at the time, but in hindsight, it was clear that the cancer was already getting its troops into formation for the final insidious battle with my dad's brain. It didn't occur to me at the time that the cancer was already taking over, not only by depleting his immune system, but also by messing with his thinking and emotions. I thought he was just being an asshole, same old story.

In the middle of that trip, while my dad was sick in bed, I made a short pilgrimage to the old ski mountain where my dad had first taught me and my sister how to ski. The mountain had already closed for the season and was completely deserted. As I slowly drove up the lonely, snaking, gravel-covered road, I started to unearth little nuggets of memories like buried treasure in the snow. Singing with my dad on the chairlift. Feeling the rush of racing him down the mountain, top to bottom. Getting treated to hot chocolate and curly fries every day because we were on vacation and mom wasn't around. Staying up late and watching movies. Those were the golden memories.

I open the window so I can feel the wind on my face, like I am actually skiing. I drive past the entrance to the big chairlift—Northstar—that would bring us all the way to the top of the mountain. Past the little brown house in the middle of the bunny slope where we used to stop for hot chocolate—the Sugar Shack. This achingly beautiful past and my present grief over losing both my dad and sister are swimming together, in me and through me. I feel my sister with me at the same time as I am missing her so terribly. I feel my dad's current pain and know it will be over soon. He will be released. But he won't get a do-over. God dammit! We deserve a do-over! We deserve so many more fun moments together. There was never enough time. It is all so bitterly sweet and beautiful. Only one language has a name for this feeling: *saudade.*

I have my sister's ashes in my hand and as I am passing the Sugar Shack, I release them out the window. The Sugar Shack was her refuge because she always hated the cold. The ashes are flying through the wind, across space and time, and they are taking my heart with them, and I am flying. Her ashes are my cosmic calling card. This practice of releasing ashes at sacred sites was the thing that always helped me deal with my grief. It kept me connected with her. It was a way for me to entrust the world with my grief. Here! Take it! I can't hold it alone. But it had been a long time since I had released them like this. I had been stingy with those ashes. What was I afraid of? That I would run out? Yes, I would run out. Eventually, every single thing that made Rebecca would be gone. This is exactly what I was afraid of.

I tried to share all of this with my dad after I got back to the ski condo, but he just didn't get it. By the time we got home the next day, I was fuming. I called my friend *Joshua* who had been coaching me through the painting of my children's book. "It was so fucking beautiful, you know! Releasing her ashes on that sacred mountain. And my dad just didn't care. All he cares about is money! He's such an asshole." I am sobbing as I try to confess all of this while sitting in the tiny attic portion of the children's playhouse in the backyard of the farmhouse. And Joshua calmly asks, "What do you know about forgiveness?" His words take my breath away and yank me back into my body. I eventually stop crying and say, "Not much."

He offered, "Do you think you could paint about it?" And I thought about that for a minute and said, "Yeah, maybe I could."

Later that evening, I sat down to paint my grief and anger and betrayal, not just toward my dad but toward those men who had fired me and all the men who kept using and abusing women.

I wanted these men to pay; I wanted them to be punished. My hatred was palpable. I hoped that whatever showed up on the paper would magically reveal some key to forgiveness, which felt impossible.

Frances and I had been using acrylic paint for the storybook, but this time I chose watercolors. As I made the first curve with the paintbrush, I remembered a similar curve I had painted many years ago. It was before my first mushroom ceremony, with Sarah in Freedom. Sarah was an artist, although it wasn't her vocation. She had created a little art studio off the kitchen in the caretaker's house where we were staying for the ceremony. Back then, the curve I painted was red and angry. I had chosen mostly primary colors, and the art medium she taught me involved using a mini blowtorch to get the paint to move and spread as it dried. The final image revealed a ferocious dragon, guarding a lake, with distant mountains in the background.

This time, the curve was purplish-blue, and sad. She wasn't a dragon this time, but a luscious, sexy, serpent creature, not unlike the Naga that ruled over that whirlpool back in Nepal. She also looked a lot like an alien I had drawn for the scene in the children's storybook where the little girl, in all her grief and desperation to find her mother, winds up so far in outer space that she may never make it back to Earth. In the outer space scene, the curvy alien showers the little girl with a special kind of medicine that sends her crashing back into her life. In the next scene back on Earth, the little girl's space capsule splashes into a vibrant, life-filled ocean off the coast of a magical island. This is her re-entry, her moment of choosing life over death.

As I am drawing this sexy water monster—and remembering the other monstrous creatures I have painted in the past—I see that my grief and anger are not ugly or scary; they are just not of this world. Alien. Foreign. The creatures of myth and legend.

And I notice that the water-goddess is holding something in her hand. Something she is ready to release.

As I paint, I remember releasing my sister's ashes for the first time, at a small nunnery perched on the edge of a cliff at 13,000 feet, just south of the Tibetan border. As the ashes escape my hand, they hang, glittering in the thin morning air, before floating down and landing in the rushing mountain spring below me. And that spring spills down the steep mountainside, eventually joining a small river. And her ashes and this water continue their descent through a sacred river valley that is home to the cave where former-criminal-turned-Buddhist-saint Milarepa retreated from the world to find Nirvana. As I walk back down the path next to this river, I see a painting of Milarepa on the side of a rocky cliff, with his other-worldly blue face, holding his hand to his ear: Listen. And my dying sister in her hospital bed is whispering in my ear, begging me: Listen. Listen. And that smaller river, carrying my sister's body and my grief, flows into a larger, raging river, the same river that will soon hold the dead body of the heroic sherpa, Tsering, and eventually, my father. I imagine that raging river merging with some great, mythical river, the one in my painting, the one in my dreams, the one I am floating along in my sacred funeral boat, in time beyond time.

I call Joshua the next day to give my report. "It's not their fault," I say. "They just don't understand me. I don't belong in their world." And he asks, "Does this have anything to do with forgiveness?" And I say, "I'm not sure. But I think I know how to take the next step."

CHAPTER 9

((

Forgiveness Garden

THE BEST WAY my dad knew how to love us was through money. Actually, money was his universal emotional language. Money was the way he shared and expressed love, pride, joy, appeasement, apology, reconciliation, grief, and guilt. It was always hard for me to see the value in what he was offering. I wanted the real thing, real connection. But money was just fine for my sister. I remember her saying, "You know, if Dad can't figure out how to express how he really feels, his money is good enough for me."

Which isn't to say that we always had money. My parents were intellectuals who had gone to Ivy League schools; they were professionally successful, but not wealthy. We always had enough, but my impression was that they both worked really hard and there wasn't a ton left over. I grew up going to public school in a typical working-class community, which included some families who were quite poor. I only became aware of the wealthier side of the spectrum when my mom remarried and we moved to a rural Connecticut town about two hours north of New York City. There, I saw honest-to-goodness mansions for the first time. Entire gated communities full of mansions! Fancy cars in the driveways, dining rooms that were immaculately decorated but never used. Many of the dads took the train to the city for work and the moms stayed home. Now this was an alien world.

It was apparent to me even as a kid that all this luxury and leisure wasn't making anyone very happy. The stay-at-home moms seemed bored and emotionally numb, and the richest kids were the ones getting into all sorts of trouble with alcohol and drugs and general delinquency. I kept their outwardly refined world at arm's length while spending most of my free time hiking and playing in the woods and exploring old Revolutionary War cemeteries with my best friend. I worked from the time I was in middle school, mostly babysitting and teaching summer sports camps. I even worked with my dad once, at the first company he joined as general counsel. Honestly, I tried, but money just wasn't that interesting to me. I would make it to use it for fun things or give it away.

But money always made my dad and sister happy. And they both had a natural genius toward success in the marketplace. For my dad, his genius blossomed when he finally accepted that job as general counsel. His longtime friend was the founder of the company, and he always joked that my dad was the only person who could keep him out of trouble. Before taking that job, my dad had always worked alone or with a small group of attorneys, mostly on civil cases—divorce, medical lawsuits, that kind of thing. But when he finally had a regular salary and a whole corporate team at his disposal, he found his power center. He oversaw the sale of that fledgling company to a big, international company, and then got hired as general counsel for the next company that his friend created. Together, they had a little phrase that summed up their approach to winning in corporate America: FMNFY—Fuck me? No. Fuck you.

For my sister, her genius was apparent from the outset. While in college, she worked alongside some of the most high-powered women in the New York modeling world. And then she moved to rural Vermont, bought a building, launched her own Subway franchise, and then got hired as part of the Subway executive management team before she was twenty-five years old. She spent a lot of time traveling and being groomed by the top two executives in the company, who both wanted her to take over for them when they retired. During one of her work trips, she was in a limo with the President of the company, and he was waxing philosophic about how to be a leader in the business world, how to hold the most powerful position at all times.

"You can't convince people to respect you," he said. "You have to embody respect, exude power, and everyone will fall in line."

And when they got out of the limo at their hotel, my sister calmly and casually says to the President of the company, "Can you get my bag for me?"

As he picks up her bag and holds open the door to the hotel lobby, she flashes her brilliant smile and says, "What was that about exuding power?" There is no doubt in my mind that, except for the breast cancer, my sister would have gone on to become one of the most successful business leaders in America.

Because I didn't care about money, I didn't really register the point when everything shifted for me, financially speaking. In the middle of my pregnancy with Ray, shortly after the Jamaica women's retreat, my dad called to tell me that the company he worked for had just sold to a huge multinational corporation for an historic sum. I could tell he was overjoyed, but I couldn't bring myself to share his enthusiasm. It was all abstract and theoretical to me. At the time, I didn't understand how IPO's or stocks worked. I just wrote in my journal: "What if this means I don't have to answer to anyone ever again? What would it look like to live my dreams?"

Several months later, when it became clear that my dad might suddenly, overnight, lose his ability to think or communicate, he spent a lot more time teaching my brother and me about finance, and how to navigate the legal structures he had set up to hold our family's wealth. As far as I could tell, the sale of the company meant that, for all intents and purposes, we would never have to worry about money for the rest of our lives. We couldn't live extravagantly, but we could be comfortable. And if we were smart about it, it even meant that our kids and their kids might not have to worry, either. I could tell that this was a huge relief to my dad. He had finally made it! He had achieved his dream. And the strangest thing was it didn't seem to matter to him that he wouldn't be around to enjoy it. Slowly, slowly, I was starting to appreciate how he viewed everything. This money was his ticket to immortality; he could keep loving us (and influencing us) forever, even after his body and mind were gone.

You'd think that all of this would have made me happy, too. But it didn't. I knew that money couldn't hold a candle to mental illness or existential dread. This level of wealth was like a poison chalice. You take a little sip, and you feel invincible; you drink the whole thing and suddenly you've lost your life. During one of the trips home from the hospital, when my dad was getting radiation treatment, I heard a song on the radio that sounded familiar from my college days when some electronic DJ had remixed the chorus. Hearing the full, original lyrics felt like a cosmic portal straight into my dad's subconsciousness. I had to look up the name of the song when I got home: *Standing Outside a Broken Phonebooth with Money in my Hand*, by Primitive Radio Gods. (Alright, Universe, you Trickster, that was a good one!)

☾

My dad was in one of his quintessentially grumpy moods when he came over to the farm to celebrate what turned out to be his final Father's Day. Those moods made me wish for the days when a simple cigarette break was all it would take for him to snap out of his funk. He stormed into the house, late, and nearly tripped over the baby gate that was blocking the doorway between the kitchen and the big hallway. Then he couldn't figure out how to unlatch it, and this was always one of my dad's triggers: inanimate objects that wouldn't bend to his will. He threw up his hands in frustration and let out a guttural "ARRRRRGH" and stormed back out of the house to wait in the backyard.

At dinner, he doted on Frances and basically ignored me and my brother. I suspected that he was also still pissed that I chose not to celebrate my birthday with him the week before, because he had given up some important plans to stay home to take me out to dinner. But of course, he hadn't told me that until the day before, so it felt less like an invitation and more like a convenience for my dad. All of this was just classic Richard, expecting the entire world to curve and adapt to fit his wishes.

What my dad didn't know is that I *did* spend my birthday with him, just not in physical form. It had been a few months since my first solo MDMA ceremony back in the Spring, and I felt like more needed to be unpacked. There was the big argument we had at the ski condo, plus my nighttime anxiety was out of control again. I still felt quite far from really understanding my dad and being able to empathize with what he was going through. I and the Father were definitely not One.

The MDMA session on my birthday was brutal. I hiked out to the Sacred Grove just before sunset and laid out my special flying carpet from Nepal. But as I burned sage and called in the spirits of the land and my ancestors to support me, I felt this nagging sensation of some supremely dark energy that was somewhere nearby, watching, amused by my foolishness. I imagined it saying, "Oh, poor girl. She thinks that sage and prayers will protect her. Well, I'm coming for you. There's no way to hide." I tried to stay with that sensation and allow the music to carry me into my journey, but it was just torture. My body, my brain, my mind, my heart, EVERYTHING hurt. Every aspect of my being knew that these rituals and meditations and ceremonies didn't amount to anything in the face of death. That final answer was coming, and there was nothing I could do to stop it.

So I turned and faced it, right? Not this time. I stood up and threw all my shamanic paraphernalia into my tent and turned to leave. Fuck this shit! I'm so done. What am I trying to prove anyway? I can't do this. And as I start striding across the farm field, intending to march all the way back to the house and bail on the ceremony, a new energy starts filling my body. It is light and joyful. I feel like I'm soaring up the big hill to Pride Rock. And I look up and the sky is simply huge! And the colors . . . it's like I'm in one of those William Blake paintings from the magical, summer day in London. At some point I literally start spinning and dancing and singing, with my arms outstretched, and I feel a bit like Julie Andrews in the *Sound of Music* (it really was that cheesy and theatrical!)

After maybe half an hour of ecstasy-on-the-hillside, I feel called to walk down toward the crypt. Oh yeah, the crypt. Did I forget to mention there was an old gravesite on the property? Apparently, it used to be full of the bodies of the settler family that had first occupied the land, but some teenagers vandalized it, so the bodies had to be moved to a local cemetery. Now it was just empty and creepy as hell. There were some large stone slabs propped up over the opening, but otherwise it was like a straight drop into the pit of hell.

But my shaman friend Patrick saw it differently. During his one visit to the farm, back when we first moved in, we toured the land to see if he felt any energies or spirits that we should address. As we stood over that gaping maw, he said that he found the darkness inviting, beautiful in its own way. He experienced it as an entrance to a sacred place, to the womb of the land. He told me that if I really wanted to understand the spirits of the land, and the people who had come before us, I would descend into that opening and spend the night there, alone. But even I wasn't that crazy.

There was so much pain and shame and mystery still wrapped up in this place that we had called home for only a few years. The farm had been a vortex long before we arrived. It had witnessed the deaths of children; suicides; even murders. Maybe the land itself was cursed ever since the first white person claimed it as their own. But I also felt like the land was blessed. The land and I had an understanding, a relationship. Once, when my pain was too much, I sat on one those hillsides and cried out, asking the land to take it. And She said, "I can't take your pain. But if you decide to commit yourself to your family, and your healing, I'll hold it with you."

I cautiously make my way down the sloping hillside to the burial ground. I notice that the trees form a natural circle around the opening, and I sit right in the middle, on top of those big stone slabs. Then, out of nowhere, I realize that I am not alone. I feel the same, threatening presence from the beginning of the trip. But it's not so overpowering or spooky this time. It feels strangely inviting.

It is the Lord of Death, himself. He isn't so scary up close.

"Hard to make friends in this line of work," Death says.

"Yeah, I bet," I reply. "Thank God for MDMA."

"You know. I don't really want to fight you anymore," I offer.

"Me neither," Death replies.

"Truce?"

"Truce."

That encounter really brought it all home for me. I wasn't going to find the answer to my nightmares and anger and messed up relationship with my dad by battling him to the death. I wasn't going to win by calling to the Mothership for a one-way ticket out of this joint (appealing as that was). For my whole life I had perfected disconnecting, dissociating, imagining, transcending—always looking for a way out. Now, I was finally starting to see a way IN. If I could befriend Death, I could befriend my dad.

The day after that terrible Father's Day dinner was when my dad called to tell me the brain cancer had come back. His mood had shifted dramatically since the day before. He sounded soft, scared, open. There were several new tumors, small, but scattered. It wouldn't be possible to do surgery this time around. They would try targeted radiation, but the overall exposure would be higher because of the number of tumors. Recovery would likely be harder this time.

My dad wasn't experiencing the same cognitive problems as before, but he was in a lot of pain, which he thought was because he had thrown out his back water skiing. He had one more trip planned—to Ireland—but he promised he would start the next round of radiation treatment as soon as he got back. The night before his flight, on the summer solstice, we all hiked out to Pride Rock in honor of Ray's first birthday. Me, my dad, my brother, John, Frances, Ray, and my niece, Anya. All of us together, on the final frontier.

With my dad in Ireland, I got to work. There was no time to waste. In the course of painting the children's book, my friend Joshua had helped me develop some daily habits that would keep me connected with my grief while also making room for joyful feelings to arise. It all started with a simple gesture that Joshua had taught me, a tai-chi type move that we called The Joy Asana, which involved bringing my hands, palms facing up, toward my heart center, and then allowing that movement to flow upward and outward as my arms opened into the space around my body. In this way, I was calling forth and releasing joyful energy. I had also recommitted to sitting in front of my altar while belly-breathing for at least five minutes every day. I decided to put living flowers at the center of the altar and hang an image of the Tree of Life in place of a rather terrifying tanka painting that I had brought back from my first trip to Nepal. I remember remarking to Joshua, "I've been bowing down in front of this red-faced, wrathful deity for years now, expecting my anger to go away. It's ridiculous! I think I need to try praying to something a lot softer and kinder." And then, there was my spontaneous painting of the water-serpent Goddess, who appeared to be scattering something into water. I combined all of these themes into one practice, which I called Flowers and Ashes. Every day, I would walk out to the pond just below the Sacred Grove and release some of my sister's ashes along with flowers into the water. This became the living expression of my personal religion, my daily sacrament.

But there was a piece missing. And that piece had to do with creation. I was sitting with flowers, picking flowers, releasing flowers, but not growing flowers. And it was a pretty hilarious moment when I finally said to my husband, the farmer, "Could you teach me how to plant a garden?" John laughed and said, "You're gonna wait until our last summer on the farm to finally learn how to grow something?"

So, while my dad was on his final pilgrimage, I planted my forgiveness garden. I had no idea how hard it was to make something grow. There was the digging and the moving of rocks. The cow poop and the layers of compost. You know that saying that farmers love? "Getting dirt under your fingernails"? Well, I hated getting dirt under my fingernails. It was one of my lifelong phobias. But I managed to dig my hands into that poopy, rocky dirt and plant my first seeds. Teddy Bear sunflowers and zinnias for joy, calendula for healing, cosmos for the Mothership, marigolds for Death, poppies for the heroine's journey (a nod to Dorothy in the *Wizard of Oz*), and finally, lion snapdragons for anger. As I pushed each seed into the Earth, I planted my grief and rage and feelings of betrayal alongside it. And as I scattered my sister's sacred ashes over the top layer of soil, I said my prayer: "Please, take this shit and turn it into gold."

My dad must have known that the trip across the ocean was his last hurrah. He squeezed in a quick visit to see his sister in France and meet her first grandchild, before continuing on to the Celtic homeland. There, he was surrounded by some of his closest friends, touring with their band through the countryside. He was in a lot of pain, but even his best friend remarked "He was a delight, a real delight to be around! I never saw him grumpy the entire trip. You know, not typical for your dad." He told me later that my dad had gone out of his way to visit the gravesite of a friend who had also died of brain cancer, as well as the site where William Butler Yeats was buried.

My dad had always been fascinated by poetry, and theatre. During the years he spent getting to know all those Irish friends, he also acted in several plays the local Irish charity put on. They always chose performances that had a direct connection to Ireland. My dad's best role was as Count Dracula, in the play adapted from the novel written by Irish author Bram Stoker. My dad was always so proud of this one photo of him, as Dracula, holding his friend Billy, who played the monstrous sycophant Renfield, up by the scruff of his neck. All those emotions that my dad couldn't seem to express really came to life on stage. He was a natural actor. And then, Billy died of cancer when I was in high school. Piecing it all together, I realized that my dad had lost two of his best friends and his dad in a short span of time, right after his son was born. Maybe our griefs weren't so different after all.

Before boarding the plane back from Ireland, my dad sent me and my brother an email with two photographs and the subject "Heading home." One image was of a large green cliff hanging over the western coast of Ireland, which I recognized from an old black and white photo that my dad had framed and hung in the main hallway of his house by the lake. The second image was of Yeats' tombstone: "Cast a Cold Eye, on Life, on Death. Horseman, Pass by!" It was easy to read between the lines, whether my dad intended it or not; "heading home" meant the final home-going: death—and whatever lay beyond.

Shortly before my dad came home, I had started reading a book narrated by a revered Tibetan Buddhist teacher, Yongey Mingyur Rinpoche, who had disappeared from his monastery one night and wandered through India and Nepal for nearly four years. When he returned, he said that he had learned everything he needed to know about enlightenment at the very beginning of his trip, when he ate some street food he was offered and got sick with food poisoning. It was in encountering death, directly, that he finally surrendered.

Two things stuck out for me as I read his account. The first was that he described Nirvana as the reunion of Mother and Child consciousness, which seemed to square with my understanding of mystical experiences and unity. His description affirmed the experience I had had on retreat, of returning to my mother's womb and experiencing perfection and bliss. The second thing that stood out was the way he talked about his lifelong anxiety disorder. Apparently, even being born a *tulku* (a recognized reincarnation of a former Buddhist saint) to a family of tulkus doesn't prevent debilitating anxiety. I was in great company. And this is what he said about how he finally triumphed in that particular battle: "When I stopped trying to destroy the wave, it stopped trying to destroy me."

Somehow, when I read those words, I woke up. I had been battling my dad, God, Death, medical institutions, my anxiety, abusive men in general, all the injustices in the world. And for what? I was in more pain and distress now than ever before. My dad was dying of cancer, for Christ's sake, and I still wanted to hold him accountable for something that happened a million years ago. I yearned to exact revenge on those assholes who fired me; they had won the battle, but I was going to win the war, God dammit! I was just stewing in hatred and anger, hoping for a miracle while actively creating the conditions that would prevent any miracle from occurring. My meditation teacher used to joke about humans in general and Americans in particular: "We would rather be right than happy."

So I decided to stop being right. I decided to love my dad, right then and there, without needing to fix him. I decided to stay by his side as he went through this final death journey, through the hospital visits and last-ditch treatments and, hopefully, if he was OK with it, hospice. I decided to stop pushing against the wave that was my dad, with all of his bravado and armor and self-righteousness. I decided to accept him and be his friend.

☾

Getting close—physically close—to my dad was one of the scarier aspects of my life. It was like he had a permanent force field up, and every time I crossed that boundary, I felt like I was in enemy territory. Or maybe I had the force field up, it was hard to tell. It's not like we never hugged, but we would greet and hug each other in a very perfunctory way. Like, let's pretend we have a normal father-daughter relationship and get this formality over with as quickly as possible.

The closest I ever got to my dad was at his father's funeral, when I was in high school. My dad wrote and gave the eulogy, and I remember how tough he still seemed and how beautiful his words were. Toward the end, he talked about how his dad used to stroke his hair as he fell asleep, the same way my dad did with me and my sister when we were little, and the same way he now did with our younger brother who was still a baby. He said that he remembered his dad's love every time he did that. When the eulogy was over, my dad came to sit between me and my sister, and then suddenly reached out to hold my hand. At first, I thought he was trying to comfort me. But then I realized tears were pouring down his face. He had his head up, eyes open, looking straight ahead, and maybe we were singing a song or something, or maybe my grandpa's WWII compatriots were performing some kind of ceremonial send-off. But all I could focus on was this new energy emanating from my dad, and the sensation of him tenderly holding my hand. It was foreign because of how normal it felt. I remember wondering, "Is this what other people feel around their dads?" I had never been near him when he was this vulnerable and soft and open.

After that funeral, I only saw my dad's armor drop one other time, when he was recovering from his first round of brain surgery. Despite being very high on opiates, he initially managed to have a normal conversation with me about the doctor's assessment of how the surgery went. And then he announced that he was going to rest, and closed his eyes and laid his head back on the slanted hospital bed. I left for maybe half an hour and when I came back in, the nurse was upset and said he had been moved to a different room. I couldn't figure out what had happened, but by the time I found him, he was blubbering and ranting and terrified, almost like he was R.P. McMurphy pretending to be psychotic in *One Flew Over the Cuckoo's Nest*. I mean, this is how strange it was to see my dad like this, without his tough-guy mask; it was more automatic for me to think he was acting than to accept he had actually lost control of his mind and feelings.

He kept saying how the guy in the first room was threatening to kill him, and that some evil messages were coming out of the TV. The nurse came in to deliver the food he had ordered, and he just looked down at his plate and started crying. He tried to pick up his fork and work a bite of mashed potatoes into his mouth, but he couldn't seem to line it up properly. And I said, as gently as possible, "Dad, it's OK. You're OK. It's totally normal to feel like this right now. Can I help?" As he let me spoon mashed potatoes into his mouth, I suddenly felt like I was caring for a little boy. A scared little boy. Oh, so that's who you are on the inside. My dad's little boy was finally feeling safe enough to make an appearance.

Of course, by the next morning, the mask and armor were fully back on, and the little boy was stuffed back into some closet deep in my dad's subconscious. This reminded me of something

I had seen before in my psychedelic work: When you lose your ego, sometimes it comes back even stronger than before.

I walked into my dad's room to find him fully dressed and ready to leave, barking orders at the nurse about his discharge papers, and cracking jokes that only he laughed at. When we got home, he awkwardly tried to hold Ray and make him sit up on the dining room table, but he was only a few months old at the time, so he toppled over and landed on the side of his face on the hard wood. "Dad, what are you doing! You're going to hurt him!" I said and went to scoop up Ray. But my dad actually grabbed Ray first, and we were literally playing tug of war with my son. My dad wouldn't let go and kept saying, "He's fine, he's fine." And I'm saying, "No, Dad, he's not fine, you need to let go." Finally, he did, and I walked out the door with Ray. I was in shock. This guy had just survived fucking brain surgery, and we all dropped everything to take care of him, and now he's an even bigger jerk than before. I texted John and said we were on our way home and that I would need to go to the Sacred Grove and scream for about three hours. The whole drive home, I could barely swallow. My therapist had been telling me to stay in touch with my anger, to find it in my body, and I kept telling her I couldn't. But when I walked through the kitchen door at the farmhouse, I announced to John, "I found my anger. It's in my throat."

When I arrived at my dad's lake house one late July morning to take him to the hospital, I found him barely able to walk, vomiting in the driveway. Horrified, I said, "Dad! What's going on?? You seemed fine on the phone!" And he said, "I think it's something with the meds. I haven't been able to eat since last week. My doctor said they're having a team meeting later today, but that I could come down early and get admitted if the pain got bad enough."

Several more rounds of vomiting and one spinal tap later, my dad was resting in a small hospital bed in the ER when I witnessed his version of a panic attack. He had been advised to lay flat for at least half an hour after the procedure, but only lasted ten minutes before he freaked out. He jolted upright and started rubbing and kicking his legs. He was screaming in this really low, guttural way and started to explain that he was just going to walk around the hallway for a bit. I had to use all of my Hopkins training plus those special tactics I had learned at psychedelic festivals to get him to stay in bed. I refused to leave until they transferred him to a real room, which finally happened around midnight. And then, as I was walking out the door, I made the mistake of glancing at the doctor's notes: "spinal tap to rule out leptomeningeal disease."

A quick Google search revealed the best and worst news: if the spinal tap confirmed this bizarre-sounding disease, then my dad would be dead in a month, tops. Why was this good news? Well, the horrific pain he had been in wouldn't last long. Bad news because there was no treatment or cure. Leptomeningeal disease used to be quite rare, because people with end-stage cancer wouldn't live long enough to experience it. But it basically means that the cancer cells have infiltrated the cerebral-spinal fluid that coats the entire brain and spinal cord. It's a sneaky and insidious final move for the cancer to pull off, because it means tumors don't show up in MRI scans. This diagnosis would explain so much about the last month: why my dad kept getting sicker and sicker even though the doctors couldn't seem to find any trace of the cancer, why his back pain was so bad, why he could barely walk.

The last full conversation I had with my dad while he was totally lucid, was, of course, about money. He had been obsessing about some deadline that was coming up and kept telling the doctors that he had to live until August 10th, which was just over ten days away. He even told me and my brother, who were his health proxies, to make sure the doctors kept him alive by any means necessary. Finally, he instructed us to contact his financial advisor, so that we could all be in the room when he described why this date meant so much to him. I suppose he needed a professional to confirm that his obsession wasn't crazy.

I gained a totally new appreciation for financial advisors that day. I had always put them in the same category as garbage collectors: a very important job, and somebody's gotta do it, but it can't be that enjoyable. But when *Brian* walked into the hospital room, after driving two hours from his home office, it felt not unlike the arrival of a chaplain or a priest. This was the man my dad had chosen to represent his deepest wishes, the man he had trusted with his most sacred life assets. This was the person who would pass us the keys to the kingdom and steadfastly guard the gate to what my dad believed granted him everlasting immortality. Through money, my dad would never die.

I came to learn that a big part of Brian's job was actually quite similar to that of a priest or trusted therapist. He mostly helps people feel as calm and secure as possible in the face of tragedy and fear.

When we called Brian to tell him our dad was sick and in the hospital and freaking out about this upcoming calendar day, he said, "OK, OK. I'll be there tomorrow. Don't worry, I'll talk him off the ledge." When he arrived, he dutifully downplayed my dad's concerns.

Brian said, "Rich, first of all, you're gonna make it 'til the tenth. And second of all, at the end of the day, it's not that much money."

I saw the gears turning in my dad's head, working out the algebra problem he must have worked out a thousand times before. He enumerated a bunch of details that only he and Brian seemed to understand and they finally both nodded, and Brian admitted, "Well, yeah. It's the difference of a million dollars, for Ed and Katherine."

And my dad goes, "Right. So I need to live until the tenth."

This amount of money was simply theoretical to me and my brother. Obviously, it was a lot of money; but it was like monopoly money, it didn't seem real. We didn't understand at the time why it was more important to my dad than the actual lived experience he was having with us, in that moment. Without understanding the full scope of what this money would eventually accomplish for us, I thought it was just an easy out for my dad. Like, here, take the money, I can't say I'm sorry. Right before the money talk, my dad told us a psychiatrist had visited him in his hospital room and asked if he had anything on his mind, any fears or regrets. And he said, "Yeah, I'm worried I haven't done enough for my kids." It was just so heartbreaking to realize that this money was the last best way he knew how to show us that he could do enough.

The doctors came in right after the conversation with Brian and confirmed what we all suspected: my dad indeed had leptomeningeal disease, and now would be a good time to "get his affairs in order," which is a hilarious thing to say to a lawyer who's had his affairs in order for years. After that, we basically just let my dad keep obsessing about the tenth of August and use it as his reason to stay alive. He could keep his eyes on the prize at the finish line, rather than feel the agony of the final straightaway. And while he was otherwise distracted by material things, I took over the job I knew how to do, which was help guide his soul through the bardos.

A couple days after my dad's final diagnosis, I hosted a beautiful womb healing ceremony at the farm with an honest-to-goodness

Celtic priestess. We gathered underneath the canopy of the big maple tree that created what one visitor called "a swimming pool of shade" throughout the backyard. With the help of drumming and singing, and accompanied by the cicadas humming their midsummer serenade, she guided us through the layers of our consciousness, first to our immediate female relatives who had died and then, further and further back through the curtains of time, to our first female ancestor. When I envisioned my mother's mother, my gram, I found myself standing beside her tiny corpse, painting red lines along her forehead and cheekbones. The burnt red color of this paint reminded me of the ferocious women of the Shuar tribe in Ecuador who had just defeated a big oil company in court as they defended their sacred forest.

As I followed the circuitous path through the eons, I was surprised when a huge turtle shell popped into my vision. I was thrilled to learn later that turtle is one of the oldest indigenous symbols for Mother Earth, the embodiment of goddess energy, the physical incarnation of the eternal Mother, from whom all life evolves.

After the ceremony, I spoke with the priestess about what my dad was facing at the hospital. I told her I was worried he wouldn't make it home, that he would die in the ICU just like my sister did. And in her soft, Irish accent, she said, "Use your voice and just be Katherine. You are strong enough to do this. You'll get your dad home." Between the visions from the ceremony and these words of encouragement, I felt confident and determined. I was a woman on a mission.

The next day was the first time I thought my dad might actually die. We had another meeting with the whole team of doctors, and they described a litany of last-ditch "treatments" that my dad could try. It was overwhelming, and none of the options seemed to grant him much quality of life. I got the feeling that the doctors just wanted to extend his life a few weeks or months in order to try out some new experimental treatments on an otherwise healthy man.

The radiation doctor, in particular, made both me and my brother think of Dr. Mengele, the infamous Nazi doctor at Auschwitz. Like, "Oooooo, another body to experiment on!" My dad came out of that first whole-brain radiation session looking like he'd had a lobotomy. Frustrated, I said to the doctors, "My dad has barely been able to talk or stay awake for more than an hour since the radiation you guys did last Friday. You said it would help, but it obviously made things worse. Why can't we just go home?" They finally agreed to let my dad leave the hospital if he submitted to one more MRI and a second radiation treatment.

I had a terrible feeling about all of this. My dad had previously had such bad panic reactions while being stuck in the narrow MRI tube that they could never get a clear picture of his spinal cord. But the doctors insisted that they needed a full-body scan in order to determine if targeted radiation could improve the pain and numbness in his legs. I said I didn't think my dad would survive full anesthesia, so they promised they would try partial sedation first. My gut kept telling me he was going to die, and that maybe that wasn't such a bad thing. It would be a peaceful way to go. He wouldn't make it to the tenth, but he would be free.

As I sat next to my dad in the pre-op room—the same room where he was last "himself" before undergoing whole-brain radiation only a few days earlier—I felt his familiar force field. His protective armor. The wall that always kept us apart. But it was weaker now, more permeable. I took a chance.

It was like my whole life I had been learning the moves to some epic dance performance, and now I was finally getting to do the dance. The moves were simple, but required all of my attention: breathe, stay in my body, feel the sensations and emotions as they arise, notice what action is needed in this moment, let go of fear. Slowly, slowly, I danced my way through my biggest nightmare: my fear of getting physically close to my dad, my fear of meeting his demons, up close. And this was the way I learned to forgive him.

I reached up and placed my right hand gently on his upper back, just behind his left shoulder. It was an unmistakably intimate expression. Not a perfunctory hug or kiss on the cheek. At first, I held my hand with the lightest possible pressure, so that he might not even notice its presence. Then I let my hand fall, just slightly heavier, resting on his body. I could feel his strong muscles beneath my hand, muscles that had been permanently contracted in self-defense for over fifty years. I kept breathing. I kept feeling. I kept letting go. Slowly, slowly, the force field dissolved. It was just me and my dad. I loved him so much. I could feel his pain, his fear, his loneliness. He didn't deserve any of it. Then, he sighed, like he had been holding his breath his entire life. In that sigh, I heard him say, "Thank you for loving me. Thank you for being my friend."

The anesthesiologist showed up and said what I knew he would say: we're going to have to go with full anesthesia, because we can't risk him moving and ruining the scan. "Can I be in the room with him at least?" I asked. "No," the doc said,"But you can wait across the hall, and I'll let you know as soon as he's awake. It'll be fine." "Yeah, right," I thought.

Sitting in the waiting room, my heart pounding in my chest, I momentarily panicked. What if this is it? How am I supposed to guide my dad through the bardos from so far away? Then I had an insight. I remembered what the Celtic priestess had told me after the ceremony the day before. She reminded me that I could yoke my consciousness to my dad's consciousness, even if he couldn't speak or recognize what was going on around him. "You can guide him through death; you can journey for him."

A big smile quickly spread across my face when I realized that the anesthesia was just the medicine we needed. My dad's mind would be naturally expanded, loose, permeable. His normal ego defenses would be temporarily tranquilized. I could slip past the guards.

With renewed enthusiasm, I set up my Cosmic Ground Control. I found a chair in the corner, facing a wall, and got into the most normal-looking but formal meditation posture I could. Back upright, eyes closed, hands resting in my lap in the mudra of the awakened one. The small room was packed with anxious family members, and the TV was on, so I put ear buds in my ears and turned on the music I had listened to during the peak of my last MDMA ceremony. I started to breathe deeply into my lower abdomen, finding that hearth center, my Mama Bear womb space. I imagined my dad lying on the hospital bed, the chemicals coursing into his veins, his surface-level consciousness slowly receding. I had no idea what his subconscious would be like, once I got in. And I briefly remembered a terrifying movie I had once watched, stoned, about a psychiatrist who was able to enter her patients' minds by lying next to them while they were both injected with a dissociative, psychedelic chemical. They would mind meld. But the horror and pain she encountered in her patient's mind was barely worth the answers it provided.

But more than the sounds in the room or this old movie memory, I was distracted by a rather mundane concern. I'm sure some of you readers have been wondering why I spent pages upon pages in earlier chapters lamenting the shitheads who fired me—ahem! accepted my resignation!—from the MDMA study. Well, let me tell you, my friends. It's all connected! Because, on the very day that my dad underwent anesthesia, I learned that one of said shitheads had removed me from the website of the program we had founded together, and refused to add me back in, even after I asked him to. I guess it wasn't enough for him to destroy my career; I also needed to be permanently erased from history. Isn't that how it always goes with powerful women? I was livid.

Try as I might, I couldn't get him out of my head. But I remembered that time at the Vermont meditation center when the teacher guided me through the first of my panic attacks, by teaching me how to use my distracting thoughts as fuel. I remembered my teacher saying, "If you can't stop thinking, just redirect the energy." And finally, I saw that my anger could be my best friend. It was just the rocket fuel I needed. Cosmic Ground Control to the Mothership! We have contact!

I felt my mind become like a laser with its focus. Before I even knew what was happening, I found myself in a barren desert landscape alongside a skeletal, insectoid creature who was scraping and crawling along the sand. I knew it was my dad. I knew it was the part of him that felt alone and unloved and misunderstood and abandoned. My first instinct was to reach out and pick him up and hold him, just like when I saw my little girl curled up in a cave years before. But this creature was too far gone. Even normal contact would be threatening. It reminded me of those old experiments they used to do on baby monkeys, raising them in empty, joyless cages to see if it fucked them up (spoiler alert: it did). The monkeys wouldn't even form normal attachments later on, when the scientists finally let them hang out with other monkeys again. They would choose an empty cage with a robot mother who supplied milk, over a real mother who supplied love and affection. Love was so foreign it was life-threatening.

Still, I tried to hug this pathetic, lonely monster. I tried to send love into him, but there was no place in him to receive it. He would rather claw at the bare earth. So, instead, I laid his body back down and started filling the skeletal spaces with dirt. The dirt wasn't sandy, like I expected. It emerged from my hands as dark, rich, fertile soil. The kind of soil that has been loved over lifetimes and has grown lives upon lives in its dark womb. As I sunk my hands into this darkness and pulled up huge mounds to pour into my dad's body, I felt that I was returning him to the Great Mother, the Earth. With each handful, his body slowly melded with the darkness, until there was more soil than skeleton.

With the final scoop, his body was just . . . gone. Completely absorbed. It got sucked into the Earth as if entering a vacuum, and I saw him speeding through some underground portal or tunnel. To my delight, he emerged literally FLYING out of the Earth, as a little boy in the green hills of Ireland. Leaping, climbing, playing. All of his life force returned to him. He didn't even look back. He didn't turn to say goodbye. He was just so gone, so done with that former life.

Just like with my sister on the night before her death, I hoped he would die right then and there. What a glorious and pain-free rebirth that would have been! But, also like my sister, my dad had unfinished business. He had committed to living until August 10th, so he had to wake up.

It took a long time for the anesthesia to wear off. Re-entry was rough. Even the Mengele doctor agreed he was too sick to undergo another round of radiation, so she canceled his session. In a moment of fate fit for the theatre, the man who came to wheel my dad back to his room was the same man who had first escorted him from the ER after his spinal tap the week before.

My dad had gotten so sick since then that the guy didn't recognize him. But my dad gave him a big handshake and a salute and said, "Thanks, Chief." Again, I was reminded of my dad's brilliant acting performances. And just like at the end of *One Flew Over the Cuckoo's Nest*, I could see that my dad was ready to make his final escape.

Back in the hospital room, my aunt and I got my dad settled in bed and ordered him some dinner. He was still quite woozy, but he knew where he was. As I was about to depart, my dad surprised me by swinging his legs over the side of the bed, slowly standing up, and taking three extraordinarily careful steps over to me. He kissed me on the cheek and hugged me and looked straight into my eyes as he said, "I love you." Nothing about it was perfunctory.

☾

There is a certain level of insanity reserved for family members trying to get their loved ones discharged from a hospital "against doctors' orders." Luckily, I was completely OK being the crazy person. It was pretty clear to me that my dad's oncologist was going to keep bluffing her way through each day until my dad died in the ICU, just like my sister had. I'd like to believe the doctor's tactic wasn't intentional, but I had read her papers. Academically speaking, she specialized in studying end-stage cancer, including the very disease that my dad was currently struggling to survive. How could she let such a great data-point—excuse me, *patient*—slip away?

I knew my dad remembered what I had pulled off with my sister when he chose me as his health proxy. And while he wasn't thrilled with me at that time, I knew he was impressed with my willingness to fight to the death for her, to protect her from the doctors and their last-minute meddling. I also knew how my dad would behave if someone was telling him he had to stay somewhere against his will. I mean, this is a man who would roll into a full-blown rage at a baby-gate blocking his path, remember?

I conjured all of my dad's rage along with my own tenacity and confidence, and I set my sights on getting him discharged. Just like I imagined my dad used to do in court, I tried polite and intelligent negotiation first. No luck. The oncologist wouldn't come down to his room to meet with us, and the nurse basically just ignored me. Then I remembered my dad's corporate motto: fuck me? No, fuck you. I did a quick internet search to make sure that my dad and I would both be legally protected with what I was about to do. Then I connected with the center of my anger, in my throat, and I made my scene.

I waited until the nurses on the floor were all gathered by the main desk for their morning meeting. This is when they would run through everyone's charts and get updated meds and doctor's orders. The halls were quiet. And I started screaming.

"I'm not gonna let my dad die here! I know my rights. I can take him out of here right now against doctor's orders. Prove me wrong!"

Well, that worked. My dad's nurse left the meeting all flustered, furious with me, and said, "In all my years as a nurse, I have never had anyone speak to me that way." And I said, "Don't worry. It's not personal. Now make sure the oncologist is down here within the hour."

When the oncologist arrived, she tried her usual tactic of fear and delay. She went through her list of all the things that my dad would have access to if he stayed in the hospital, some of which would be impossible to replicate at home. "Listen, I get where you're coming from," I said. "You kind of remind me of myself when I used to work at Hopkins. But my dad is dying.

He deserves to be at home, with his family and his dog. I'm going to give you 24 hours to sort out all those issues you just outlined and discharge him. And if you can't, I'll take him out of here anyway, and we won't return for any follow-ups. You can cooperate, or not, it's up to you." And she came to see my side of things.

The following morning, the portal opened, and my dad made it home. By noon, he was back in his sanctuary—his beautiful house by the lake—with his best friend, Teddy, the golden retriever. Against all odds, we even managed to return for a follow-up the next day, just to surprise his doctor. After that, my dad cruised. Which isn't to say the ride wasn't bumpy. But he was home. What was the worst that could happen? He would die?

I have to hand it to the doctor, because she was right about how hard it would be to replicate some of the medical treatments that my dad was receiving at the hospital. We hired a 24/7 home health aide, but she wasn't allowed to directly administer medication, and also wasn't really up to the task of dealing with my dad, especially at night. She left after a few days, after my dad called her "bossy." I tried to explain to her that, given my dad's personality, he probably meant it as a compliment. But she went on her way, hopefully to find a sweet, frail, old lady to take care of instead.

Those final nights were beyond stressful for my brother and me. We had almost made it to the finish line, but if my dad died even a few hours before midnight on August 10th, it wouldn't matter. And if my dead sister could throw a huge trampoline into the woods over a minor disagreement about her final wishes, can you imagine what Dad-the-Ghost would be capable of? No way was I inviting that haunting into my life.

My brother stayed with him all night the night of the ninth, and then I stayed with him all night the night of the tenth. He was quite disoriented and agitated at night, and we were exhausted. He could barely speak, but he made it clear he was not happy with all the medications and treatments and restrictions on his movement. It was a grueling slog through the mud, those final 48 hours.

But around 4 A.M. on the morning of the 11th, my dad woke up and suddenly seemed like himself again. He was actually able to speak coherently.

I said, "Dad, do you know what day it is?"

"I do," he said.

"You made it."

"I know I did."

"So now you have to make a new decision."

"I know I do." And the next part was the hardest.

"Do you want to know my opinion?" I asked.

And he said, "Sure."

"I think we should consider transitioning you to hospice. I don't want to see you suffer any more than you already have. I don't think the treatments are going to help."

And he said, "I understand. OK."

The next morning, I was in shock. I felt like I was stepping out of a long nightmare. I couldn't believe we had survived the last ten days. I looked at my brother and laughed, shaking my head, "Well, Ed, we made it. Don't ever let anyone say we didn't work our assess off for our first million bucks."

CHAPTER 10

(

Hakuna Matata Tea

What is to give light must endure burning.

—Viktor Frankl

My dad's real death journey began the day he accepted there was nothing left for him to do. And the last thing he needed to do was make one final trip to the hospital. As we went through his normal routine of checking in and sitting in the waiting room, I could see that he was showing up in his best form (limited as it was) to say a formal and respectful goodbye. He insisted on standing on his own and claimed he didn't really need the wheelchair he was using. It was actually quite beautiful to watch as each of the staff who knew him said, "Hello Mr. MacLean! Lookin' good! We'll see you again soon!", all the while knowing he was about to die. I don't have a great deal of sympathy for how the medical system treats terminal cancer patients. But in that moment, I felt deep compassion for the nurses and staff who have to say goodbye to the people they have come to know and love, while keeping their own emotions suppressed and hidden.

During the final meeting with the oncologist, I was proud of my dad when, in the face of all the forced optimism and pressure to keep going with last-ditch treatments, he literally stood up and walked out the door. We were shocked. My uncle chased after him to make sure he didn't fall, and the oncologist called out, "I don't think that's a good idea!"

And with his back toward her, already halfway down the hallway, my dad snapped back, "It's all bad ideas."

This was classic Richard. When he was done, he was done. I can't tell you how many times I have been on the receiving end of just such a walk-out. It's brutal. But as an observer, I could appreciate its theatrical brilliance. I looked at my brother and said, "Well, I guess we know how he really feels. Let's get out of here." And that was my dad's final goodbye. On his terms.

The days really blended together after that. Everything was a swirling blur of home-ness and summertime: family dinners on the porch and delicious French wine, jigsaw puzzles and rolling around on the ground with baby cousins and grandkids. My dad and his siblings had always made a point of gathering together for at least one week every summer, and it surprised no one that my dad had managed to arrange his final weeks of life to line up with the annual family reunion. I mean, honestly, who gets to die with all of their brothers and sisters and their kids and grandkids at a freaking gorgeous lake house at the peak of summer? For all of my dad's fuck-ups and foiled attempts at real relationship, I couldn't help but feel that he really deserved this beautiful, perfect death.

And I wish I could've fully enjoyed the celebration. But I was distracted and stressed out by all sorts of annoying logistics, all the things you don't think about when your loved one is dying miserably in a hospital. Let me tell you, home death sounds nice, but it's hard. My brother and I were going insane trying to keep track of the nurse's schedules and all the different medications, how to get my dad showered and dressed, how to keep him safe at night when he got agitated. Do you know how hard it is to get a comfortable hospital bed delivered at a moment's notice? Or a fucking bottle of morphine for a dying person? Good luck if you think it's gonna be any easier to get prescribed psilocybin or MDMA. The labyrinth I navigated just to get a doctor to prescribe liquid morphine for my dad convinced me once and for all that the corporate medical pathway to legalization will absolutely ensure that amazing drugs stay far away from everyday people.

The hardest part, though, was trying to get my dad formally entered into home hospice. I knew from my previous volunteer training that people often get only a week or two in hospice care before they die, and I could never understand why families would wait so long. Now I understand. No matter how clear your convictions and written instructions—and my dad had signed legal documents clearly indicating that he didn't want any form of resuscitation or artificial life extension—it's bound to bring up all sorts of intense feelings. Mainly doubt and guilt. It can feel like you're giving up, like you're signing their execution papers. Rationally, it was a relatively easy decision for me and my brother, because we had already spent the last year with our dad learning how he felt about everything and seeing how much pain he was in. He was an avid sportsman and had taken us all out on the lake waterskiing the week before he went into the ER. He didn't have any interest in living a few more months if he couldn't walk or talk. But it was hard for the family to accept that this was really the end. They knew my dad as a fighter, and they wanted to give him every last chance to survive. Finally, my uncle asked us the right question: "Is this the decision you can live with? Is this the decision you can feel OK about for the rest of your lives?" Absolutely. I told him I would make the same decision for myself in the same circumstances, for my children, for anyone I loved.

Even after that conclusion, I kept wondering if I was doing the right thing, mostly because my dad often wouldn't (or couldn't) communicate about his needs. I remember seeking council from two women I greatly admire. The first was my friend Sarah, the amazing Buddhist death chaplain and mushroom companion from Freedom. During our conversation, she mostly listened, but then finally offered, "I think this may be the point where you have to get OK with not knowing." And that was such a relief, because it took the pressure off needing to be right about any particular decision, even the biggest ones. The second woman was my cousin *Ali*, whose mom had struggled for many years with a degenerative condition that left her completely dependent on her family and caregivers. At one point during the week, we were hanging out by the little beach next to my dad's house, watching Frances play. I looked at Ali and said, "This is just so hard. How do you do this?" She shared about what it was like when her mom first got sick, and the mistakes they made, and the subsequent realizations, and the learning curves. Most importantly, she knew how to procure the perfect automatically oscillating air mattress to go on top of the hospital bed so that my dad wouldn't develop bed sores. Between Sarah's gift of not-knowing and Ali's expertise in comfy beds, I could let go of the enormity of the reality we were confronting as a family: my dad was now traveling down a one-way road with no detours.

By the end of the week, my brother and I felt like we could finally relax a bit. We were sitting out on the back porch with our cousin from Paris. It was a perfect midsummer evening, and the sun would be setting soon. Ed and I were joking about how we had really wanted to get Dad out on the boat one last time, but it was almost impossible to even get him out of bed. And we looked at each other, and I said, "We have to try. Right now. There's no other time."

Everyone sprang into action. Ed went into the house to see if my dad was awake and willing to get into his wheelchair. I ran to the driveway to get my dad's truck lined up right next to the stone steps leading from the front door. I told my aunt and uncle to let everyone know to head down to the dock, and my brother texted my dad's neighborhood waterskiing buddies to head down too.

We didn't have any ramps or anything, so Ed and our cousin had to basically lift my dad, in his wheelchair, down each stone step, to get from the house to the car. Our cousin had always had a close relationship with my dad and had lost his own dad to cancer several years earlier. He was a master at using humor and deflection to deal with difficult, grumpy fathers, so it was fitting that he and my dad could do this particular dance together. I hated laughing but there was nothing else to do, as I watched them fumbling their way down the steps, with my dad facing backwards in his wheelchair, almost dropping him on one of the taller steps. I watched the expressions of fear and amusement move across my dad's face and thought, this is how the man will finally let go, after sixty-five years. Because he has to.

With my dad safely in the passenger seat, I drove the short distance up the driveway and then down the hill to the community dock. As I pulled the truck up to the little beach, I saw everyone waiting on my dad's pontoon boat, ready for the perfect send-off. We briefly considered wheeling my dad across the dock to the boat, but my dad's friends decided to physically carry him instead. It was heart-wrenching and beautiful as they slowly and carefully maneuvered him along the wobbly dock, holding him upright in a throne made of their arms. As they lowered him into his seat on the boat, a wave of triumph and relief moved through my body. We did it! I felt my dad beaming with love and pride. And it really was the perfect sunset cruise. We drank champagne and ate stinky French cheese and slowly motored around that mystical lake one last time, the whole family, all together.

Two days later, the hospice director arrived to initiate my dad into hospice care. I was nervous that, in spite of all our conversations, my dad still wasn't totally on board with the decision. As she approached the door to his bedroom, I said, "Dad, remember the hospice director is here this morning. Is it OK if she comes in . . .?" And he interrupted me in a gruff voice, "Absolutely not!", and my heart sunk into my stomach. But then he jokingly turned to the director, hand outstretched and said, "Oh hi, *Charlene!*" in a really pleasant, charming way. So not only could he speak when he wanted to, but he even remembered her name. I was pissed off at his little joke, but also relieved to see my dad once again holding court and playing the room the way he used to. After two weeks of barely getting a forced "yes" or "no" from my dad, I was surprised to find him suddenly able to converse relatively normally. Charlene explained what the hospice decision meant, and my dad was able to verbally confirm that he understood and was ready for it. As Charlene placed the red do-not-resuscitate bracelet around my dad's wrist, I felt like he was being knighted. It was a simple, noble act, a final theatrical flourish marking a life's worth of great accomplishments—battles won and lost— now all behind him.

Back home at the farm, the first flower in my forgiveness garden bloomed that day: calendula, a super-healer and member of the marigold family. Marigolds, with their pungent aroma, are the flowers that call the dead back to their families on *Dia de los Muertos*. They are also the flowers offered to Ganesha. Oh yeah,

Ganesha. Remember that guy? I haven't said much about him since the first chapter. I guess I forgot to mention how I tried to throw him into a whirlpool in Scotland to end the curse of all the trauma from my sister's death and Tsering's drowning in Nepal and everyone's lung problems. How I took him off my altar and replaced him with a very peaceful white Buddha, hoping I could just cure myself with extreme positivity. But he kept coming back. He can't help it; he loves hard cases. He knows you can't just chop someone's head off and banish them. You can't stuff your monsters in the closet and tell them never to come out again. You have to heal in relationship, even if your dad is kind of a stubborn jerk. So how could I not pay attention when this magical marigold bloomed on the very day my dad entered hospice? How could I not accept that forgiveness was happening, whether I liked it or not.

The next morning was the last time I saw my dad alive. It was a rough goodbye, and certainly not the one I had hoped for all my life. John and I had planned a week-long vacation in Rhode Island with my mom, which was another annual tradition going back to when me and my sister were kids. Of course, the timing turned out to be terrible but karmically appropriate, because it forced me to choose between my mom and dad, something I had been doing (whether I liked it or not) my whole life. I felt like I had done everything I could for my dad, and it was now my turn to step back and let go of control. His sister had decided to change her return flight to France so that she could stay and help out, and between her, my brother, and the nurses, my dad was in good hands. He had a few close friends checking on him, as well. Ultimately, I thought we would both have a much more pleasant week apart than together.

Of course, I couldn't totally let go of control, and bills were piling up while my dad languished, so I was determined to get him to sign over his power of attorney to me before I left. Can you imagine trying to convince the best lawyer you know to sign away his rights? What a joke. But there we were, with three highly paid professionals in my dad's bedroom, watching and waiting as my dad reviewed the document that his estate attorney had drafted at my request. It was the first time he had put on his reading glasses in weeks, and it suddenly occurred to me that I didn't even know if he could read anymore. But he took the right amount of time with each page, silently scrutinizing each sentence, clicking his pen. His assistant Jess, whom he often referred to as his "other daughter," was there in her capacity as notary public, and she later told me that my dad would use the pen-click trick as a stalling tactic during important meetings to make sure everyone knew he was in control.

My dad slowly flipped pages. The attorney described the restrictions she had included to limit what I could do with his money. We waited. His financial advisor explained that the document would help me take care of important business expenses. *Click click, click click.* I was growing impatient; the waiting was torture.

I said, "Dad, if it doesn't feel right, we can just call it off. I'll figure out another way to get the bills paid."

He wouldn't acknowledge any of us. Not even a nod of his head. It felt like an eternity. Jess did her best to remain professional as she held back tears in the corner.

Finally, the attorney said, "Richard, you don't have to produce your full signature if you're unable to. You can just make a mark with your pen." And my dad held the pen a few centimeters above the paper, totally still. Game over.

It felt stupid to have wasted our time on such a futile exercise, but I also learned a lot about my dad during that seemingly pointless meeting. I witnessed how hard it can be even for the most powerful man in the room to say "no" when a bunch of smart people are waiting for you to say "yes." I felt like he was teaching me what the business and legal worlds are really like. As he sat there clicking his pen, I felt like he was saying, "Don't sign anything unless you're really sure it's a good idea." I came to appreciate later that he probably thought he was protecting me. He knew that as soon as he signed that paper, people could come after me instead of him. He had already spent years drafting the exact documents that would provide his dream of financial security for his kids, while also preventing us from making stupid decisions or giving away money to anyone who might show up asking for it. I remembered when he first described his whole plan to me, shortly after the first brain tumor, and it just seemed so convoluted.

I said, "Dad. Don't be ridiculous. We'll be fine. We can make good decisions," but now I'm not so sure. I think most people, myself included, are pretty dumb with money. We don't even know what good decisions are, so we can't translate the power of money into lasting happiness. And I hate to say it, but the real world seems to match up a whole lot better with my dad's perspective than the one I have hoped for on meditation retreats and dreamed about during MDMA ceremonies. I want to believe the world is a safe place full of well-meaning, trustworthy people. I want to believe that what you give away comes back to you. But my gut tells me we have a long way to go. And man, that pen trick. Solid gold. I'm totally going to use that one day sitting around a table with a bunch of VIPs.

I thanked the professional folks and escorted them out the front door, and then chatted with Jess for a bit in the kitchen. The scene in the bedroom was very emotional for her, and she said, "It's just so hard to see him that way. He was always the smartest guy in the room."

And I said, "Well, clearly, he still is." We both laughed. She promised me she would spend a couple days with him during the week I was away. Honestly, I wish I felt worse about leaving, but it was actually a relief. I had to accept that my dad could be better cared for by people who loved him less conditionally than I did.

After Jess left, I went back in my dad's bedroom to see if he would talk to me about the power of attorney thing.

"Dad, I'm sorry. We're trying really hard to manage everything. It's just a lot."

Nothing. I explained that John and the kids and I were going to Rhode Island with Mom, and it was really important to me that we go. He wouldn't say anything, wouldn't look at me, instead keeping his eyes fixated off to the side. He kept making this sound through his teeth that usually meant he was contemplating something serious, or trying to find the right words for bad news. *Tsch tsch tsch tsch.*

Finally, his eyes moved to find my face and he said, "How come?"

I asked, "You mean how come I tried to get you to sign that paper? How come I'm going to Rhode Island instead of staying here?"

He said, "No."

I waited. And waited. But that was it. No more words. Our last conversation. It breaks my heart to this day that this is what my dad left me with. After a lifetime of waiting for two little words: "I'm sorry." Maybe five words: "I'm sorry I hurt you." Actually, eight words: "I'm sorry I hurt you. Please forgive me." How hard could that be? For the man with such an expert grasp of the English language that he was always correcting everyone else. The man who could conjure all the energy he needed to have a lovely conversation with a total stranger just the day before. Pen click. *Tsch, tsch, tsch, tsch.* How come. Yeah, Dad, how come.

John and the kids came in for one last goodbye. Ray had just started calling my dad "Pop" the night before, which was beyond adorable, and he seemed a lot more comfortable being close to him now that he was bed-ridden. Ray kissed my dad on the cheek, and Frances (always "Frankie" to my dad) gave him a big hug and said "*Je t'aime,*" which was always the way my dad and I would say "I love you." We left John alone with my dad for his own goodbye, and John later told me that my dad was still struggling for the right words. He said something about "the girls." John wanted to believe he said, "Take care of the girls, for me," but he said the tone in my dad's voice was more along the lines of exasperation, like, "These girls, huh? What're we gonna do with them?"

(

Point Judith, Rhode Island was one of my happy places growing up. It was always a refuge from the stress and confusion of home. My mom tells me that we first started going together as a family, all four of us, but I only remember the years when it was just me, my sister and my mom. The Girls Trip. It was one way I got to act out my fantasy of fleeing my dad for good, just packing up and heading to the coast (Atlantic or Pacific, it didn't matter). I was always dreaming of my new life near the sea, free of the unpredictable monster in the background of my life that I could never seem to tame. My mom, ever the peacemaker, thought it was important that we grow up close to my dad, so we could have a real relationship. It was clear at the time how much my sister hated going to Dad's house, because she would wail and clutch onto Mom during every goodbye, and then she would fall asleep staring at a photo of her and Mom together, right next to her bed. But I guess I put on a good show, pretending I didn't mind it. By the time I was an adult and had had a few years of therapy, I was able to tell my mom how hard it had been for me, how much I hated going to Dad's house on the weekends. How I always got so sick there; how I couldn't breathe because of his stupid cat; how I always went to school on Monday morning—late, because of Dad—with a pit in my stomach after two straight days of walking on eggshells and trying not to wake the monster. She admitted that she would also get physically sick the whole weekend; it was nearly impossible for her to trust him with us. He was reckless, neglectful, prone to temper tantrums, like a teenager. She said she didn't have a choice; the visitations were required as part of the divorce agreement. Life could have been so different, if I could have just told her what was really happening, if she had had the awareness that leaving was OK.

But for two weeks every summer, we could pretend we were free—just the girls. We stayed in a tiny wooden cottage on the edge of the Great Salt Marsh, almost to the end of a long, stony, dirt road. The ancient couple who owned the property lived in the house at the very end of the road, and Mr. Kenyon would take us sailing around the marsh in his boat. My sister and I got such a kick out of this adventure that we would re-enact all manner of sailing escapades in the bathtub, pretending the boat had capsized and screaming, "Save me, Mr. Kenyon!" while clawing at the sides of the tub. Being next to the salt marsh in the middle of summer, the air was always thick with moisture and mosquitoes. And there was nothing to do. There was no TV, no internet (remember when there was literally no internet?). We played a lot of Yahtzee. And I would stay up late reading the creepiest Stephen King novels I could find, just to freak myself out imagining all sorts of ghouls and vampires and sea monsters tapping at my bedroom window.

And the ocean. Oh, the ocean! I didn't have a fancy cosmology back then, but my body knew its faith. The water was cold, even at the height of summer. I would dive in with no fear and swim far out, way past where my feet could touch the rocky bottom. Huge waves floated my body several feet up and down again as they cruised past on their way to the shore. I would swim almost out to the big orange buoy, but not beyond, so that the lifeguards wouldn't blow their warning whistle. Looking back toward shore, I could barely make out my mom with her hat and sunglasses, hiding her pale skin from the sun under her big beach umbrella. And my sister, playing on the blanket or building sandcastles or tanning (in later years). She would never join me in the water. Out in that deep ocean, at the liminal edge where domesticity ends and wildness begins, I would float on my back and imagine sharks lunging up from the depths to devour my body. Way before I ever heard the words "ego dissolution," I knew how to do it. It's so easy when you're a kid.

The last Girls Trip was the summer after my sister finished her first full round of chemo and surgery and radiation. My sister's daughter had just turned two and was equally fearless and in love with cold water as me. Looking back at the photos of me and Anya in the surf, all you can see is radiant joy emanating from both of us. I still can't understand why my sister trusted me to take her little girl out into those big waves, without a life preserver. My kids are six and three now, and I wouldn't do the same with them. It's hard to remember that I used to not have debilitating anxiety. It's hard to remember that I used to completely trust the ocean. That I used to completely trust myself.

If Point Judith was our Mecca, then the Point Judith Lighthouse was our Black Stone. The center of our faith. Our annual pilgrimage wasn't complete until we had had lobster dinner at Aunt Carrie's restaurant and then continued on down the winding path to the lighthouse for sunset. Back in the day, the area around the lighthouse was totally open, and you could walk along the nearby beach covered in perfectly round, smooth stones, each one as big as your hand. We would each try to find the flattest one and skip it into the waves. One, two, three, four skips if you were lucky. Our arms would ache the next day from whipping those heavy stones into the surf. And if the conditions were right, we'd get to watch daring surfers dance along the cold, crashing waves, wondering in awe how they managed to avoid a fatal collision with the huge rocks at the edge of the land.

The last trip with my sister was also the last time I found the lighthouse open. After that, the government put a big chain link fence around the whole tip of land surrounding the lighthouse and the stone beach. "Coast Guard Area. Keep Out." You can't play here, anymore. Sorry. Show's over. Every time I went back, I hoped that the fence was a mistake. Maybe they sometimes left it open? Maybe there were visiting hours posted somewhere? Nope. It was always locked.

It kind of reminded me of another special place where I used to seek refuge. It was a garden at the edge of my college town that a couple had created in honor of their teenage son who drowned in the river that flowed past their house. A little sign on the gate welcomed visitors during daylight hours only. But on certain mysterious, sparkly nights, floating in my bubble of sacred, psychedelic protection, I would wander down that quiet street to find the gate open, like an invitation. With goofy reverence, I would make my way through the trees and shrubs down into that beautiful, lush glen. I would sit on the little seats carved from tree stumps, or swing on the wooden swing that the boy's parents probably intended for little kids. And I would feel that boy's soul sitting with me, enjoying the garden. It was his garden, after all.

But it wasn't my lighthouse. I thought it was, just like I thought the ocean was my ocean. Like I thought my sister was mine, too. Forever. That final summer, I was joyfully, stupidly ignorant of the storm that was about to take over my life. We played in the sand and swam in the waves and ate our lobsters and skipped stones at sunset. How could it ever be different than this? I didn't know I was about to lose my sister, and then watch a friend drown and lose my trust in the water. I didn't know my happy place was about to disappear. I didn't know a person could get locked out like that.

So, how could I have ended up anywhere other than at that lighthouse on the final morning of my dad's life? Like a homing beacon drawing my soul back to its place of worship, the lighthouse was calling me to remember my center. How limited of me to think that it mattered whether I was physically next to my dad as he was dying.

The morning was so windy I could barely push Ray up the final hill in his stroller. I wanted to feel composed and graceful, but I felt frantic, like the wind. We were packing up to head home, and I wasn't ready to confront what was waiting for me. So I did the only thing I knew how to do, which was release my sister's ashes and hope for the best.

When I got to the top of the hill, as Ray napped in his stroller, I took out the little plastic bag that held her ashes and tried to take out a handful to release over the rocky shore. But the wind just grabbed them and scattered them all over the grassy hill behind the bench where I was sitting. I couldn't help but think of the scene in *The Big Lebowski* where they are trying to do this really sweet, sacred thing by scattering their friend's ashes over the Pacific Ocean and all the dust just blows back in their faces. This is exactly how my religion feels, most of the time.

That morning was also my mom's birthday. We had taken her out for dinner the night before, and after too much wine, we were both able to open up about Dad. My mom had chosen not to see him at all since he went into the hospital at the end of July; she said she couldn't stand to see him so sick. She said she already suffered too many losses and didn't want to remember him that way, the way cancer just devours every recognizable thing about a person.

I couldn't imagine making the same decision, so I demanded, "Don't you want to see him one more time? Isn't there anything you still want to say? Any final words?"

I guess I wanted to believe that my mom hated him as much as I did. That she also held him responsible for Rebecca's death, and for all those years she cried herself to sleep at night, a single mom, working her ass off trying to provide for her daughters and keep them safe.

I imagined her standing by his bedside saying, "Fuck you, Richard. You ruined my life." And if she knew what really happened to me, maybe she'd kill him, too.

As these dark fantasies played out in my mind, there was no way for me to be prepared for what she actually said.

"I remember looking into your dad's eyes for the first time. I remember getting married in the backyard of Grandma and Grandpa's house, right after we graduated college. We were really in love, you know? Of course, he broke my heart. But we lost a daughter together. For all the mistakes your dad made, all the harms done in the past, it's all water under the bridge. There's nothing left to say. All is forgiven."

We had just started driving when I got the phone call from my brother.

"Hey, Kath. How far are you from Connecticut?"

"We just left, a little over two hours," I said. "Why?"

"Well, just get here as quickly as you can. The nurse said it could be hours." And I barely had time to take a few deep belly breaths before he called again. "I guess it was minutes."

The shock of this still reverberates. That there was no sign my dad was about to leave. That the hospice nurse got it wrong. That my brother was in the kitchen making coffee and I was in the car, and despite the fact that at least one of us had been with my dad every minute of every day all summer, he just snuck out the back door while neither of us was looking.

The first physical sensation I remember was an intense wave exploding up from my heart into my throat, like my breath or life force leaving my body. I called my mom, who was driving behind us, and she already knew what I was about to say.

I asked, "Are you OK to drive?"

"Yes," she said. "I'm OK. Let's just get home."

And I couldn't help myself, but I said, "Well, Mom. Happy Birthday. I guess Dad thought this was the best present he could give you."

We both knew that the words she had uttered the night before—"all is forgiven"—had cleared the path for him to safely depart.

☾

When I walked into my dad's bedroom, the hospice nurse was taking care of paperwork.

She said, "I'm so sorry for your loss. I'll give you a moment alone, and then I can call the funeral home for you."

A moment? I'm gonna need a whole lot more than a moment, hon.

And I responded very matter-of-factly, "You don't need to call the funeral home. I'll be keeping his body here. It's for religious reasons."

I felt bad when she got all flustered. She really was so sweet. Nervously, she said she'd have to call her supervisor. I stood politely just inside the door frame, listening to her end of the conversation out in the hallway.

After she hung up, she said, "I'm sorry. I wasn't sure if you were allowed to do that, but my supervisor says it's fine."

The nurse had me sign a document confirming the time of death and then made a bee line for the door. She wouldn't even help me move my dad's body from the hospital bed to his normal bed. Isn't it fascinating how death freaks everyone out? Even the professionals.

I was momentarily quite proud of myself, but then I suddenly realized I was way out of my depth. Who was I kidding? I didn't know how to take care of a dead body! I needed at least a few Buddhist friends with me, or better yet, a whole Buddhist village. Heck, even a bunch of drunk Irish people dancing around the body would be fine. But it was just me, alone with a corpse. I was beginning to understand why the nurse had been so reluctant to leave the body.

On the drive home, I had called a trusted friend out on the West Coast, a hospice aide, and asked her to talk me through everything I needed to do when I got home. She was the one who encouraged me to say that the request to keep the body was for religious reasons, to avoid any pushback. She said I should make sure the room stayed very cold, and if we wanted to wash or dress the body, we'd have to do it quickly before rigor mortis kicked in. "OK, I can do this," I thought.

I turned down the central AC to fifty degrees and asked my uncle and husband to help me move my dad's body into his bed. His body already felt rigid. My uncle said, "Careful, he's naked from the waist down, so just make sure to hold the blanket in place as we lift." And I knew as he said this that we were so not the family who was going to lovingly bathe his body in some kind of graceful ritual. I had picked out the outfit that I wanted to dress him in, but even touching his body to get him dressed seemed beyond my capacity. So we just left him in one of his favorite tee shirts that he was already wearing when he died. We placed a water-absorbent pad under his body and layered a few more blankets on top.

After John went back to the farm with the kids, I was once again alone with my dad. I gingerly arranged a cream-colored *khata*—a Buddhist cloth—around my dad's neck, making sure not to touch or move his head. He had worn that sacred cloth during my wedding ceremony, and he had draped it over the lampshade in his bedroom, just next to the photo of us that hung over his dresser. The photo was my Christmas gift to him that year: both of us dressed in our fancy wedding attire, beaming our mirror-image smiles at each other. We even had the same smirk in our eyes. The photographer, bless his soul, had managed to capture a fleeting moment of real authenticity and connection between us. Looking around at all the photos on the walls, I realized that my dad's refuge was us, his kids. Our faces filled the room. Every night he went to sleep and every morning he woke up, there we were. His pride and joy.

I lit a candle and placed a stick of burning incense on the make-shift altar next to my dad's bed. I filled a glass bowl of water and placed it next to the incense. I refreshed the flowers with ones that my friend had brought from the garden at the farm. They were many of the same flowers I had planted in my forgiveness garden, which had yet to fully bloom. As I went about these simple acts—lighting fire, pouring water, arranging flowers—I could appreciate all the fancy rituals I had seen monks perform at Buddhist and Hindu temples. The rituals kept my mind focused. I could momentarily ignore the body that was the true centerpiece.

Each time I left and re-entered my dad's room, I had to actively practice greeting his body, recognizing he was dead, getting over the spookiness of being in the vicinity of a corpse. I was now in the land of the dead, slowly rowing my dad across the River Styx. This was not human territory.

The strangest thing was I could see all this subtle, wavy energy appearing to move in my dad's body. Like a very delicate wind moving across a still lake, or electricity just under the surface of the skin. If I tried to ignore it, my mind would play tricks on me and convince me that my dad was about to sit up or speak. If I looked too intently, it would stop. It was like one of those optical illusions you can only see if you look off to the side of the drawing; or like how stars twinkle more brightly when you can only see them in your periphery. The Buddhist admonishment to stay with the body until ALL of the energy had dissipated was no longer theoretical for me. I knew it was necessary. I remembered the disorientation of leaving my sister's body with strangers only an hour after she died. I remembered Tsering's mother wailing, demanding, "Where is his body? Why haven't they found his body?" There was no way I was letting this one go.

Tibetan Buddhists believe that a person's "spirit" or life force sticks around for a while after the last big physical breath leaves the lungs. They say it is important to speak with the person, attend to their body, remain calm, and avoid big displays of grief. As you are guiding them through the stages of transition, your intention is to remind them that they are, in fact, dead, and help them make the best possible "choice" for their next incarnation. Of course, I put "choice" in quotations because choice in the Western sense of "free will" has very little to do with it. Most people are simply propelled into their next life through the force of karma—all the actions and consequences of actions across their lifetime. And for uninitiated people—people lacking a strong meditation practice—fear and confusion regarding attachment to their physical body or past memories (even good ones) can lead to rebirth in "lower" realms. Fortunately, even the Buddhists left room for magic. They say that the liminal space of the death bardo is so supercharged with possibility that any person, even a criminal or a non-believer, can achieve enlightenment in that space. Or, as Carlos Castaneda put it, "All of us . . . have a cubic centimeter of chance that pops out in front of our eyes." If this was my dad's last best chance at a golden ticket to Nirvana, I didn't want to screw it up.

Thankfully, I had great support. My uncle and aunt had stayed at the house with my dad the night before he died, and they insisted on staying the next day and night, just to make sure my brother and I were OK. Shortly after dark, we all went down to the lake and lit a fire. I drummed my hand-made deer-skin drum. And my brother sang and played guitar. He was always very private about performing musically, but that night he let his achingly beautiful, baritone voice soar through the fire and out across the lake. When the first sound escaped his lungs, my mind couldn't even process what I was hearing. It was alien, supernatural, thousands of years old. I let the gift of his grief move through my body. He sang about losing loved ones to disease and losing contact with his own mind. And then he sang our favorite song from when he was a baby—*You Are My Sunshine*. It was the first time since returning to the house that I allowed myself to feel heartbroken.

As we slowly walked back up the wooded path to the house, my heart started beating hard in anticipation of what was coming. My mind was like a courtroom, as I tried to debate and bargain my way out of what I knew I had already committed to: a few uninterrupted hours with my dad. In the Mazatec tradition, the nighttime mushroom ritual is called a *velada*, or vigil. This was the vigil I had been waiting for my whole life. I knew that this was my last chance to forgive him, or rather, specifically, to forgive his body. I'm such a materially oriented person that I knew I needed to see his body and actually speak to it, even if he couldn't say anything in return. I once told my therapist that the only way I could forgive my dad would be if he was mute and unable to move, so that I could say exactly what I needed to say without fearing how he would respond or react. I guess I got what I asked for.

But I was so freaked out to try mushrooms again. I couldn't imagine anything spookier than being in a dark room with a corpse, tripping on mushrooms. Let alone the corpse of the most intimidating person I knew. Besides, mushrooms had already given up on me; they just didn't work anymore. I tried to convince myself that they would make me sick because I'd had pizza for dinner. I tried to pretend it was important that I remain sober, like a good Buddhist. But I wasn't a Buddhist. And mushrooms weren't even my favorite ritual substance anyway. My tried-and-true sacrament was MDMA.

Earlier in the summer, after my dad returned from Ireland and when he was still "himself," I gave him a special goody bag. I told him there was everything in it that he needed to have a safe, healing solo journey, including instructions and musical suggestions.

He laughed, "You know, I still have those mushroom chocolates you gave me years ago. They're just sitting in my freezer. Sometimes I take them out and look at them, but I always end up putting them back."

"Why not try it, Dad?" I asked. "What do you have to lose?"

His reply was telling, "I don't think my life can stand up to the scrutiny."

He never told me if he actually took the journey, but I guessed not. So I found my brother downstairs, getting ready for bed, and said, "Ed, where do you think Dad would keep drugs, if he had drugs?"

And Ed said, "Right next to the vape pen he never uses because pot just makes him anxious now."

And there it was. The special goody bag. Right where my brother knew my dad would put it, because he knew my dad better than anyone. And I said, "I gave this to Dad when he got back from Ireland because I thought it would help him realize all the shit he's done and apologize to us before he died. It's from the same stash I wanted to give him last Christmas, because I thought he needed to take it for me to forgive him. I had it all backwards. I'm the one who needed to take all of it."

We cracked up and Ed said, "Have fun!"

"You're sure you don't want to join the goodbye party?" I asked.

"No, I'm good," he said. "I'll see you in the morning."

I can never shake that feeling that psychedelics give me: that my very life is on the line—that I'm about to die. As I slowly prepared the room for the ceremony, I almost bailed another five times at least. I turned off all the lights except for the candle still burning on the altar. I lit a stick of sage and wafted it around the room, over my dad's body, over his hospital bed, over my body. My dad's dog Teddy was almost thirteen years old but still managed to jump up onto the hospital bed to help see me through the ceremony. He wanted nothing to do with my dad's body. I guess the hospital bed smelled more like the person he knew than that lifeless thing across the room.

I had the playlist all set—a new mix of the songs I had been listening to all year in my solo ceremonies. As I went to turn it on, I thought how much my dad would hate this kind of music, but at least he was dead now, so he couldn't complain. And then the electronics glitched and turned off. I tried several times to turn it back on, but it wouldn't work. So I stood up and went over to my dad's body. "Dad. This is my show, tonight. I get to pick the music. You get to sit back and watch. I want to show you what I can do." And then the music turned on, no problem.

The first hour was hard. All I could do was pace the room and breathe deeply into my stomach. I kept shaking my hands downward to send the energy back into the Earth. I hardly looked at my dad. I knew that I needed to successfully navigate this first part of the journey alone. The previous solo ceremonies had shown me that my trauma landscape was a gateway. There was no bypassing it. I had to walk through it in order to enter the deeper territory of Mind. In my early mushroom ceremonies, the trauma landscape was the whole trip, save the final hour or so once the drugs were almost out of my system. Now it was just the first forty-five minutes to an hour. But it was still just as brutal. If you are a trauma survivor, you know this feeling. Like you're walking through a desolate hellscape, alone, and if you just stay real quiet and keep putting one foot in front of the other, you might make it through alive. Just don't wake the demons, because then you'll be stuck for good.

I kept moving. I was going to make it, dammit. I had to make it. And the final step was unmistakable. That grand, gracious space opened up. I had arrived. I looked over at my dad's body. "Hey, Dad. Thanks for being here." Which was a funny thing to say, because I didn't really know where *here* was. All I knew was we were together, just BEING together, and that he was definitely no longer his body. The body that was the center of so much of my fear. The body that I could never trust. The warrior's body that had inflicted so much incidental harm on so many. I was no longer afraid of it. There was nothing this body could do to me anymore.

I went over to the bed and sat down on the edge. I took a deep breath. I had been thinking that healing and forgiveness were about finding the right words. The right words to tell a trusted adult what had happened to me when I was little. The right words to tell my mom and my brother now, so they could see how much pain I'd been hiding my whole life. The right words to say to my dad to make the pain go away. The right words to make this story make sense, finally. All of these right words, stuck in my throat for nearly forty years. Slowly choking me, terrorizing me, holding me hostage.

I let the music carry me: the soundtrack that my friend Eileen had created and gifted to the women in her life who were trying so hard to heal their trauma. "Mother Magic." I felt held by the legacy of defiant mothers, of women who had borne the burden of unprovoked violence and still managed to create and nourish life. I felt into my Mama Bear identity, my soul space. I felt the current of my life extend beyond me and into my children. I once told a somatic healer that my children must have seen how much agony I was in and incarnated just to help me survive it. And I could easily see how I might not have even been able to have children without first starting down the path of recognizing and healing my sexual abuse. They were the living reminder of my healing, the unexpected gifts of my trauma.

Then one song grabbed my attention, evoking memories of gifts at Christmastime. My dad's favorite holiday. He always went over the top with gifts, like he was making up for something. It was the one day a year he could prove to us that he really loved us. It was the one day a year when there was no doubt that he really did.

I thought more about this idea of a gift. I suppose I had always thought that forgiveness was something you could choose to do, like offering a gift, and it didn't matter how the person received it. But sitting there, regarding my dad's body, letting the memories of our shared life flow in and through me, I knew that forgiveness was an energy. An exchange. It cannot be one-sided, despite all of those lovingly cheesy affirmations about how forgiveness doesn't have to be received to work, that forgiving a person is really for you, not for them. Of course it is for them! How could it not be? It is an unavoidable mutuality—a mutuality originally born of harm and then, eventually, lovingly allowed to die with the release of blame. It's not something one person does, but something that happens between people when the conditions are right. And in that exchange, I couldn't help but appreciate my dad and everything he had given me. The love I felt for him, and that he felt for me, was truly greater than the violence we had endured together. I didn't deserve what he did to me, and he didn't deserve a lifetime of shame in the aftermath.

My life started to feel like one great *koan*, with a totally obvious yet inexpressible answer. Ever since the first confusing memory of my sexual abuse bubbled up to the surface in my late twenties, I had an inkling that that violation was also a spiritual initiation. Coming to terms with it almost killed me, but it forced me to confront reality as it is, in its totality. It was the reason I started meditating every day. It got me to sign up for all those week-long silent retreats. It compelled me to stay in my body while I worked on my anger. It urged me to take my vow of nonviolence. And it was still trying to teach me about forgiveness, the true jewel of a spiritual life.

Here I was, sitting next to my guru, knowing he loved me beyond lifetimes, and yet still wondering why he chose such harsh methods. But now I could also see him as he truly was: a simple, imperfect human being who could do nothing other than be himself. Yet, the unanswerable question remained.

"Why would you hurt me? How could you hurt me?"

No words came back. It was his turn to be silenced.

Then, something inside me said, "Katherine. This is what you need." Just like my dad's ego had stepped back to allow the music to turn on and the ceremony to begin, my own ego now took its back seat. My somatic wisdom took over. The forgiveness exchange was making its terms known. My right hand reached out to touch my dad's bald head. It was bony and cold. Then his shoulder. Then his chest. The lack of breath movement was disorienting. But I trusted what was unfolding. My left hand joined the right and stayed there for a bit, over his cold, cold heart. And then slowly, in the way that maybe all those very wise and compassionate death doulas suggest that you bathe your loved one's body after they die, I washed away my fear. I let my hands slowly and respectfully move over my dad's body, hovering just an inch or so above the blanket we had draped over him. Down the right side and back up the left. Checking. Making sure that nothing remained that could hurt me again. Nothing left that could haunt me in the middle of the night. No residue of the monster. As my hands moved, I felt like I was calling back my power. I was calling back all of my parts that this body had taken from me.

Once the body scan was complete, I sat back and knew that it was over. I had taken back what I needed to start my life again. With luck, my dad would get his next life, and it would be a good one. But I would be damn sure to get mine. I wasn't going to wait until I was on my deathbed to claim it. With the balance of power restored, I could finally say the words I thought I would never say to him out loud: "Dad. You sexually abused me. It wasn't OK. You really fucked up my life. I'm not ready to forgive you, but I'm going to get there."

"Oh, and one more thing. I'm going to write this story, and

I'm going to tell the truth." Immediately, I felt him push back, the part of him that was still attached to his body and his personality and his legacy. I persisted. "Dad. This is important. It's not about you. I'm scared to do it, but I know it has to be shared. I think it's going to help people. You have to know that no matter what I say, I promise to say it with compassion and respect." I felt him waiting, contemplating the terms. Pen click. *Tsch tsch tsch tsch.* And then, the echo of him taking a big breath and letting it out, "OK." The biggest and most genuine OK in the whole word. He wasn't thrilled about it, but he understood.

The next morning, I ate a bowl of Cheerio's and drank a perfectly boring cup of coffee on the back deck, watching the summer sun rise through the trees over my new life. I was free. I was ready to say goodbye to my dad's body.

My Buddhist friends—Chris and Kiana—were on their way back from Rhode Island and agreed to stop by the house to help me with the ritual I wanted to do. They had just led a Buddhist-inspired retreat on Block Island and had dedicated the merit to my dad. Chris had been an honest-to-goodness monk when he was young, and he was now the parent to two amazing kids. He and his family had come up to the farm several times for our backyard parties and camping. Chris was one of the only men in the psychedelic community who really stood by me when every-one else decided to kick me to the curb. He and I had taught a course together at the New School while I was pregnant with Ray, and then worked together to launch a community-focused exploration of consciousness called Psychedelic Sangha. I had met Kiana at the inaugural Psychedelic Sangha gathering, which my brother had also attended, back in the Spring right before my dad got really sick. I remember being surprised by her at first, because she had this powerfully sensuous air about her, like a modern-day dakini. She definitely stood out from the typical intellectuals and academics and nerdy psychonauts that usually showed up to these kinds of events. I remember Kiana sitting next to my brother in the front row while I led the group into deep contemplation of death and rebirth, and I had a hunch that maybe she was a long-lost family member. She hardly knew me, but never hesitated when Chris asked her to change her plans to help me and my dad out that day. This is the definition of a true spiritual friend.

When they first arrived, we sat and chatted in the living room for a bit. We were all glowing from our various contemplative endeavors of the past few days, and it was joyous to be sharing the first, fresh hours of my new life with friends. But the clock was also ticking. After about half an hour or so, I said, "Well, alright. We should probably get to work. I know you guys have to be on your way soon. And the funeral director is coming at four." I continued, "So, my dad's body is in the bedroom, just down the hallway. You probably noticed how cold it is in here, and that's on purpose, so his body doesn't start to decompose. And I'm also not sure if you noticed, but it still smells a bit like decay, so just kind of prepare yourself for that as we go in the room. I have incense burning, so it shouldn't be too bad."

As we were about to stand up, I said, "Do either of you have any concerns or questions before we go in? Are you guys OK with this?" And they both said "yes." "It should be fairly straight-forward," I said. "But I should probably ask. Have either of you seen a dead body before?" Chris had, but Kiana shook her head. She later told me that that day with me and my dad was her initiation into the death vortex.

The three of us walked into the room, and Chris sat, and Kiana kneeled at the foot of the bed in a meditative posture. Teddy the dog sat with them.

I stood up and recited the words as they came to me, "Richard, we are here to say goodbye to your body. Please remember that you are dead, and your body is of no use to you anymore. You are not your body. It is now time to say goodbye, to let go, and to be on your way into your next life. Soon, a man will come and take your body to a morgue, and then it will be cremated. I will make sure your body is well cared for, and I will be there when it is cremated. You have nothing to worry about."

And then I turned my attention to the body itself. I wasn't sure what the Buddhists had to say about it, but my scientific and somatic training encouraged me to acknowledge the body for everything it had given and taken.

"Thank you for bringing Richard into this world and carrying him through his life. Thank you for everything you have given to others, all of the joy and laughter and entertainment you have allowed Richard to share with the world. We forgive you for all the harms you have done to others, any act of violence or violation or disrespect. Thank you for being so strong for Richard, for propelling him and protecting him through his life of work and athletics and especially this final journey with cancer. Oh, great body, you have endured so much pain and suffering. You have known true joy. You have completed your mission. You are free to go."

Then I sang the *metta* sutra I had learned at my first silent retreat all those years ago, the same one I sang for my sister as she was dying and for Tsering by the riverside and for each cow on the farm before they were slaughtered. May all beings be free of suffering. May all beings be happy. *Om mani padme hum.*

After the ritual, we walked down the path to the lake. It was a glorious summer morning, and as we stood out on the dock surveying the beauty that surrounded us, Chris couldn't help himself, "Wow. This is all yours now, huh? You have boats!"

I laughed and said, "Actually, the boats go to Ed. But yeah, what a trip. I just inherited a corporate lawyer's retirement dream. Certainly not what I envisioned for myself. I guess I'm a card-carrying old white man now."

Chris said, "You're a *player* now. Fuck all those guys who don't want you to speak at conferences or work at their clinics. You don't have to answer to any of them anymore."

Kiana was quiet and reflective as Chris and I bantered, but then suddenly burst out, "Oh my god. I love your dad SO much. I feel so lucky to be here."

I remember the feeling in my body when she said that. It felt disjointed, out of place, inappropriate. Her words didn't fit with my conflicted feelings about my dad. How bizarre that a complete stranger who had only known his dead body could love him that way, when I couldn't. I felt myself pushing back against her words, wanting to say, "Well . . . you know . . . he wasn't a very nice person." But then I remembered the feeling of just being with my dad the night before, without the confusion of our past or our personalities or our "issues." The tension in my stomach softened and the resentful words in my throat dissolved and I allowed myself to just appreciate what she had said. Her words were pointing to my path, like, "Hey, just up ahead! I hear there's an amazing vista." In my mind, I said, "Dad, please help me. I don't know how to do this. I want to get to the place where I can say what Kiana just said, and really mean it. I want to forgive you. Please help me get there."

After the Buddhists left, I had one final ritual I wanted to do. Seeking to cover all of my spiritual bases, I had asked the Celtic priestess from the womb ceremony at the farm to help us release my dad's soul to the stars. I also invited my dad's best friend to join us, hoping he wouldn't be too freaked out. He was part of the crew that had just been in Ireland with my dad, and his partner had been married to one of my dad's close friends who had died of cancer (it was this gravesite that my dad had gone out of his way to visit on that final trip to Ireland). Thank God for the Irish crew. They had come by the house one day while I was in Rhode Island and sang and played and drank and made sure that my dad was surrounded with good cheer.

We all gathered around my dad's body, standing in a circle— all the humans, and Teddy, the dog. Nadiya, the priestess, called in the directions, the spirits of the North, South, East, West, Below, and Above. As we turned our gaze upward, she said, "Our dear brother, Richard, we are here today to send you back to the stars." We sang and drummed and rattled and whistled and did everything we could to move the energy upward, to get his soul to fly. As we called him "dear brother," it reminded me of his favorite lullaby that he would always sing, "Lay down, my dear daughters." I knew he would approve.

Then, at the last moment, a family friend who was originally from Brazil arrived unexpectedly to say her final goodbyes. She knew my dad and sister and had also lost her own sister to cancer. Still, I was surprised when she texted me to ask if she could come say goodbye, and I had no idea if she would really show up or not. Toward the end of our ritual, I heard a knock at the door, thinking it was the funeral director. When I opened the door, she literally launched herself through it, wailing. The rest of us emotionally repressed Americans just stood there in awe of this public display of raw vulnerability and grief. Nadiya could perhaps sense my concern that we hadn't finished the ritual and that I was worried the pagan-ness of it all would freak out our wailing friend. So she went over to her and put her hand on her shoulder and asked her what her religion was. When the woman said Christian, Nadiya didn't miss a beat, and explained how we were releasing my dad's body back to the Great Mother in the sky, whom Christians call Mary.

And then Nadiya said, "In a traditional Irish wake, the 'wailers' are women who walk through the streets of the village, crying and screaming, to help others release their grief."

Nadiya thanked our friend for showing up and making sure that this part of the tradition could be honored. Without planning it, we had managed to cover all the roles for my dad's final scene.

After all was said and done, and Nadiya had taken her leave, we had maybe fifteen minutes before the funeral director was set to arrive. We each cracked open a Guinness on the back deck, and my dad's friend, who was a brilliant musician, gave us all critical feedback on our performance. We joked and laughed. The mood was bittersweet, but mostly sweet. I couldn't have asked for a better send off for my dad. My only disappointment was when my brother denied my final, insane request, which was to burn my dad's body on a floating pyre at the center of the lake. Sadly for me, everyone agreed with him.

"Fine!" I said, "I can settle for a normal cremation. But just so you know, I'm totally getting my own Viking funeral when I die."

And there was one final, unexpected blessing. The local funeral director ended up being the most respectful, understanding, compassionate person I had encountered in the entire process of my dad getting sick and dying. He showed up with reverence, and without a hint of judgment about us keeping my dad's body for an extra day. I told him I was nervous about not staying with my dad's body, and he promised me that he would be personally accountable for it. I told him I didn't want any chemicals put on him or any embalming done to the body, and he said, "Absolutely not. Not a problem at all." I handed him the outfit that I had wanted to dress my dad in and asked when the cremation would be. He said he was planning for first thing Wednesday morning, which would be the third day after death. *Perfect*, I thought. And I asked if I could be there.

He didn't hesitate: "Of course."

The funeral director called me the next day to explain how things would go.

He said, "You have to understand, not many people want to attend a cremation. Hardly anyone asks to. The people who run the facility aren't really . . . ummm, 'people people.' They're very nice, but they're just not set up to provide support for grieving families. Anyway, they're fine for you to be there to begin the process but they asked if you would agree to leave right after. Also, you should know that your dad's body will be in a cardboard box, but by law, you aren't allowed to open it one last time to check to make sure it's really your dad, which is often what people want to do. You have to trust me, and I promise that I will make sure your dad is dressed the way you want and that he's in there. If that sounds OK to you, I think we're all set. I'll see you tomorrow morning, 7 A.M."

☾

The morning was quiet on the farm as I got into my sister's car—the Girl Rocket—to carry me on my sacred mission. I turned on the radio and Bone Thugs-N-Harmony greeted me: "See you at the Crossroads, so you won't be lonely," and I had to laugh and shake my head. Yep, still in the bardo. But at least my sister was here with me. "Hey Bec. Thanks for showing up."

I texted my friend Sarah and asked if she would talk to me as I drove. I don't remember our conversation, but it helped me stay focused. I lost reception about five minutes before turning onto the back road to the cremation facility. I was in no-man's land.

As I parked the car, I saw the funeral director standing nearby. He greeted me and invited me inside the small, square, cement building. He introduced me to the cremation guy, whose skin was almost translucent from spending all his time inside with dead people. The director explained the process to me, reminding me that I couldn't look in the box, and then said, "I'll step outside to give you a moment with your dad."

I stood next to the box and said my final prayers.

"Well, Dad. I guess this is it. You deserve to be free. I love you. Everything's going to be fine."

The guys came back in.

"Are you ready?"

"Yes, I'm ready."

And they slid my dad's body into the retort (you do not say 'oven' in a crematorium).

My heart started pounding in my chest, like the beginning of a panic attack. I suddenly felt the trapped-ness of that huge metal box. Oh shit. He hates confined spaces. He's gonna freak out. I started deep breathing and talking to my dad in my mind.

"Hey Dad. It's OK. I'm here with you. Remember, you are completely safe. You are not your body. Your body will be set on fire, but you are not your body."

Oh Jesus, there was no way to make this sound good. No wonder they don't let people come here.

"I'm sorry, Dad. I promise everything is OK."

Then I heard my brother's final request in my mind: "If they let you push the button to start the fire, you should totally push it."

I pushed the button. A heavy metal door dropped down, covering the space where my dad's body had entered. A huge sound took over the room. I tried to stay present as two memories competed for space in my consciousness, demanding my attention. First, I saw the scene playing out from an early therapy session, the time I purposely envisioned my dad burning to death alone in a huge forest fire. My rage was unquenchable then. I relished in the burning. What does it feel like, Richard, to have no one to save you. What does it feel like to be all alone, tortured by the flames. But this time was different.

"I'm here with you, Dad. I won't leave you alone."

And the second memory, an ancient dream I had had over and over when I was a kid. Of my dad driving me and my sister to some remote outpost, like an abandoned wild-west saloon. Him leaving us on the bank of a swampy river in the custody of a creepy, amphibious tollkeeper while my dad took a row boat across to tend to a raging fire on the opposite bank. He told us to wait. He said he'd be right back. But I knew he wouldn't return.

"God speed, Dad. *Je t'aime,*" I said out loud over the deafening roar.

Standing outside in the parking lot with the funeral director, he said, "You know, what you did in there was very brave. I came here with my dad, but I couldn't stay in the room."

And I replied, "Well, I've seen open-air cremations before, when I spent time in Nepal. It's a really important ritual. They say that only the most spiritually pure practitioners can be entrusted to do it correctly."

"That sounds amazing," he said. "I'd love to go to Nepal."

"Just curious," I asked. "Over the course of your career as a funeral director, how many people have asked to keep the body?"

"You're the first one."

"Wow," I said, "Thank you for not making me feel weird about it."

As I got in the car, I thought I was totally fine. But as I started driving, I felt a powerful energy start rushing through me, like fire without burning. I was crying and laughing uncontrollably, just feeling the amazing release of all of this SHIT. It was exhilarating. But a part of me also realized that I probably wasn't safe to be on the road, so I used my phone to search for the nearest diner. "Leo's Diner" popped up and I just followed the GPS, not even thinking where I was going. As I pulled into the parking lot, I realized that I had driven past this place easily a hundred times, going back and forth to therapy. How had I never seen it before? I was so disoriented. I kept driving around the parking lot but not seeing the entrance to the diner. I finally parked and just breathed and tried to calm down. I turned on the song that had supported me during my vigil with my dad—the Christmas-y one that sounded like *Carol of the Bells*. I was in the vortex, standing in the center of the fire with my dad, and it was just fine.

Once I got my bearings, I stepped out of the car and decided to find the diner on foot. There it was, tucked away in a little grassy corner on the lower level of what appeared to be a mixed-use office building. Hiding in plain sight. Back in college, usually the morning after taking too many drugs, I would call this a *Truman Show* moment. Like obviously this diner was not a real diner. It was full of actors who had been quickly called to the scene because I had deviated from the usual script and shown up in a new place unannounced. I walked through the door and was immediately greeted by the face of a lion and a sign that said: "Today's Special! Hakuna Matata Tea."

Have you ever heard of Hakuna Matata Tea before? Yeah, me neither. Because it's not a thing. It never existed in the Universe before that moment. I knew right away it was my dad, now free of his body and getting to have a bit of fun with the cosmos.

We always joked that "Hakuna matata" was his motto, like in Disney's *The Lion King*. I think my mom was the one who said it first, but it caught on with the rest of the family. It was classic Richard: no worries. Even when he was causing distress for everyone else, none of it seemed to affect him. Like water off his back. And now here he was, no longer Richard and yet somehow still exactly Richard, reminding me: there's nothing to worry about. Everything's going to be fine.

I sat down and ordered my favorite breakfast—eggs Benedict—and sipped that damn tea. It was iced tea with an Italian lemon ice dropped into it. It wasn't very good. I bet they'll never serve it again. It was just for me.

When I got back to the farm, I was still in a pleasant state of goofy after-shock, but at least I felt like I was back on planet Earth. As I walked toward the kitchen door, Frances came running out and said, "Mom! Mom! Look! Your sunflower is blooming!" And there it was. My first sunflower. Physical proof that my miracle was real. My forgiveness garden had worked. I was ready for my afterlife.

EPILOGUE

☾

My Island

BERMUDA IS A TINY, fishhook-shaped island in the middle of nowhere—nearly a thousand miles from any other land mass—situated at the northwestern edge of the mysterious Sargasso Sea, which is itself a swirling vortex of golden seaweed in the middle of the North Atlantic Ocean. Many a myth has been told about sailing vessels and aircraft being lost through that portal, the infamous Bermuda Triangle. Perhaps it is by standing guard at the edge of this vortex for millions of years that Bermuda has developed such resilience and fearlessness. My daughter was the one who pointed out that Bermuda looks more like a mermaid than a fishhook, and my son is enraptured with Bermuda's origins in the mouth of a volcano. These are the myths we tell in our family. It brings me great pleasure to think of Bermuda as a bad-ass mermaid, born out of a volcano, presiding over an entire ocean. She's my kind of girl.

After my sister died, Bermuda was the place that convinced me that joy was still possible. We came on a family vacation during the week leading up to Easter. On the last day of our trip, while my dad was ironically sick in bed, my brother and niece and I took a walk to Horseshoe Bay beach and discovered thousands of people flying kites. It was a huge celebration! We had no idea that Good Friday was such a big deal in Bermuda. And the Gombey dancers! Parading and drumming and whistling their way along the pink sand in their outrageously beautiful, shiny headdresses and Mardi Gras-like costumes. It was straight out of a dream. A dream of a new way of life. A dream where it is possible to be exquisitely happy even when you have lost your most important person. I thought of Rebecca, and of Jesus, and smiled. I saw the radiance of it all, beyond the shadow of death. And I felt a wise presence say, "Well, Katherine. It is certainly true that life can be hard and miserable. Even if you try to embody love and forgiveness, you may still be betrayed by your friends, and your father will still hurt you. In the end, you might even be tortured to death. But please, in the meantime, go fly your kite anyway!"

Seven years have passed since that first, fateful trip. I am now sitting in a cozy writer's studio on one of the highest points on the island, looking out over a huge expanse of deep blue water, feeling into the unbelievable miracle of finally living my dream. I've been in Bermuda for half a year, and it still hasn't completely sunk in yet that I have claimed my new life. Perhaps it's because Paradise isn't exactly the way I imagined it. I still suffer through waves of chronic pain and insomnia and trauma flashbacks. I still worry about my kids' safety. The majority of my days are not pleasant or easy. I'm still trying to befriend and release my anger, and sometimes it feels like a bottomless pit, an eternally seething volcano that will never exhaust itself of fuel. Nevertheless, I persist. I've started somatic therapy again. I keep noticing more moments of joy. Most importantly, I've come to accept that life-after-death—whether it's your own annihilation through trauma or the loss of a loved one—is an ever-unfolding process of opening and revealing and enduring the rawness of each new layer. I survive by writing. And by swimming.

Bermuda is the perfect place for cold-water swimming. The water around Bermuda is warmed by the Gulf Stream to tropical levels during the summer months, but in the winter, it reaches the same brisk temperature as the summer waters off Rhode Island where I first developed my cold-plunge spirituality. After living here for nearly four months, lacking the courage to brave the cold, it was my friend Kiana who finally convinced me to start my practice again. She came to visit in the middle of winter, during my month off from writing, and made a commitment to go in the ocean every day, no matter the weather. About halfway through her visit, I started going in with her. I didn't enjoy it; I endured it (kind of like my life). This wasn't how I remembered it from when I was a kid. Why was I so scared to go out into the deep? Where had my trust gone? And then, to my surprise, after about two weeks of near-daily plunges, I suddenly remembered my original love. I sent a message to Kiana back in the States: "I no longer feel like the ocean is something I am swimming in, something separate from me. I am the ocean. It is an extension of my body."

Cold-water swimming was also how I first began to trust my dad. We had gotten certified in scuba together back when I was only eleven years old, and he took me on an epic trip to St. Lucia over Christmas break as a way to celebrate. He had invited me to get trained again a few years ago, the day after that big mushroom ceremony with John. Then I got pregnant with Ray, so we couldn't. But shortly after my dad was cremated, a good friend gave me the opportunity to take one last deep dive with my dad.

I had gone into the city to lead a psychedelic integration circle the night before, so I thought I was just stopping by Behike's place to say hi before jumping on the train back to Connecticut.

But when I walked into his humble apartment, I discovered that he had laid out a beautiful ceremonial altar on the rug in the middle of the floor. My friend motioned to the altar and gently said, "There's no pressure at all. But the offer stands." And I knew what offer he meant. He was one of the only people I still trusted, and he was skilled in administering the exact medicine that had thrown me into the middle of the vortex during my winter of despair after my sister died; the medicine that had shown me the other side of Death.

We chatted for a bit to ease my anxiety. I shared some of what my brother and I had gone through with my dad. "One morning, after my uncle and brother had given my dad a shower and dressed him, I came in to find my brother holding my dad in his arms, laying him ever so gently down on the bed so that his head would come to rest on the pillow without any discomfort. My dad's head was cradled in the crook of Ed's arm, and it was like watching a mother lay her precious child down to sleep at night. I mean, this is a twenty-two-year-old kid for Christ's sake. And there were times he seemed even more angry at my dad than I was."

Behike started quietly weeping and said, "Oh, what you have seen, Katherine. Your brother is one of the lucky ones. What a gift that he could set aside his anger and show such compassion for his father. I have seen men in ceremony who have tried to hold onto their hatred, who have punished their parents by withholding pain medication or refusing to even visit them on their deathbed. It eats them up inside afterward. Their suffering is so deep."

We sat down on the floor facing each other, on either side of the altar. I was terrified to do this medicine again. I had been putting it off for six years. He said, "Why don't you just draw a card and see if that helps with your decision." I looked down at the cards lying in an arc. I sat and breathed and finally turned one over: "The Traveler." The woman on the card even looked like me. I knew I had no choice. Death and Fate were already waiting.

My friend began preparing the room, burning herbs and laying out his musical instruments. As I sat in meditation, heart pounding, I caught a glimpse of a framed image of two dolphins playing and said, "I've always loved dolphins. That picture makes me feel safe."

My friend said, "Oh, that's kind of a joke. I was going to take it down because people think it's silly."

"Well, it's perfect for me," I said. "It makes me think of my dad and scuba diving. You know, it's crazy. After he died, I found his dive log with all his notes from our first dives. I really wanted to scuba dive with him again, even once. This feels right."

My friend wafted burning smoke around my body to cleanse me and splashed a bit of *agua de flora* on my face and upper body. I laughed as the droplets hit me. I remembered motoring out on a little dive boat into the crystal blue-green sea. I remembered the thrill of adventure; the freedom of being able to breathe underwater; the dazzling visions of rainbow-hued corals and anemones and fish. Looking back, I now realize that my Bermuda dream and the possibility of forgiveness were first seeded in those Caribbean waters so long ago.

Behike asked me if I was ready. I moved from the floor to the edge of the couch and took a deep breath, "Yes." I reminded him, just like I had reminded the first friend who had offered me this gift, that I was dumb about smoking, so he would have to coach me through each in-breath and out-breath.

First breath. The acrid, burning, grape-syrup-smelling smoke enters my throat and lungs. Exhale. Second breath, and before I know it, I'm in. I lay back on the couch. The ceiling swirls. I briefly panic and flail, reaching backward over my head for my friend's hand. He moves just out of reach and starts singing. I feel held by the music. In his voice I can hear both natural talent and years of practice. I feel like such an amateur in his presence. My final, rational thought is, "How can all these clinicians pretend that they know how to guide psychedelic sessions? You need a real shaman."

Suddenly, I am lying in the hospital bed in my dad's bedroom, looking out the big glass door that leads out onto the deck, and then onward through the trees down to the lake. I am taking my last breaths. I am dying. I am completely aware of and present in my body and yet also clearly in-between worlds. My dad is standing off to one side, but I can't see him. I am otherwise alone. I know that this is how I am going to die. I am scared. I keep breathing but each breath takes so much effort and feels like it could be my last. I sense the world beyond this one opening up. I don't know if I'm ready. Telepathically, like with my sister in the hospital, I hear my dad say, "Remember how it feels to die. This is how I felt. I was scared, and I endured it. But it could have been easier. I wanted music. I wanted you there." I feel regret, but no guilt. He isn't judging me, but simply showing me. Like, "Look, you *know* how to help people die. It would have been nice for you to be there." Then I understand with my entire being that this IS how I will help others die: by knowing exactly how it feels. By dying myself, over and over, until it is no longer a fearful, foreign thing. I can practice death and show others how to do it. I can help guide people across because I am a denizen of both worlds. Death has given me a special exception to come and go.

☾

I decided to be the officiant at my dad's funeral because, as I joked at the time, "My dad and I share the same unwavering belief: that we know the right way to do things." I pulled off an amazing, respectful, beautiful ceremony. And then at the end, inspired by my DMT-dive in the city, I decided to take a chance and tell a very personal story, about my dad training me to hold my breath and swim underwater so that I could pass my scuba test. I recounted:

"The rest of the people in our class were adults, and I wasn't even technically old enough to get a certificate, but my dad had lied about my age on the application form, because he never believed the rules applied to him. The underwater swimming test—fifty meters, no push-off, one breath—was physically challenging, even for the adults. I had tried to pass once already and failed. So I only had one more try. I trained every weekend at the pool at my dad's apartment complex, with my dad coaching me. He kept telling me it was like a wall, I just had to swim through it. It was brutal. Every time I tried to make it from one end of the pool to the other, I would come up for air a few feet short of the finish line. I kept running up against that wall.

But on the evening of my final test, a small miracle occurred. I reached that same point where I would normally come up for air, and just . . . kept swimming. Suddenly, I felt like I could swim forever. I had unlimited air! I could breathe underwater! I swam way past the finish line and when I came up, I saw my dad and everyone else cheering. I did it! I broke through.

"And Richard has broken through, too," I said to all the folks gathered to honor my dad. "He has finally done what he never believed was possible." The part I didn't say out loud was, "He has broken free of his body. He has made it to his afterlife."

As I was concluding my story, I suddenly noticed my friend Sarah, sitting in the funeral audience, signaling and pointing to the space behind me. I thought she was urging me to wrap up the personal stuff and let the musicians play their final piece, but she said, "No! Look!" I turned around to see a huge rainbow around the sun. It was a bright, cold, blue day. Not a single drop of moisture. There was no mistaking it. It hung in the sky for minutes. Every single person saw that rainbow. I knew that my dad was saying, "Yes. Believe her. She is telling the truth."

About a month after my dad died, my brother and I traveled to Bermuda for a different kind of funeral: releasing our dad's ashes at my favorite, secluded beach. As I made my way down the rickety wooden staircase, dodging tiny lizards along the way, I spied an ancient Bermudian man who appeared to be drawing something in the sand. When I arrived at sea level, he revealed himself to be kind and joyful, but warned, "Make sure to keep an eye on your kids. The ocean is unpredictable here." And I thought, "A man after my own heart," because I always appreciate when people prioritize safety. After he left, I walked over to where he had been so focused on the sand. There it was, a mystical message just for me:

Be Well, Charon.

I wasn't exactly surprised by the message, as my brother had already been going on about how Charon was like my alter-ego. You see, Charon is the name of the ferryman who rows the dead across the River Styx on their way to their final judgment in the underworld. After witnessing everything I did to help my dad die, my brother had remarked, "You should name your book, "Becoming Charon." But I think it might be the other way around: maybe Death becomes me.

I let the message in the sand sink in. "Be Well, Charon." Truly, don't worry. It's all going to be fine. You know how to do this. I laid out a make-shift altar along the jagged edge of a huge, dragon-headed boulder that stands guard in the middle of the beach. Tiny pink nuggets of coral and little limpet shells with their perfect fractal designs. Pink oleander and red hibiscus flowers I had plucked along the walk. Blue and green marbles of sea glass, smoothed by the ocean herself. I carefully positioned the little blue buffalo totem that my dad had been given for good luck, along with a red stone heart and an ellipse of golden metal that came from the last pair of sandals my sister bought and that I had worn every day after she died until they broke. Around the edge I draped travel-size Tibetan prayer flags. And at the center of the altar, I placed Ganesha: a perfect little blue version of him that made me think of psilocybe mushrooms and the ocean. I was no longer afraid of him. I had accepted my fate, my vortex. I prayed to Ganesha to help clear the path forward as I navigated the first year of my afterlife. I asked him to help the grief move through me more quickly this time, so that I wouldn't be sick for years and years like I was after my sister died. I asked my dad to help me, too. In life, it was always hard for me to admit I needed his help, but now that he was an ancestor, I didn't hesitate to put him to work on my behalf. Finally, I bowed in deep gratitude for the Spirit of Bermuda, that mysterious and powerful deity who had inexplicably called me into her womb for safe keeping. She told me I could stay as long as I wanted.

I didn't know it at the time, but my prayer would be answered in the strangest of ways. A global pandemic hit about six months after my dad died and forced us into isolation. We all had to renounce normal life overnight. My family and I were some of the luckiest ones, living in a comfortable, beautiful home by a lake, surrounded by trees and far from other people. But my anxiety was out of control, because I had always been a bit of a germaphobe, and I wasn't ready to deal with even more death and loss. On top of everything, my brother and I were ensconced in a labyrinthine prison of estate attorneys and probate courts and business documents and financial advisors. It was truly a nightmare, that so many people and official agencies stood between us and the financial freedom my dad had worked so hard to provide. By the end of the summer, when it became clear that the brilliantly destructive virus wasn't going anywhere anytime soon, I knew I had to make my escape. There was no way I was going to survive another cold, sunless winter trapped in my dad's house 24/7 with two little kids, negotiating with lawyers and analyzing spreadsheets.

And it just so happened that, in addition to being my dream island, Bermuda was also one of the only countries that had figured out how to deal with that crazy virus. Through rigorous testing, mask wearing, and quarantine procedures for travelers, Bermuda had emerged as a reliable shelter from the storm. This was my chance! My cubic centimeter! I begged Ganesha to open the portal for me: "Please, help me and my family make it safely to mystical, mermaid island!" And he did, with the help of some great friends. The path was cleared. Bermuda even manifested a totally new residency certificate to allow foreigners to move to the island to "work from home." It was the best decision I've ever made.

Before I moved to Bermuda, I never knew that this is how much safety I needed to heal my trauma: an entire ocean between me and everything else. I had tried so many different strategies: somatic therapy, massage, climbing mountains, getting baby goats, quitting alcohol, sitting in silent meditation retreats, and all the psychedelic journeys. The only time the pain went away completely was in the middle of my pregnancy with Frances; her healing energy is the most powerful thing I have ever known. Still, the relief was temporary. I begged the land at our farm to help me. I even briefly considered handing my life over to Jesus since he, like Ganesha, was quite the expert in painful wounds and difficult fathers. During one of my lowest points, I remember a meditation teacher telling me that I was suicidal because I was still too attached to my own story.

"If you would just do the techniques the way I'm teaching you, you would be free of suffering," he said.

Well, in case you couldn't guess, that didn't help at all. Trauma is more powerful than any technique because it is embedded in the nervous system. For many trauma survivors, it's nearly impossible to tell where the trauma ends and your "real self" (or selves) begin. For me, total physical separation—from my dad (because he was dead) and from the world (by living on an island)—was the thing that finally helped my nervous system calm down.

The other thing that really helped was meeting people who had survived childhood abuse. Shortly after my dad died, I presented a talk at a conference out in California that was focused on science and spirituality. There, I encountered two wise women who inspired me to tell my own story. The first woman came up to me after a workshop on how to uproot and heal sexual abuse in spiritual communities.

As we chatted, she told me very calmly and matter-of-factly about her own abuse.

"I was sexually abused by my dad when I was little, but with the help of psychedelics, I was able to forgive him."

The way she said it was really that simple and straightforward. I was amazed. "You mean you actually forgave him, in person?"

"Oh yeah," she said. "I confronted him about it, and he admitted what he had done and said he was sorry, and I forgave him."

I stood there in shock. I felt like I was looking at a real-life superwoman. How had she done the thing I was so scared to do? How had she said those words out loud and actually received the apology she had been looking for?

I felt so defeated, like a total failure. What a scaredy-cat I was, that I had to wait until my dad died to have that conversation; that I needed to be on drugs to do it. I went back to my hotel room and sobbed. I felt wretched.

The next day at lunch, I sat with a friend I had met earlier in the year at a conference on Orcas Island, another fantastical refuge like Bermuda. She shared with me about how she was caring for her elderly mother while writing her first book, and how she had confronted her estranged father and made him apologize and take responsibility for abusing his wife and kids. I couldn't help it, I just started crying in the middle of that sunny, crowded lawn of happy conference-goers. "Well, I could never confront my dad," I said. "I was too scared that he would ignore me or claim it never happened or make me feel bad for even trying. It was better to never get an apology than to try to get it and have him deny me." And she said, "Well, I'm not so sure you didn't get it. Look around you. Look at these palm trees waving in the breeze, and this beautiful, sunny day. Listen. Maybe your dad is saying it now. 'I'm so, so sorry. Here, take everything I have. Live in my house. Use the dishes in my kitchen. Take it all. It's yours. I'm so sorry.'" And I just sat there happy-crying and thinking, hoping, that maybe she was right.

There's a way in which our cultural taboo around abuse convinces you that you are making up what happened to you, that maybe it never really happened because all the adults are acting like it didn't. Considering that childhood memories are often composed of confusing, fragmented visual snapshots or body-based sensations, it becomes very easy to disbelieve your own story. I've even had alleged experts in the psychedelic community tell me that people fabricate memories of sexual abuse while high on mushrooms or ayahuasca. It's mind-boggling how many moments of my life I have spent trying to disbelieve what my body has been telling me. How many times I've tried to rewrite my own story in my mind, to edit out the parts that included the reality I just couldn't rationally accept or explain. I even tried to edit this book to make the story more palatable for readers, and to protect my dad. Many times, I wondered, "Wouldn't it be better to hold onto my secret? Wouldn't it be easier for me to keep suffering alone rather than force others to suffer with me? Wouldn't it be better for everyone if I could just forgive and forget?"

The answer I finally came to was "no," it is not easier, and it is not fair for anyone to suffer with this reality alone. The shame, the fear, the daily anxiety, the nightmares, the insomnia, the physical symptoms . . . these are not things that can be treated at the individual level. They must be held and healed in community. No one wants to believe that little children are physically and sexually violated by members of their own family, by people who are also nice and smart and generous. I don't want to believe it! And yet, here we are. We must deal with it, together. Including the perpetrators, who are more often than not victims themselves. This is the curse that must end. And I believe that MDMA and psychedelics will help, as long as people can heal on their own terms and in relationship with their friends and loved ones. The kind of healing I experienced could not have been completed in a medical setting. I suspect that there are many other survivors who would also feel safest having psychedelic experiences in their own homes, with the people they choose (or alone, which was ultimately my preferred method). I believe that our homes are the perfect setting for this kind of healing, partly because it is where so much of our living takes place; it is exactly where many of us must learn to battle our demons, or better yet, make friends with them. We must clear out the curse at its root, and kindly but firmly show the trauma that it no longer has a place to hide.

☾

Toward the end of my time in Bermuda, only a few weeks after I finished writing the last chapter of this book, a new variant of the virus emerged that forced the entire island to "shelter-in-place." And, because the Universe enjoys a dramatic flourish, I ended up coming down with pneumonia.

As I drove myself to the hospital—struggling to breathe, with deep pain in my right lung and anxiety coursing through my body as I worried about what would happen when I arrived at an emergency room in the middle of a pandemic— a strange peace came over me. I felt my sister with me, reminding me that it would be OK. I remembered that her final journey had begun in a similar fashion: driving herself to the hospital because she suddenly couldn't breathe. Same, same.

I spent about half a day in the ER, receiving excellent drugs, and was discharged once they confirmed I didn't have the virus that was wreaking havoc all over the world. The doctor said she had never been so relieved to inform an otherwise healthy, young person that they "*only* had regular pneumonia." It was also Earth Day, which I felt was cosmically appropriate for another re-birth.

That evening, the kids and John and I made it down to the beach and drew our names in the sand and thanked Bermuda for carrying us in her womb for so many months. I wasn't ready to leave, but I knew my time was up. Still, I felt that perhaps Bermuda was asking if there was something I needed to leave behind.

The night before our departure, I went down to my favorite beach—my church—one last time, planning to offer some of my sister's ashes as a gesture of gratitude. As I pulled the small glass vial out of my pocket, I thought back to the first time I had handled her ashes. Using a small, silver kitchen spoon, I had prepared to scoop her ashes out of her elegant, black, crystal urn into a little plastic baggie so that I could bring some to Nepal with me. As I carefully removed the glass lid and peeled back the interior lining, I was wholly unprepared for what I would encounter. It wasn't just dust. It was coarse and textured. It was Her. Her body. The tiny, jagged pieces of bone were what broke me. I didn't make it past the first scoop. I started sobbing. I kept looking at the bones, thinking I would recognize her. Where is she? Why can't I see her?

As I knelt into the thick, cake-batter sand next to the huge dragon-headed rock, I suddenly knew that I would leave her there. All of her. I was ready to entrust my most important person to this island.

I dig a deep, narrow hole next to the boulder and drop the vial in. Out loud, I pray, "It has been the honor of my life to carry you for nearly forty years, but I am going to put you down now. I trust Bermuda to hold you. I know where to find you. Thank you for coming to find me."

Along with the ashes, I bury some glitter that my daughter gave me for the ceremony—magenta pink, of course, my sister's favorite color. I also bury my guilt. Guilt about not doing the right thing or not doing enough to save her. Guilt about what she might have experienced or witnessed when we were kids. Guilt that we never talked about it, and guilt that all of the silence contributed to her cancer.

After filling the hole, my grief overcomes me. I let the screams escape, hoping that the roar of the ocean waves will drown them out. As the wind whips salty sea spray into my face, mixing with my tears, I look up and see an osprey diving elegantly and fiercely toward the water. Just before she reaches the surface, she swoops upward and circles directly over me, looking me straight in the eyes. I am briefly very confused, because ospreys belong in Connecticut, not Bermuda. And then, I recognize her. Rebecca. I have been seen and witnessed. My intention has been fulfilled.

Rebecca and Katherine in 1987.

ACKNOWLEDGMENTS

I WROTE THIS BOOK to save my life, but the truth of the matter is that many people helped me stay alive until I was ready and able to write it. Before I start thanking all of those people, I want to send up a prayer of deep gratitude and respect for all of the indigenous medicine carriers who have been the stewards of sacred plants and mushrooms for thousands of years before people like me came along. Thank you, especially, to the original mushroom godmother/grandmother, María Sabina; your gift to the world was the gift I needed, and I owe you my life.

I like to talk about *Midnight Water* as a labyrinth; each time I entered the maze I wasn't sure I would make it back out again. I always expected the monster to eat me alive. So, thank you to my editor, Rose Alexandre-Leach, for encouraging me to take one last, intense journey into this labyrinth. The book is immeasurably better for you believing in me and being so compassionate and skillful with your feedback. Thank you to my proofreader, Reid Bartholomew, for your careful eye to detail. And most of all, thank you to my publisher, Dede Cummings, who is a kindred spirit in forging her own path of healing and who understands deeply that certain books simply must be published, even if you are the only one (for a little while) who knows that truth.

Thank you to my family, especially my mom, Julie, and husband, John, without whom it would have been literally impossible to write this book. At the end of the day, only these two humans will ever really understand the grueling slog of the past ten years, the deep love we shared through it all, and the steadfast desire for liberation from suffering that we are still praying for.

Thank you to my mother-in-law, Debbie, for all of your support and love. Thank you to my (little) brother, Edward, for confidently walking your own labyrinth and helping illuminate my own with your inexplicably old wisdom and huge, huge heart. Thank you to my brother-in-law Ryan and his daughter, my niece, Anya. You have been a shining light through the darkest parts of this journey, and I am so thankful that Rebecca chose both of you to be a part of our lives. Thank you to my sister's extended family in Vermont, especially Tom, Meri, and Michele, and her best friends in Connecticut, Ashley and Nicole. Thank you to my dad's best friends, siblings, and coworkers who showed him such love and devotion, and who have helped me gain a new appreciation for what an amazing person he was. I should also thank my children, Frances and Ray, but I hope the book itself makes it perfectly clear that they are my saving graces.

I was blessed to work with amazing scientists, meditators, and psychedelic experts along my path. Thank you to my first mentor, Yale Cohen at Dartmouth College, for helping me learn how to act and write like a real scientist; I apologize for returning to my original flowery and overly dramatic style. Thank you to my mentors at UC Davis—Ewa Wojciulik, Ron Mangun, and Cliff Saron—for launching the project of a lifetime and helping me find my niche in it. Thank you to the entire Shamatha Project team, especially my first (formal) meditation teacher, Alan

Wallace; my fellow campmates/researchers, Stephen Aichele, Anthony Zanesco, David Bridwell, Brandon King, and Tonya Jacobs; and to everyone who did the hard work back home while we were up in the mountains, especially Baljinder Sahdra, Erika Rosenberg, Phil Shaver, and Emilio Ferrer.

My time at Johns Hopkins was certainly a spiritual crucible, and I am grateful that I had a few guardian angels there with me to make sure I didn't become entirely engulfed in the flames. First and foremost, thank you to Maggie Klinedinst, study coordinator extraordinaire and one of the coolest (and most multi-talented) humans I have ever had the pleasure to be near. I still have the magical necklace you made me, and the appropriate/inappropriate hand-sewn sign you created for the short time I occupied an office with a window. Thank you to my mentors— Mary Cosimano, Roland Griffiths, and Bill Richards—and the female faculty at Hopkins who kept my faith alive—Gwenn Smith, Annie Umbricht and Jeannie-Marie Leoutsakos. Thank you to all of my fellow postdocs, researchers and assistant guides for laughing with me through hell, especially Dan Evatt, Porche Henry, Denis Antoine, Shauna Acquavita, Brian Richards, Haley Sweet, and Fred Reinholdt. Thank you to my wild and crazy Baltimore friends who helped me understand my psychedelic work from a far less objective lens. And of course, thank you to the psychonauts themselves, especially Twig Harper, for teaching me so much about the human mind and heart.

Unfortunately, it is not possible to fully name all of the people who helped me on my path of healing, mostly for safety/privacy reasons. Thank you to everyone who walked with me in Nepal, especially Tsering Paljor Lama, Pema Gyalpo, Challen Clarke, and Prem Dorchi Lama; you changed the entire course of my life. Thank you to my meditation and yoga teachers, my psychedelic guides and shamans, my midwives and doctors (especially my pulmonologist, Dr. Larry Wasser), and every single somatic healer, chiropractor, acupuncturist, and massage therapist who helped convince my soul to stay somewhat close to my body, particularly in the midst of pain. I especially want to thank Kevon Simpson, Lori Sommerville, Colleen Olphie-Lippmann and Laura Ahern for gently guiding my body on its return path.

Thank you to all of the amazing women I met after my sister died, who first heard my stories, witnessed my grief and pain, and showed your solidarity, especially Eileen Hall, Alicia Danforth, Maria Mangini, Boa Cowee, Cassandra Vieten, Mica Estrada, Angela Beers, Oriana Mayorga, Carmen Otto, Jennifer Thetford, Linnae Ponte, Bénédicte Mannix, Leia Friedwoman, Annemieka Neenan, Gretchen Krampf, Katie Gray, Ines Andrade, Leslie Bernstein, Nadiya Nottingham and Gaurī Rasp. And to my lifelong friends, who somehow have stuck by me through the many iterations of Katherine: Gabrielle Steinhorn, Katie Skartvedt, Ilona Lorincz, Jared Ray, Peter Rapp, Ryan Higgins, and Erin Sullivan.

While this book was conceived in New York City (January 2013) and gestated in Connecticut (2013-2020), it was birthed in Bermuda (2020-2022). I would not be who I am today without the tremendous love and support of so many Bermudians, plus a few brave Americans who ventured into the Bermuda vortex with me. Thank you to Marlene and Anthony Bicchieri for helping me discover home(s) away from home; Mr. and Mrs. and Keeivin Bailey for safely transporting my family all over the island; the amazing staff at The Reefs, especially Antonetta (Toni), Lena Mae, Andrea, Shani and Donna; Amanda Temple (photography) and Mia Chambray-Gregory (makeup) for capturing the essence of my Bermuda self for posterity; Ruth-Anne Outerbridge of Spirit House; Charles Lawrence; Chris "Doc"

Kelley; Serena Malkani; Kiana McCourt; Becca Summers; Erik Davis; Jennifer Dumpert; Ixchel Yaah; David Bodycombe; Sara Johnson; Helen Orchard; Lucy, Viktor and Maria of Belgarde; Jenn and Chris of Fiddlers Green; Dionne, Beth, and all of the teachers, babysitters and friends who supported me and my family while I wrote this book. Of course, we should all thank author Andrew Stevenson of humpback whale fame and Paul Shapiro of Brimstone Media who refused to let me print only a few hundred copies of my book and call it a day.

Finally, thank you to the early fans and readers of my story, who believed in me and continually encouraged me to take the next step, especially Julie Holland, Elias Dakwar, Joseph McKay, Sandy Hockenbury, Robin Gunkel, Michael Hughes, Margaret Cullen, Amishi Jha, Erik Storlie, Robert Forte, Jules Evans, Michael Sapiro, Stephen, Jennie, Laura, Prescott, and Janeth Hall.

RESOURCES

CREDITS

Note: Portions of the story told in *Midnight Water* have previously appeared in: *Death: An Oral History* by Casey Jarman (chapter on "Katherine MacLean: Psychedelic Scientist"), and *Good Chemistry: The Science of Connection* by Julie Holland M.D. ("The Final Retort" section that ends the book).

BOOKS

Meditation

The Fruitful Darkness by Joan Halifax
After the Ecstasy, the Laundry by Jack Kornfield
In Love with the World by Yongey Mingyur Rinpoche
The Places that Scare You by Pema Chödrön
The Attention Revolution by B. Alan Wallace, Ph.D.
Be Here Now by Ram Dass

Caring for People with Trauma

The Ethics of Caring by Kylea Taylor
Healing the Fragmented Selves of Trauma Survivors by Janina
    Fisher, Ph.D.
The Empath's Survival Guide by Judith Orloff, M.D.

Women's Perspectives on Abuse/Trauma
The Apology by Eve Ensler
Her by Christina Parravani

Psychedelics
The Psychedelic Handbook by Rick Strassman, M.D.
The Wild Kindness by Bett Williams
Secret Chief Revealed, Revised 2nd Edition: Conversations with Leo Zeff by Myron J. Stolaroff
The Healing Journey: Pioneering Approaches to Psychedelic Therapy by Claudio Naranjo
María Sabina: Selections, edited by Jerome Rothenberg with Texts and Commentaries by Álvaro Estrada and Others; University of California Press
Now is the Time to Open Your Heart by Alice Walker

Death
Being Mortal by Atul Gawande, M.D.
Love and Fear: Stories from a Hospice Chaplain by Renshin Bunce
Smoke Gets in Your Eyes & Other Lessons from the Crematory by Caitlin Doughty

WEBSITES
Shamatha Project:
https://saronlab.ucdavis.edu/shamatha-project.html

Johns Hopkins Center for Psychedelic and Consciousness Research:
https://hopkinspsychedelic.org/

ABOUT THE AUTHOR

KATHERINE MACLEAN, PH.D. is a research scientist with expertise in studying the effects of mindfulness meditation and psychedelics on cognitive performance, emotional well-being, spirituality, and brain function. As a postdoctoral research fellow and faculty member at the Johns Hopkins University School of Medicine, she conducted clinical trials of psilocybin, the primary chemical found in "magic mushrooms," and other psychedelic compounds. Her groundbreaking research on psilocybin and personality change suggests that psychedelic medicines can enhance openness to new experiences and promote mental health and emotional well-being throughout the lifespan. Dr. MacLean co-founded and directed the first center for psychedelic education and training in New York, was featured in the *New Yorker* article entitled "The Trip Treatment" by Michael Pollan, and her TED Talk has been viewed nearly fifty thousand times.